TEJANO PROUD

NUMBER ONE

Fronteras Series

Sponsored by Texas A&M International University
Jóse Roberto Juárez, General Editor

Tejano Proud

Tex-Mex Music
in the Twentieth Century

GUADALUPE SAN MIGUEL, JR.

TEXAS A&M UNIVERSITY PRESS • College Station

Library of Congress Cataloging-in-Publication Data

San Miguel, Guadalupe, 1950–
    Tejano proud : Tex-Mex music in the twentieth century /
Guadalupe San Miguel, Jr.—1st ed.
        p. cm.
    Includes discography, bibliographical references, and index.
    ISBN 1-58544-159-7 (cloth : alk. paper) —
    ISBN 1-58544-188-0 (paper : alk. paper)
    1. Tejano music—History and criticism.   2. Mexican
Americans—Texas—Music—History and criticism.   I. Title.
ML3481.S26   2002
781.64'089'68720764—dc21   2001005013

Contents

List of Illustrations   VII

List of Tables   IX

Preface   XI

Chapter 1. Música Tejana: Its Essential Elements   3

Chapter 2. Diversity and Change in the Initial Recordings, 1927–41   20

Chapter 3. Post–World War II Developments, 1946–64   37

Chapter 4. Before the Arrival of the Major Record Labels, 1964–89   60

Chapter 5. The Era of Corporate Involvement, 1989–99   92

Chapter 6. Trends in Música Tejana during the 1990s   113

Conclusion   129

Appendix A. Discography   137

Appendix B. Tejano Music Awards, 1981–2000   143

Notes   153

Bibliography   183

Index   185

Illustrations

Los Rancheros from Benavides   *page* 11

Lydia Mendoza   40

Hermanas Guerrero   43

Chelo Silva   44

Eugenio Gutiérrez   49

Isidro López y Su Orquesta   51

Conjunto Bernal   61

Tony de la Rosa   63

Steve Jordan   65

Los Relámpagos del Norte   67

Ramón Ayala   68

Los Dinos   72

Los Dinos and the Caravanas Tejanas   75

Los Kasinos   79

David Lee Garza y Los Musicales   80

Country Roland   82

Los Fabulosos Cuatro   84

Laura Canales   87

Emilio at National Council de la Raza   95

Intocable   100

Michael Salgado   101

Selena y los Dinos   109

Jennifer Peña   127

Los Kumbia Kings   133

Tables

Table 1. Orquestas Tejanas, 1927–41   *page* 25

Table 2. Selected Dance Halls, 1948–64   56

Table 3. Selected Orquestas Tejanas, 1950s–70s   76

Table 4. Selected Organ-based Grupos, 1970s–80s   86

Table 5. Selected Grupos Tejanos, 1980s–90s   103

Table 6. Types of Songs Recorded by Mazz, 1977–98   107

Table 7. Selected Discography of Mazz, 1977–99   108

Table 8. Selected List of Women in Música Tejana, 1970–99   119

Table 9. Attendance at the Go Tejano Rodeo, 1990–2000   121

Table 10. Music Awards Programs, 1974–99   124

Preface

Let me begin by stating up front that I am not a musician. I do not play a musical instrument, although at brief, very brief, moments in time I have wanted to take some lessons. I also do not sing. My only experience singing was with my high school choir. But even then I could not carry a tune. On the other hand, I *am* a dancer—a hard-core Tejano dancer. In fact, most of my relatives on my mother's side are dancers. My *sobrino* (nephew) from Corpus Christi, Victor Manuel, swears that music is in our family genes. But I think it is primarily in family traditions. Even to this day, my mother, Sixta, is an avid dancer on the weekends, and, at the writing of this book, she was eighty years young. My sister Lily (in her late fifties) as well as my *tías* (aunts), *primas* and *primos* (cousins), *sobrinas* (nieces), *sobrinos*, and so many others, are all fabulous "fancy" dancers in their own right. Whether dancing is in the genes or not is unimportant for the moment. Of importance is the fact that I come from a multigenerational family of dancers. This is how I became interested in *música tejana*.

Ever since my middle-school years in the 1960s, I have been dancing to the beats of música tejana. Polkas, *rancheras, cumbias, huapangos,* two-steps, and many other dances have been integral parts of my life. In those early years, I attended countless dances at *quinceañeras* (coming-out dances for fifteen-year-old Mexican American girls), *bodas* (weddings), social clubs, graduations, and public dance halls. During my high-school years I belonged to an informal group of Tejano dancers. Our goal was to be the best and most colorful dancers in Corpus Christi. We would make up complex turns, spins, and whirls to the simple dance steps of polkas, *baladas,* or cumbias and attend as many dances during the week and on the weekends as possible.

After high school I left Texas to attend college, first on the East Coast and then on the West Coast. While in these areas I picked up other popular dance steps, including salsa in the early 1970s and disco in the late 1970s. But I never forgot my passion. I kept coming home during holidays and summers to visit family and friends and to go dancing. Even after I was married and had several beautiful children, my passion for dancing did not end. Because of family obligations, I ventured less often to the public dance halls, but I continued my fancy dancing at family gatherings and private functions.

Sometime in the 1980s, while in California, I began to give lectures in Chicano Studies classes on Tejano dancing—on its complexities, its similarities and differences to Mexican dancing in California, and its music. In the 1990s I spent more time lecturing than dancing. These lectures eventually led me to write about the varieties of music played in the Tejano community and their origins. Thus this book on música tejana.

Música tejana is not a single music but a complex set of musical groups, styles, and genres.[1] Although its roots can be traced to the Spanish colonial period, little is known about its origins and development. Much of this history is still to be recovered, discovered, and reconstructed. During the past several decades, however, a few scholars have investigated significant aspects of its history. Américo Paredes, for instance, has published several works on the evolution of particular *canciones* (songs) found in música tejana, especially the *décima* and the *corrido*.[2] Manuel Peña, in turn, has focused on the evolution of two types of musical groups found within the Tejano community—the *conjunto* and the *orquesta Tejana*.[3] Both emerged as distinct musical forms in the immediate post–World War II era and reached their height of popularity in the 1960s and 1970s. Ramiro Burr has provided essential information on many of the groups that have recorded música tejana in the twentieth century.[4]

Although insightful, these studies provide an incomplete and slightly inaccurate picture of the music's evolution, especially in the 1900s. Existing scholarship, for instance, suggests that corridos have been a significant part of música tejana. The evidence from Tejano recordings indicates that this is not so. For most of the twentieth century, *canciones típicas* and *canciones románticas,* not corridos, have formed the core of this music. And orquestas Tejanas and conjuntos are not the only types of musical ensembles in the community, nor do they exist in isolation from each other or from the larger society. Other ensembles to be discussed later have arisen at different points in time, influenced each other in the process, and competed for dominance in the Tejano music industry. Música tejana likewise is composed of an evolving repertoire of dance forms that differs across time. None of the current studies has investigated this aspect of the music, or how and why this repertoire changed over time.

PURPOSE

This book refines the existing interpretation of música tejana and provides a comprehensive, although brief, history of its most important musical developments and adaptations during the twentieth century. More specifically, it describes and explains the origins of the diverse, distinct, and dynamic groups, songs, and dances that compose recorded Texas-Mexican music and how this music has evolved over time. This study synthesizes the existing scholarly and popular literature on the history of música tejana and goes beyond it by utilizing the actual recordings of Tejano groups as a primary source of data from which to draw its conclusions. For this reason, it begins in the 1920s with the rise of recorded music and ends in the year 2000.

I argue that música tejana is complex, diverse, evolutionary, and reflective of the historical realities and ethnic identity of the Mexican American population in Texas. For most of the twentieth century, it experienced significant changes and went from a regional musical style to an international one. It also assumed different forms that changed over time. The best-known expressive form was the conjunto, an accordion-based musical ensemble. In addition to the conjunto, however, at least five other types of ensemble were common—the vocal tradition of the *solistas* and the *duetos,* the orquestas, the progressive conjuntos, the *grupos Tejanos,* and the Chicano country bands. These ensembles originated at different historical periods, at times competed with each other and with non-Tejano musical styles for popular attention, and, in some cases, declined in popularity. Among these ensembles, the only one that maintained a continuous presence in the Tejano community during the entire twentieth century was the conjunto. All the others emerged and declined as viable ensembles in the recent past or were on the verge of declining in the contemporary period.

Despite the emergence and competition of a variety of ensembles, música tejana remained rooted in Mexican music and in the Spanish language. It also continued to reflect the diverse historical experiences and the distinct but constantly changing identity of the Tejano population. For these reasons, música tejana has been and continues to be viewed as *nuestra música* (our music) by those who perform it and by those who dance to its intoxicating rhythms.[5]

ORGANIZATION

Música tejana, or "Tejano," as it came to be known in the 1980s and 1990s, became extremely popular during the latter decades of the twentieth century. Despite this popularity, there was a great deal of misunderstanding and confusion about its definition. Chapter 1 tackles this issue and provides a comprehensive overview of its essential historical and musical components. It argues that Texas-Mexican music is a particular form of border music developed by Tejanos for Tejanos. Because it is an indigenous creation, this music reflects the entire spectrum of Tejano life. Música tejana is anchored in selective Mexican musical traditions but has been constantly updated and modernized over the years. Vocal groups of varying sizes and at least five different types of musical ensembles, likewise, play this type of music.

Although música tejana has been around for centuries, no recordings were made until the late 1920s. For thirteen years, from 1927 to 1941, major labels recorded this music for a national audience. By 1941 they abandoned the genre because of its limited market and the increasing scarcity of materials for the making of records during the war years. Chapter 2 describes the diverse forms of music recorded during this period and how Tejano audiences responded to them.

After World War II, local companies assumed responsibility for the recording of música tejana once the major labels abandoned the genre. Chapter 3 discusses the role they played in the emergence of two new types of musical ensemble—the female duet and the orquesta Tejana—and in the reemergence and dominance of conjuntos during the years 1946 through 1964.

During a twenty-five-year period, from 1964 to 1989, música Tejana evolved in new directions and expanded beyond South and Central Texas. The conjuntos and orquestas continued to be an integral part of the community's musical heritage but subsequent changes occurred in them. Furthermore, three new distinct musical ensembles—the progressive conjunto, the chicano country bands, and the grupo Tejano—emerged and evolved in competition with each other, with the conjunto and orquesta, and with other non-Tejano styles found in the Mexican American community. These new developments are discussed in chapter 4.

During the last decade of the twentieth century, música tejana again experienced significant changes in its ensembles, its musical repertoire, and its artists. Many of these changes were due in large part to corporate influences. Chapter 5 discusses these developments and shows how progressive conjuntos became influential, how traditional conjuntos enjoyed a renaissance, and how grupos Tejanos extended their dominance.

Several other significant musical trends emerged in the 1990s. Chapter 6 discusses three of the most important ones—the mainstreaming phenomenon, the increased role of women in Tejano and Latina music, and the fluctuating popularity of música tejana.

The conclusion reiterates and reinforces the three major ideas covered in this book. First, música tejana is a form of border music reflective of the historical experiences, internal differences, and ethnic identities of Mexican-origin individuals residing in Texas. Second, it is a complex array of evolving musical forms and styles based on traditional Mexican music but continually updated and modernized over time. Third, it is played by a variety of musical ensembles or groups. In addition to the conjunto and the orquesta, it includes vocal groups of different sizes as well as progressive conjuntos, grupos, and Chicano country bands.

The appendixes include data used in the book, especially a list of Tejano Music Award winners from 1981 to 2000, and a selective discography.

TEJANO PROUD

Chapter 1

Música Tejana

Its Essential Elements

Música tejana, or Texas-Mexican music, is contagious; it makes you want to dance. It can have the beat of a polka, *cumbia, bolero,* or *ranchera.* It can also have influences from other musical styles, such as disco, pop, rap, country, and reggae. Its sounds come from a variety of instruments, including accordions, synthesizers, electric guitars, congas, and *pitos* (horns). This type of music, known as Tejano in the contemporary period, is extremely popular in Texas, in other parts of the United States, and in Mexico.

Despite its popularity, there is still a great deal of misunderstanding and confusion about this music and its definition. Is música tejana, for instance, a particular form of music that has lost its ability to "connect" with its audience because of its commercialization or is it still "culturally meaningful" to Tejanos? Is this music, in other words, an "organic" symbol of Tejano culture or has it become a "superorganic" commodity to be consumed by an anonymous mass disconnected from the history and cultures of Tejanos?[1] Also, is música tejana based on the accordion, the saxophones, the keyboards, or a mixture of these? What types of songs comprise this music? Some commentators have argued that Tejano is *conjunto* or accordion-based music that has been "urbanized" and modernized. By modernization, these commentators generally argue that the traditional conjunto sound incorporates more instruments, especially keyboards, and borrows heavily from other music forms, like rock and country.[2] Others argue that Tejano is either an extension of Mexican music in general, a modified form of *música norteña*—that is, conjunto music from northern Mexico—or a mixture of conjunto music and country and western sounds.[3] The scholar Manuel Peña argues that Tejano can be distinguished as "synthesizer-driven" music.[4] Vilma Maldonado, a journalist for the *McAllen Monitor,* states that Tejano music also includes the styles popularized by *orquestas* and *grupos Tejanos* of the 1960s and 1970s.[5]

Which of these is a more accurate definition of this complex music? Is música tejana culturally significant for chicanos and chicanas? Is it based primarily on the sounds of the accordion or the synthesizer? What about the pitos, i.e., the "brassy sound" of older groups such as Little Joe, Sunny Ozuna, and the Latin Breed? Also, what is the relationship between música tejana and norteño music in particular or música tejana and Mexican music in general? What about American musical forms? How do they relate to música tejana? The following is aimed at answering these questions.

Before I begin let me clarify several key terms. One of these is "Tejano," the other one is "Texas-Mexican music" or "música tejana," its Spanish equivalent. Tejano is not quite the same as música tejana. "Tejano" is a term of recent vintage and refers to the music played by Tejano artists in the latter part of the twentieth century. It came into common usage in the 1980s, but most commentators do not agree on what it means. The term "Tejano," then, generally means whatever one chooses it to mean.[6] In my view, it is not a useful term for understanding the historical complexity and diversity of this music. Música tejana, on the other hand, is not specific to any particular time period. It is much broader and more inclusive than Tejano and allows for the existence of other musical forms and styles. As used in this book, "música tejana" comprises all the musical genres, forms, and styles that have existed in the Tejano community since at least the nineteenth century.[7]

Other terms that need defining are "Tejanos," "Mexican Americans," and "Anglos." Tejanos are individuals of Mexican descent who were born and raised in Texas. The term "Mexican American" refers to individuals of Mexican descent who are born or raised in the United States. Tejanos are all Mexican Americans, but not all Mexican Americans are Tejanos. Anglos generally are individuals of northern European descent, but, as used in this study, the term refers to the entire white population residing in Texas. The definition of

"Anglo" varies throughout the Southwest. In New Mexico, for instance, "Anglo" was used to denote anyone who was not Indian, Spanish Indian, or of Mexican descent. According to Richard Nostrand, even blacks were considered Anglos.[8]

BORDER MUSIC

Música tejana, as noted above, is not a single music but a complex set of musical forms, styles, and genres, composed of five distinct essential elements. Tejano is a particular form of border music. Its unique sounds were created or performed by Tejanos living along the Rio Grande border, and by those on the metaphorical border of two distinct cultural worlds. The concept of the border, as used in this study, includes two dimensions, physical and metaphysical.

The physical notion of the border refers to a particular location encompassing those communities along both sides of the Rio Grande. It includes the areas of South Texas and northern Mexico. The latter includes the northern Mexican states of Tamaulipas and Nuevo León.[9] The former encompasses a geographical area of Texas that extends from Corpus Christi in the east to Laredo in the west and from San Antonio in the north to Brownsville in the south. From the Spanish colonial era in the mid-1700s to the mid-1800s, South Texas actually encompassed the region from the Nueces River to the Rio Grande border. According to the historian Armando C. Alonzo, this area was considered a part of the *govierno,* or government, of Nuevo Santander (1797–1824) and later Tamaulipas (1824–45). Spanish/Mexican authorities and colonists, in turn, generally viewed the smaller territory occupying the space from San Antonio to the Louisiana border as Texas. After the signing of the Treaty of Guadalupe Hidalgo in 1848 and the establishment of an international border, San Antonio came to be recognized as part of the South Texas "homeland."[10]

Música tejana, although originating along both sides of the border, was nurtured mostly in South Texas, especially in the twentieth century. Distinct areas of this region contributed in their own ways to the development of its content and style. The lower border region, for instance, became the music's historical breeding ground. It produced the originators of the conjunto ensemble, such as Bruno Villarreal, Narciso Martínez, and Valerio Longoria, and created many of the *corridos* popular in the Tejano community. The San Antonio area became a center of strong support and active promotion of the various forms of música tejana, especially conjunto music.[11] Sam Suniga, archivist and researcher for the Tejano Music Awards, also argues that San Antonio historically has had one of the highest per capita of Tejano composers and song writers in the state.[12] Alice and its surrounding communities, including Corpus Christi on the Gulf Coast, on the other hand, became the creative center of this music.[13]

The Alice area contributed significantly to the shaping of música tejana. In addition to consolidating the conjunto style of playing, musicians from this area created two distinct types of ensembles—the orquesta Tejana and the grupo Tejano. Alice was also the home to Ideal Records, one of the most significant Tejano recording companies of the post–World War II era. From 1946 to the 1960s, it popularized the various forms of música tejana and recorded many of the leading conjuntos, orquestas, and female musicians. In the 1970s Corpus Christi expanded this rich tradition of musical recordings. In the early years of this decade, it became the home of Freddie Records and Hacienda Records, two of the most influential forces in the Tejano music industry during the 1970s and 1980s. Together, these three studios recorded most of the major artists that shaped the contours of música tejana during the twentieth century. Among the most influential musicians recorded by these companies were Lydia Mendoza, Laura y Carmen, Beto Villa, Isidro López, Tony de la Rosa, Conjunto Bernal, Los Relámpagos del Norte, Ramón Ayala y Los Bravos del Norte, Los Fabulosos Cuatro, Carlos Guzman, Laura Canales, Sunny Ozuna, Freddie Martínez, Agustín Ramírez, and Selena.

Música tejana has also been created or performed by Tejano musicians who no longer live in South Texas. Two of the most popular Tejano musical groups of the 1980s, La Sombra and La Mafia, for instance, were from Chicago and Houston, respectively. Despite their distance from the "homeland" region of South Texas, these musicians continued to play border music because they were on the border of two clashing cultures. The border refers to more than simply a geographical or physical space; it also refers to a series of "sites" that are present "wherever two or more cultures edge each other, where people of different races occupy the same territory, where under, lower, middle, and upper classes touch, where the space between two individuals shrinks with intimacy."[14] Those who live on the border, then, include those living the contradiction of being socially and culturally distinct in a society that despises differences. It also applies to those trying to negotiate the ever-present pressures of assimilation and ethnic loyalty. An example of this is the orquesta Tejana of the post–World War II era and the music it developed in response to the Tejano's "middle" position between an unappreciative dominant society and a large group of working-class Mexicanos.[15]

MÚSICA TEJANA AND TEJANO LIFE

Música tejana is a Tejano creation; it has been created, adapted, or performed by Tejanos to meet the musical sensibilities of other Tejanos. As early as the 1920s, Tejanos were demanding that traditional Mexican music reflect their sensibilities by including instruments and singing styles that they could identify with and appreciate. In the early part of the twentieth century, much of this focused on the sounds of the accordion. In the post–World War II years, Tejano musicians continued to adapt Mexican music to meet the musical sensibilities of Tejanos in several ways. First, they incorporated vocal singing in general and female duet singing in particular into música tejana, which had been mostly instrumental. Second, they supported the continued use of the accordion and the *bajo sexto* instrumentation in conjuntos. Third, they incorporated the unique sounds of the saxophone and the trumpet (los pitos, or the horn section, as it came to be known years later) to create the orquesta Tejana. In the second half of the twentieth century, Tejanos continued to adapt this music by adding organs, brass instruments, electric guitars, and keyboards. Additionally, they played and sang the lyrics of these songs in a style unique to them.

Because it is an indigenous creation, música tejana has reflected this community's unique historical experiences in the state. Prior to the middle of the twentieth century, most of these experiences were based on a rural economy, a subordinate social status, a traditional patriarchal culture, and constant conflict with Anglos. In the second half of the century, the Tejano community became more urbanized, acculturated, occupationally diverse, and less patriarchal. Tejanos also experienced better relations with the dominant Anglo group and with mainstream institutions.[16] Música tejana, its various forms and content, reflected these experiences.

Corridos, for instance, played a key role in expressing and reflecting the historical conflict between Anglos and Mexicans in South Texas in the late nineteenth and the early twentieth centuries.[17] Corridos, as several scholars have noted, are narrative ballads that typically tell the story of a hero and are sung to simple tunes.[18] They emerged and developed during a time of profound and violent change along the Rio Grande and in South Texas that embraced the years from 1836 to the 1930s.[19] In many ways, corridos were the product of a subordinate society whose only means of fighting the dominant Anglo powers was symbolic.[20] Representative of this type of corrido and its hero was "The Corrido of Gregorio Cortez," an individual who single-handedly fought the Anglo law and won.[21] After 1930 the corrido remained culturally significant but declined in popularity. It shifted its focus from the cultural hero to the helpless victim. The newer corridos aroused sympathy for the victim and spurred Texas-Mexican communities to take collective action for the benefit of all. The real hero in these corridos was the organized and politically active community as a whole, not the individual.[22]

Canciones, or traditional Mexican songs, reflected both the continuity and change of Mexican culture in the state.[23] Canciones comprised several types of songs and, in addition to corridos, included, among others, *canciones típicas, canciones rancheras,* and *canciones románticas.* Throughout most of the nineteenth century, the canción típica and the corrido dominated the vocal music of Tejanos.[24] By the latter part of the 19th century, the canción romántica, a canción "subtype," emerged and began to compete with canciones típicas and corridos for popularity among Tejanos.[25] In the twentieth century, the canción ranchera emerged as a dominant type of song among Tejanos and, in effect, replaced most other types of songs in the community.

Canciones in general dealt with a variety of themes, most of which focused on nonpolitical topics, especially love. For this reason, they tended to reflect the continuity of traditional Mexican rural culture in the state. They rarely reflected the profound changes within Mexican culture as did corridos. Although canciones tended to reflect the traditional cultural practices of Tejanos, in some cases this was not so. The "treacherous woman" theme popular in the canción ranchera, for instance, consistently portrayed Mexican women as traitorous and unfaithful to men. Reality, however, indicated that men were more likely to be unfaithful. These types of songs did not accurately reflect gender norms in the Tejano community.[26]

Música tejana also reflected the emerging social differences among Tejanos. Instrumental dance music, for instance, reflected the growing class distinctions of this community. The orquestas and grupos reflected the rise of the Tejano lower and middle class, whereas the conjunto and chicano country bands reflected the dominance of the working class.

Likewise, canciones, especially the canción típica and the canción romántica, reflected social differences within the Tejano community. The former was associated with a working-class aesthetic and the latter with a middle-class one. Stated differently, the former was generally of a folk nature, with simple tunes and lyrics, anonymous in composition, and often of ancient origins. The latter was more specifically associated with modern Latin American urban culture and its attraction to European music imported to the Americas, especially Italian music. These distinctions remained among Tejanos until the 1920s, when the canción típica acquired a new label and became known as the canción ranchera. The new ranchera then became the property of the

disfranchised masses on both sides of the border.[27] After World War II the
canción ranchera and the canción romántica solidified their positions within
the social-class structure of the community.[28] Despite these differences, there
was never a rigid dichotomy.[29]

Finally, música tejana reflected the specific ethnic identity of the Tejano
population. This music was more than simply a response to subordination or
a reflection of social differences. For many, it was also an expression of pride
in the Mexicano ethnic identity as it developed along the border and throughout the state of Texas. The use of distinct ingroup labels for this music reflects
this pride. In the nineteenth and early twentieth centuries, and under pressure to assimilate, Tejanos used Spanish-language terms such as *fandango* and
baile to indicate pride in their music. In the post–World War II period, they
called their music by distinct labels such as "conjunto," "orquesta," or, more
generally, "Tex-Mex music" or "música tejana." In the 1960s and 1970s, Tejanos
referred to the diverse styles of music as "la Onda Chicana." Recent uses of the
term "Tejano" and all its derivatives—for example, "Tejano proud," "totally
Tejano," and *puro Tejano* reflect this ethnic pride. "Tejano [in the 1990s] is, as
much as anything, an attitude," argues Héctor Galán, the noted Mexican
American cultural videographer. "It's as if to say: 'This is us.'"[30]

MEXICAN MUSIC AT ITS CORE

Música tejana is mostly Mexican music sung in Spanish. Because it is based
on Mexican music, it is rooted in the history of the Americas. More specifically, its roots lie in the musical heritage of Spain and indigenous America
and in the historical interactions between these two groups.

Música tejana also is intimately related to norteño, or northern Mexican,
culture. Between the 1700s and the mid-1800s, this music was an integral part
of the Spanish and Mexican culture brought by settlers to the northern frontier of Mexico and shaped or influenced by local and regional conditions. In
the period after 1848, however, northern Mexican culture was fractured as a
result of the establishment of the Rio Grande as an international border. Although this culture was similar on both sides of the border, commentators
soon began to make distinctions between the Mexican culture found in South
Texas and the Mexican culture found in northern Mexico. The former eventually came to be known as Tejano culture, the latter as norteño culture. Both,
however, came from one primary source—central Mexico. This phenomenon
helps to explain the presence of similar cultural and musical forms on both
sides of the border.

Unfortunately, little is known about how this music (and the culture of which it is an integral part) was brought to Texas, how it was played, or what instruments were used to play it. The little information available on this music is primarily for that played in the last one hundred years. Thus, many of the following comments are based on the music's development since the latter part of the 1800s.

Generally speaking, Texas-Mexican music has been composed of a diverse and changing repertoire of songs and dances. In the nineteenth and early twentieth centuries, polkas, huapangos, *valses* (waltzes), *schotises* (schottisches), and mazurkas were the major dance forms accompanying música tejana. Since the 1940s new dances, such as boleros, *mambos, danzones,* and cumbias, as well as fox-trots, rhythm and blues, soul, funk, rock, country, and pop, have been added to Tejano music. Tejano music is also composed of a variety of song types, such as canciones típicas and románticas, corridos, and rancheras. These canciones are sung to a variety of beats, including polkas, valses, *baladas,* and cumbias.

Despite this diversity, música tejana in the twentieth century has been based primarily on a polka beat. Polkas, like other Mexican folk dances, such as the vals and the schotis, are European in origin. They were brought to Mexico by the elite in the early nineteenth century and to the Southwest by the German, Bohemian, Italian, and Czech immigrants who settled in Central Texas and northern Mexico during the first half of the nineteenth century. Sometime after the 1850s, Mexican musicians on both sides of the border appropriated these dance forms and made them their own. The French invasion of Mexico in the 1860s most likely reinforced these and other European musical and dance traditions throughout northern Mexico and the southwestern United States.[31]

The polka emerged as a dominant form of Tejano dance music sometime in the early twentieth century, probably as a result of the rise of recorded music and of desires for dancing among the Mexican-origin population. The dominance of the polka is reflected in the historical recordings made by Arhoolie Records in the early 1970s. According to these comprehensive and representative recordings, 37 percent of all conjunto music recorded in the years 1927 to 1941 were polkas. The schotis and vals composed 19 percent and 12 percent of recordings, respectively.[32]

In the post–World War II period, the polka continued its dominance; all types of groups constantly played it. The polka beat also became more popular during these years with the rise of the ranchera Tejana. This type of song is quite different from the ranchera Mexicana. In Mexico, the ranchera is a particular type of rural-based canción that became popular during the early twentieth century.[33] The content of these songs spoke about male notions of honor, love, and life in a rural environment, usually the *rancho*.[34] Mexican rancheras were sung to a variety of beats and played mostly by mariachi groups. The Texas ranchera retained its traditional content, but the rhythms and the type of groups that played this music were different. Unlike the Mexican ranchera, the Tejano version was sung mostly to a polka beat. It was performed by the three major types of Tejano groups: female duets, accordion-based conjuntos, and saxophone-based orquestas.

In the post–World War II period, the ranchera—that is, the polka with lyrics—as well as the instrumental polka, became the dominant form of song and dance in música tejana. The increased demand for dancing among the Tejano population and the easy steps accompanying the polka probably led to its dominance. Despite its popularity, by the end of the twentieth century the cumbia became a strong competitor with the ranchera and emerged as the most popular type of song and dance in the community.[35]

Another essential element of this music is its language. Although a few Texas-Mexican songs have been recorded bilingually or in English only, the vast majority are sung in Spanish.[36] The Spanish language in association with the polka and ranchera keeps this music rooted in Mexican culture. Moreover, Spanish-language music is the most important means for preserving Tejano culture in the United States. Although Spanish-language institutions,

Los Rancheros from Benavides, mid-1940s. *From right:* Fernando Caballero (piano), Efrain Vela (guitar), Leandro Palacios (saxophone), Regelio Benavides (drums), unknown (accordion and second guitar). *Courtesy Oscar Rivera*

such as those associated with the press or broadcast media, are readily found in Tejano communities throughout the state, most of these are aimed at the immigrant population. Tejanos, most of whom are native to the United States, are exposed to and socialized by English-speaking institutions such as public schools, FM radio, or the English print media. Tejano music is the only means currently available within the English-speaking Tejano population that promotes Spanish. For this reason, this music has become crucial for preserving the community's link to its cultural heritage in a country that is rigidly assimilationist and often not appreciative of ethnic differences.

MODERNIZING INFLUENCES AND TOUCHES

Although música tejana is traditionally Mexican music, it has consistently been updated and modernized over the decades. The notion of modernization has changed over the years and has depended, in many cases, on what has been popular in American or Mexican music at different points during the twentieth century. The modernizing of música tejana has occurred in complex ways involving several overlapping processes.[37] One of these was the selective incorporation of American, Caribbean, and Latin American rhythms and instruments into this music. Another included the creative combination of these diverse types of music with Mexican music. Some of these processes will be discussed below to illustrate their complexity. It should be noted that this is only an effort to illustrate the diverse ways in which Mexican music has been modernized, not a comprehensive list of all possibilities.

Incorporation of Different Types of Instruments to Play Traditional Mexican Tunes

Some groups utilized instruments and styles associated with American or Latin American groups to play Mexican music. During the post–World War II era, for instance, Beto Villa and Isidro López utilized the saxophone, trumpet, and other instruments associated with both American and Latin American orquestas of that period. Little Joe, Sunny Ozuna, and Freddie Martínez in the 1960s and 1970s also used saxophones and trumpets but added organs and electric guitars to the instrumental mix. These musical instruments were associated not with orchestras of that era but with rock and soul groups. Grupo musicians of the most recent period—for example, Mazz, Selena, and La Mafia—modified the instrumental mix but generally added keyboards to their ensembles. In the 1970s a few groups, such as Country Roland and Country Roland, Jr., utilized the violin, the steel guitar, and the vocal singing style of country music to perform Tejano tunes. Despite the diversity of instruments associated with various musical styles, these groups continued to play mostly traditional Mexican music. The addition of these instruments, as well as the unique ways of playing them, led to the creation of an evolving Texas-Mexican sound over the decades.

Incorporation of Other Musical Rhythms into Mexican Tunes

Throughout the twentieth century, a few innovative performers took selective rhythms from diverse musical styles and incorporated them into Mexican music. They chose from a wide variety of styles and from the songs, and dances associated with them. Most of these rhythms came from two major strands of popular music in the United States—rhythm and blues and rock and roll—and from Latin America and the Caribbean. These rhythms were creatively incorporated into traditional Mexican tunes, resulting in jazzy boleros, rock-influenced polkas, pop or rap cumbias, bluesy baladas, and big-band-style rancheras.

Occasionally, Tejano musicians provided only touches of music from other styles. Their incorporation into Tejano music was brief enough so that it did not interrupt the beat of the song. Two examples come to mind—one from Letty Guval and the second from Conjunto Bernal. In the mid-1990s, Guval, a popular Tejana performer, recorded a ranchera called "Sentimiento." At key points in the song and for only a few seconds, she incorporated some *banda* rhythms. The banda rhythms were played by a tuba, an instrument not usually associated with música tejana. Because this ranchera had only touches of banda rhythms in it, it was not a banda song, nor was it a tuba-based ranchera.[38]

In the late 1970s Conjunto Bernal recorded a balada with touches of rock and roll. In the song, entitled "Senda Sin Luz," Bernal opened up with a couple of seconds from the Doors' popular song "Riders on the Storm." Bernal continued using the well-known organ rhythms of this popular rock group throughout the song, without losing the flavor of the balada.[39]

Appropriation and Adaptation of Other Rhythms

Most Tejano groups were quite diverse with respect to the music they played. In addition to polkas, rancheras, and baladas, they also appropriated and adapted dance tunes from other musical styles. Again, the tunes appropriated and played by Tejano groups were diverse and varied between groups and across time. Beto Villa, for instance, took a variety of Latin American tunes such as mambos, boleros, danzones, *porros,* and *guarachas* and made them part of música tejana. He also recorded several fox-trots and ragtime tunes.[40] During the 1950s Little Joe and Sunny Ozuna took rhythm and blues and rock and roll songs and played them in such a way that they appealed to Tejanos.[41] In the last several decades, grupos Tejanos such as Mazz, Selena, and Emilio recorded a variety of mariachi, banda, disco, rock, dance, and country music and adapted them to the musical sensibilities of Tejanos. In many cases, American pop songs were sung in Spanish or bilingually, and at times, in English. Conjunto groups were not as experimental as orquestas or grupos, but they occasionally recorded boleros, cumbias, and rock and roll songs.[42]

Although Tejano musicians were quite versatile and both appropriated and played all types of music, non-Mexican tunes composed only a small percentage of the total songs they performed. This distinguished them from Mexican American musicians in other parts of the country. In Los Angeles, for instance, Mexican American groups played mostly English songs and either ignored, rejected, or grudgingly played Mexican music.[43]

Reinvention of Non-Mexican and Mexican Tunes

The more creative artists sometimes recorded tunes from various styles but reinvented them in order to meet the musical sensibilities of Tejanos. They "Tejanoized" this music for their fans.[44] Steve Jordan, for instance, recorded a Buck Owens song, "Together Again," and added the accordion so that it could be danced in Tejano nightclubs.[45] Mingo Saldívar, a conjunto artist popular in the 1960s, took the popular Johnny Cash song "Ring of Fire" and rearranged it as a ranchera, adding bilingual lyrics.[46] Priscila y sus Balas de Plata took the popular disco song "I Will Survive" and transformed it into a cumbia.[47]

Traditional Mexican songs, on occasion, have also been reinvented for a Tejano audience. For instance, in the late 1990s Ricardo Castillon, lead vocalist for La Diferenzia, took a popular Juan Gabriel ballad, "Querida," and rearranged it as a ranchera for Tejano audiences. It was extremely well received throughout the state, as indicated by its constant play on Tejano radio stations in cities such as Corpus Christi and Houston.[48]

Fusion of Ensembles and Styles

Under some circumstances, Tejano groups fused or blended diverse vocal traditions, ensembles, and musical styles. The orquesta and conjunto musicians of the late 1940s and early 1950s combined the vocal singing tradition with the social dance music of Tejanos to create contemporary música tejana. A few bands, such as Conjunto Bernal, the Royal Jesters, and Los Dinos, incorporated three- and four-part harmony into Tejano music in the 1960s and 1970s.[49] In the 1950s, on the other hand, Isidro López blended the conjunto and the orquesta ensembles to create a new sound he called "Texachi" (a mixture of mariachi and Tejano).[50] In the 1970s Roberto Pulido blended the orquesta and the conjunto sounds to create the progressive conjunto.[51] In 1989 Emilio added a new element to this progressive conjunto sound when he incorporated the grupo sound of the synthesizer.[52] In the 1970s Country Roland and others combined the country music of Anglo America with Mexican music to create Chicano country.[53]

Local Rhythms

Not all the musical traditions incorporated or combined with música tejana were "foreign" in origin. A few of them were indigenous to Mexico. The best known of these traditions in the contemporary period, I would argue, is the huapango, a dance form and song type from southern Tamaulipas and northern Vera Cruz. The drums of the early twentieth century likewise were of indigenous origins.

The incorporation, appropriation, adaptation, or fusion of ensembles, styles, instruments, and rhythms, as shown above, has occurred throughout the twentieth century and led to the distinct sounds known as música Tejana.[54] Undoubtedly, more research needs to be conducted on these processes if we are truly to understand its complex nature.

DIVERSITY OF ENSEMBLES

Música tejana comprises several musical ensembles, not simply conjuntos. In other words, different types of groups using particular mixes of instruments and vocalists play this music. It includes vocal groups of varying sizes and five distinct ensembles—conjuntos, progressive conjuntos, orquestas, grupos, and country bands.[55] Most of this music is meant for dancing. The only exception to this is the vocal tradition. Music of this tradition, unlike the other forms discussed later in the book, is sit-down or listening music, not dancing music. Historically, singing has taken place in intimate family settings, in theatrical productions, and at various community gatherings.[56]

"Vocal singing," as the name implies, was based on individuals or groups singing a variety of songs, including lyrical hymns, children's songs, *canciones de amor,* corridos, and rancheras. The number of individuals who have sung these lyrics has varied between one and three: the solista, dueto, and trio. Prior to the 1940s, singing in Texas was usually a male-dominated form and was accompanied by a guitar, violin, or, on occasion, accordion. After the 1940s, females were added to the mix of singers. Female singers, both duetas and solistas, were accompanied by a variety of instruments, including accordions and saxophones or trumpets. Beginning in the late 1940s, the vocal singing popularized by *las mujeres* (women) was incorporated into existing musical ensembles such as the conjunto or orquesta. This, in effect, led to its decline as a viable tradition in Tejano music. Tejanas were excluded from the recording industry, since most vocal singers for orquestas and conjuntos were male.[57]

Although música tejana encompasses the vocal singing tradition, it is mostly made up of musical ensembles devoted to social dance music. Over the last century and a half, five distinct ensembles have played Texas-Mexican music—orquestas, conjuntos, progressive conjuntos, grupos, and country bands. The Spanish terms "orquesta," "conjunto," and "grupo" generally make reference to a group or association of musicians, but, in Texas, each term has a distinct meaning.[58]

The orquesta of the nineteenth century was based primarily on string instruments, such as the violin, psaltery (an ancient musical instrument resembling the zither, usually having thirty to forty strings over a shallow horizontal soundboard and played with pick and fingers), *vihuela* (a medieval type of guitar), mandolin, guitar, and contrabass. Occasionally, other instruments, such as the trumpet, trombone, clarinet, or tuba, were used. If brass or wind instruments were used with the former, the ensemble was called an *orquesta típica*. If only brass and wind instruments were used, they were *orquestas de pitos* (wind/brass orchestras) and called bandas. Those that used only string instruments were known as *orquestas de cuerda* (string orchestras). Bandas emerged in the latter part of the nineteenth century; they were not as popular as the other types of orquestas, especially among Tejanos. The other two types of orquestas, on the other hand, were readily found among both elite and working-class groups in Mexico and South Texas during the 1800s. Orquestas in general, however, came to be identified with the middle classes in Mexico by the latter part of the nineteenth century and in Texas by the early twentieth century.[59] In the post–Word War II era, orquestas changed as some musical instruments were either dropped or replaced by new ones.[60] In the two decades after World War II, saxophones, among other instruments, became extremely important in the modern orquestas. Organs and electric guitars were added to this particular type of ensemble in the 1960s and 1970s.

The conjunto was divided into two structurally distinct groups. One of these was known as the traditional conjunto, the other as the progressive conjunto. The difference between these two types of conjuntos was not in the type of music they played but in the type of instruments they used. The traditional conjunto was based primarily on the one-row or two-row button accordion; it also typically used two guitars, one of which was a bajo sexto, and a drum. Several theories as to the origins of the use of the accordion have been proposed. One of these is that German and Czech immigrants who settled in San Antonio introduced it to Mexicans in the mid-1800s. The popularity of this instrument then spread southward. Manuel Peña, a scholar of conjunto music, says that most likely German immigrants introduced the instrument to Mexicans in Monterrey in the same time period and that it traveled northward.[61] Another scholar, Chris Strachwitz, states that it was probably introduced to Mexicans in the Rio Grande Valley during the same time and that it traveled both north and south.[62] Still another scholar argues that it came by way of the Gulf Coast.[63] The other important instrument of the traditional conjunto was the bajo sexto, a twelve-string bass guitar. Scholars are unclear about how the bajo sexto reached Texas. Unlike accordions, which for the most part are made in Germany or Italy, bajo sextos are made in Texas and Mexico.[64]

The progressive conjunto adds one or more instruments to the basic four-instrument ensemble. Among the instruments added, especially in the last three decades of the twentieth century, were pitos (a set of saxophones and/or trumpets) and keyboards (organ or synthesizer). Roberto Pulido initiated the progressive conjunto in the 1970s when he added two saxophones to his traditional conjunto group. Emilio Navaira added a new sound to the progressive conjunto ensemble in 1989 when he deleted the horns and added keyboards, especially the synthesizer.

The grupo Tejano, a relatively new innovation, is anchored in keyboards, especially the organ and synthesizer. Additionally, it utilizes a variety of string and wind instruments, drums, and vocalists. Prior to the early 1990s, these types of groups did not utilize the accordion in their music. The grupo Tejano is slightly different from the grupo phenomenon in Mexico. In Mexico grupos are keyboard-driven as in Texas, but the musicians specialize in romantic ballads or in cumbias.[65] In Texas, the grupos do not specialize in baladas only; they also sing and play a variety of other tunes, such as cumbias, rancheras, and country and pop songs. Their repertoire, in other words, is more diverse than that of grupos Mexicanos. Grupos Tejanos originated in the 1960s with the formation of Los Fabulosos Cuatro, but they did not emerge as a powerful force until the 1980s. The number of grupos expanded significantly during the last two decades of the twentieth century. Among the most popular grupos Tejanos in the 1990s were Mazz, La Mafia, and Selena y Los Dinos.

Chicano country bands are unique to música tejana. These groups have at least three general characteristics. First, they are small, with between four and six persons in the ensemble. They also depend on two important instruments for their sound—the violin and steel guitar. Second, the vast majority of vocalists sing with a country twang. Third, these bands play traditional country music and traditional Mexican music—but in their own style. For the most part, they "Mexicanize" traditional country music and "countrify" traditional Mexican songs, such as "Los Laureles" or "Las Margaritas." The former is done by singing the lyrics in Spanish or bilingually, the latter by playing Mexican tunes with the aforementioned instruments and by singing them with a country twang.

Little is known about Chicano country bands or where they originated. The earliest recording of country music by a Tejano artist was in 1949. In that year, Johnny Herrera from Corpus Christi recorded the country-music standard "Jealous Heart" in English and in Spanish for the Melco label. Two years later, he recorded the same song as "Corazón Celoso" for Decca Records. Herrera's recording, however, was done with saxophones, trumpets, and the accordion—instruments associated with the orquesta style popularized by Beto Villa in the late 1940s.[66] He did not utilize the steel guitar and violin of traditional country groups.

Chicano country bands—those that sang with a country twang and used the violin and steel guitar in their recordings—probably originated sometime in the 1950s or 1960s in the Lower Rio Grande Valley and became popular in the following two decades.[67] One of these groups, the Country Roland Band, became extremely well known in the early 1970s and influenced other Tejano groups, such as Rudy Tee González y Sus Reno Bops, Snowball & Co., Roberto Pulido y Los Clásicos, and Mazz.[68]

The popularity of these ensembles has varied over time as a result of important social forces, such as shifting aesthetics within the Tejano population, the introduction of new technologies, urbanization, and commercialization. More will be said about these groups and their changes over time in the following chapters.

CONCLUSION

Música tejana is a particular form of modernized Mexican music that developed in one region of the state and was created or performed by Tejanos for Tejanos. The core of música tejana for most of the twentieth century has been the Mexican polka. Over the decades Tejano artists have incorporated other influences and rhythms into this music to fashion a sound that reflects the sensibilities and experiences of Mexican Americans who have lived in Texas. The following chapters document the multiplicity of forces contributing to the emergence and evolution of these different ensembles, genres, and styles in the twentieth century. They also explore how this music is related to the many issues facing the Tejano community. Some of the most important issues reflected in música tejana are gender relations, ethnic identity, racial injustice, and the impact of immigration and Americanization. Although references will be made to nineteenth- and early twentieth-century developments, this book will concentrate on the period from 1927 to 2000. Several dimensions of Tejano music will be explored, including the following: performance practices and contexts—manner of performing and places where Tejano groups have played; stylistic features—how musicians play the instruments; vocal combinations—the number of singers in an ensemble; instrumental combinations—the number and use of wind, brass, string, and percussive instruments; song types—canción, ranchera, balada, etcetera; and dance forms—polkas, rancheras, huapangos, and cumbias.

Chapter 2

Diversity and Change
in the Initial Recordings, 1927—41

In the late 1920s, música tejana was commercialized by major labels for a national audience. This phenomenon lasted for approximately thirteen years, from 1927 to 1941. By 1941 the major labels abandoned this music because of its limited market and the increasing scarcity of materials for the making of records during the war years. No additional recordings were made until after World War II. Little is known about these initial recordings or about the musicians and the types of songs and styles of music they recorded. Less is known about the changes that occurred in this music over time. This chapter will shed some light on the diversity and changes in recorded Texas-Mexican music from the 1920s to the early 1940s.

THE INITIAL RECORDINGS, 1927–41

In the 1920s national recording companies such as Victor, Brunswick/Vocalion, Columbia, and Okeh began to record Texas-Mexican music in particular and Mexican music in general. Their hope was to profit from this emerging

industry by targeting Mexican-origin audiences in the United States who preferred listening and dancing to their own music. They employed regional
talent scouts to identify local groups or individuals for recording purposes.
The majority were often associated with music stores or furniture stores, where
record players and phonographs were sold.[1] In the first phase of initial recordings, largely from the late 1920s to the early 1940s, these companies recorded
hundreds of songs.[2] Most of them remain unaccounted for, but in the last
several decades a significant number have been found and preserved. At least
fifty-five of these songs have been reissued as a five-volume set of historical
recordings by the Arhoolie Record Company (see appendix 2).

These initial recordings reflect the diversity of música tejana in the early
twentieth century. They show that different types of musical groups and individuals used a wide range of instruments to play a diverse number of songs
and dances during this period. Despite this surface diversity, only three fundamental types of musical ensembles existed in this period: vocal singing with
guitar accompaniment, orquestas of various sizes and styles, and rudimentary
conjunto groups.

DIVERSITY OF MÚSICA TEJANA

Vocal Singing

Vocal singing was strongly represented in the initial recordings. Historically
this had been the dominant form of musical tradition in the Tejano community, primarily because of its low cost and simplicity.[3] Individuals, usually
accompanied by one or more instruments, such as a guitar, violin, or accordion, sang a variety of songs, including canciones típicas and románticas,
rancheras, and corridos.[4] Rarely did dancing accompany vocal singing. The
texts of these songs, in many cases, reflected the political, social, and cultural
experiences of Mexican-origin individuals on both sides of the border.

Although many types of songs existed within música tejana, argues Manuel
Peña, the canción típica and the corrido predominated in the latter part of
the nineteenth century. This changed by the end of the century due to the
rise of the canción romántica, a particular type of canción típica.[5] In the
twentieth century, the canción ranchera emerged as a dominant type of song
among Tejanos.[6]

The canción típica, or lyrical song, had been around for centuries. It was a
rather diffuse genre that seemed to be in constant flux. It subsumed a broad
array of forms and themes just as it often merged with other genres, especially
dances, such as the bolero, vals, and polka.[7]

The canción típica focused on several themes, ranging from unrequited love to critiques of the various ways of modern life—for instance, new modes of dress. One of the most popular themes, as noted earlier, was that of the treacherous woman.[8] However, not all Tejana women willingly accepted this theme. Lydia Mendoza, for example, occasionally challenged the negative image of women and provided a female perspective: in some of her songs, men, not women, were the treacherous ones.[9] For instance, in "Mal Hombre," a song recorded in 1934, Mendoza calls her lover a coldhearted man because of the way he took advantage of her innocence and then callously left her. "Mal hombre," she sang, "tan ruin es tu alma que no tiene nombre / eres un canalla, eres un malvado / eres un mal hombre." (Coldhearted man / your soul is so vile it has no name / you are despicable, you are evil / you are a coldhearted man.) She further claims that all men treat women poorly: "Luego hiciste conmigo lo que todos / los que son como tú con las mujeres." (Then you treated me like all men / of your kind treat women.) Men, in other words, were not to be trusted. The theme of male treachery was also covered in another of her songs, "Pájarito Herido" (Wounded Bird). In this song she talks about finding a wounded bird that reminded her of the hurt she had experienced recently after falling in love with someone who was full of flattery and deceit ("un hombre salamero y engañoso"). Although she finally broke off the relationship, his unfaithfulness left her disillusioned and brokenhearted.[10]

Canciones románticas, unlike canciones típicas, did not have such a negative view of women. Like their counterparts, they dealt with a range of themes, from unrequited love to passionate betrayal, but they were more muted in their treatment of unfaithful female lovers.[11] For the most part, then, canciones focused on nonpolitical themes and emphasized themes of unrequited love. Although a few displayed elements of change—that is, they reflected the increasing importance of romantic love in the Tejano community—the majority reflected the continuity of traditional Mexican rural culture in the U.S. Southwest.[12]

Corridos, on the other hand, were songs that demanded to be heard. They usually expressed and reflected the economic upheavals experienced by Mexicans and the interethnic conflict between Anglos and Mexicans.[13] In most cases, their primary emphasis was on the virile, male hero. This was especially the case in the late 1800s and early 1900s. One example of a well-known corrido hero was Gregorio Cortez, a simple Mexican worker who killed an Anglo sheriff in self-defense. In 1901 Cortez eluded the much-hated Texas Rangers for several days before he was captured, tried, and eventually pardoned.[14]

Corridos evolved out of the romance tradition imported from Spain by the Spanish conquistadores and settlers.[15] In Texas, however, the corrido emerged as a viable and distinct form in the years after 1836 as a result of the coming of Anglo settlers and the emerging pattern of violence between them and Mexicans.[16] It became an important type of canción by the first decade of the twentieth century.[17] Its height of popularity was the period after the Mexican Revolution and during the rise of nationalism in art during the latter part of the 1920s.[18] The popularity of the corrido corresponded with immigration to the United States, the rise of Spanish-language radio, and the recording of Texas-Mexican music by national companies. The initial recordings reflected its dominant position within música tejana. Approximately 38 percent of all the songs in Arhoolie's five-volume set of reissued songs, for instance, were corridos.[19]

Vocal singing was popular with elites, with the working classes, and with religious groups. Elite forms of vocal singing were common in operas and operettas and usually performed in concert halls. None of this music was represented in the historical recordings. Popular or working-class forms of vocal singing were performed in open-air pavilions or in common gatherings in rural and urban areas. *Trovadores* (troubadours) and *cantadores* (songsters) popularized this form of music by traveling from market to market singing their songs and selling cheaply printed copies of their lyrics to those willing to buy them. These roving songsters accompanied the traveling merchants on the Chihuahua and Santa Fe Trails and other trade routes. It is very possible that the increase in trade after the Mexican American war led to an increase in the number of trovadores and cantadores that visited Mexican-origin villages and towns in the Southwest.[20] Vocal singing was occasionally a part of traveling entertainment groups, theatrical companies, and circuses. The latter two had acting groups such as clowns, comics, and acrobats as well as musical groups. Some of these performed instrumental songs, others sang. Historian Arnoldo De Léon refers to some vocal music in a theatrical company that visited San Antonio in 1888, a Monterrey Band that visited Corpus Christi in 1884, and some musical concerts that took place in these cities in the 1880s.[21]

In some cases, villages, towns, and families had their own *cantantes* who sang at family celebrations or public gatherings such as *mercados, fiestas,* and *cantinas.*[22] Their numbers most likely increased over time. Vocal singing was likewise popular in religious circles. Churches, for instance, organized choirs to sing Latin lyrical hymns and secular songs at church ceremonies or in religious dramas and plays. Musically oriented religious dramas, such as *los pastores* and *las pastorelas,* however, were popular only until the turn of the century.[23]

The historical recordings bear out the dominance of secular vocal singing as a musical tradition in the Tejano community. Approximately 52 percent of all the songs found in them were sung.[24] The vast majority of these recordings were by male-based vocal duets, such as Santos Guerrero y Quirino García ("Buscare Quien Me Consuele"), Flores y Montalvo ("La Cucaracha"), Pedro Rocha and Lupe Martínez ("Corrido de Pennsylvania"), and Andres Berlanga y Francisco Montalvo ("Ella es Mi Delirio").[25]

Among the recordings was one by a female artist who became extremely influential and popular among the working-class Tejano population, Lydia Mendoza. From 1928 to 1934 Mendoza recorded with her family in a band called Cuarteto Carta Blanca. Gradually she assumed a leading role in the family group. In 1934 she went solo and, as noted earlier, recorded "Mal Hombre," her biggest hit of this early period and one of the most endearing songs of the twentieth century. During the late 1930s, she acquired the name "La Cancionera de los Pobres" (The Songstress of the Poor). In her early recordings, Mendoza usually sang to the sole accompaniment of her own twelve-string guitar.[26]

Another pioneer recording artist of significance was Andres Berlanga. He started his singing and recording career in the 1930s with his partner, Francisco Montalvo. Unlike most other artists, especially those involved in duetos or trios, he recorded with an accordion. In some respects, he was part of a new generation of artists who laid the stylistic basis for the emergence of what later came to be called conjunto music.[27]

Orquestas

Close to forty different orquestas were represented in historical recordings (see table 1). They ranged in size from two to fifteen members and included trios, quartets, small string groups, and full-fledged ensembles.[28]

Some of these groups recorded vocal music, but most recordings were of instrumental dance pieces. Their repertoire was diverse and included valses, huapangos, polkas, mazurkas, *pasodobles, marchas, danzas,* schotises, *sones,* one-steps, and a few other lesser-known dances.[29]

Orquestas initially appeared in Mexico in the 1600s, but they were not associated with social dancing until the latter part of the eighteenth century. Over the centuries at least three distinct types of orquestas have appeared in Mexico and South Texas—orquestas típicas, orquestas de cuerda, and orquestas de pitos.

Orquestas típicas initially appeared at public shows in Mexico known as "Coliseos de Comedios" as early as the mid–seventeenth century. In these

TABLE 1
ORQUESTAS TEJANAS, 1927–41, BY TYPE

Trios:

Andres Huesca Y Su Trio Huracan
El Trio Alegre
El Trio Crudo
Jose Maria Arrendondo Trio
Trio Alamo

Cuartetos:

Cuarteto Carta Blanca
Cuarteto de Cuerdo de F. Facio
Cuarteto Monterrey

Quintetos:

Eulalio Sanchez y Su Quinteto Mexicano
Quinteto Los Desvelados
Quinteto Típico Mexicano

Mariachis:

Mariachi Acosta
Mariachi Coculense
Mariachi Coculense Rodrigues
Mariachi Tapatio de Juan Marmolejo

General Orquestas (size/instruments unknown):

Santiago Morales
Los Alegres
Medina River Boys
Trovadores Tamaulipecos
Los Norteños
Los Desvelados
Los Cuatezones
Santos Guerrero Y Quirino García

Orquestas:

Orquesta Acosta-Rosette
Jóse Perches Enríquez Orquesta
Orquesta Fronteriza
Orquesta Mexicana Calvillo
Típica Martínez
Orquesta de Alfredo M. Garza
Banda Chihuahua
Orquesta de Guadalupe Acosta

TABLE 1 *(cont.)*

ORQUESTAS TEJANAS, 1927–41, BY TYPE

Orquestas:

Orquesta Tomas Nuñez
Orquesta Colonial
Orquesta Pajaro Azul
Orquesta del Norte
Orquesta de la Familia Ramos
Eva Garza con Orquesta de Manuel S. Acuna
Emilio Caceres y Su Orquesta del Club Aguila

Source: Texas-Mexican Border Music, Vol. 5: The String Bands—End of a Tradition, Folklyric Records LP 9007, n.d.; *Texas-Mexican Border Music, Vol I: An Introduction, 1930–60,* Folklyric Records LP 9008, n.d.; *Mexican American Border Music, Vol. 4: Orquestas Típicas—The First Recordings, 1926–38,* Arhoolie CD 7017, 1996.

popular theaters, small companies would put on performances that included singers, dancers, comics, and musicians. The latter would interpret traditional Spanish songs and dances such as *coplas, décimas,* and romances. They would also occasionally perform local and regional songs and dances. The small orquestas usually included violins, harps, guitars, flutes, oboes, and sometimes cornets.[30]

Over the next two centuries the small orquestas were appropriated by the indigenous and mestizo population and mixed with indigenous traditions, such as the *sones Mexicanos.* Their appropriation and syncretization eventually led to the development of distinct regional musical ensembles and styles. By the mid-1850s regional orquestas típicas, based on what were at that time known as authentic folk instruments, songs, and dances, became extremely popular throughout the various parts of Mexico and the American Southwest. These musical ensembles often consisted of whatever instruments were available. The majority, however, utilized mostly string instruments, such as violins, psalteries, Hawaiian guitars, bajo sextos, harps, *guitarones,* and mandolins.[31] Occasionally, a wind instrument, such as a clarinet or flute, was used.[32] In most cases, the lead instrument was a violin, especially if the orquesta performed at an event where dancing took place. Because of their popularity, orquestas típicas were usually associated with peasant and working-class events.[33]

In the second half of the nineteenth century, the folk-based orquestas típicas were appropriated by the elite and made part of their middle-class culture. This process occurred largely under the Porfirio Díaz regime in the 1880s. During these years Mexico experienced a mild form of "romantic" nationalism that encouraged the ruling elite to flirt with folk forms, including music. This eventually led to the financial support of a nationalistic popular music based on the regional folk-based orquesta típica. "State-supported" orquestas often used both regional folk instruments, such as the mandolin, harp, *marimba,* psaltery, violin, guitar, and guitarone, as well as classical instruments, such as the violin, cello, contrabass, clarinet, trumpet, and other brass. In order to appeal to the masses and probably to give them a stamp of authenticity, these musicians occasionally wore traditional folk outfits such as the *charro* costume.[34]

Orquestas típicas appeared in some of the larger cities of Texas during the late 1800s and early 1900s. In El Paso, for instance, at least four such orquestas appeared between 1893 and 1917: Santiago Olguin Laredo and his Band (1893), Trinidad Concha's Band (1907), Rito Medina's Band (1916), and Raymundo S. González's Band (1917). Concha's Band was the best-organized orquesta of that city in the early 1900s and was Porfirio Díaz's "touring band." By 1907 it had forty members. Its repertoire comprised classical tunes enjoyed by both Anglo and Mexican elites. The band also most likely performed some type of folk music but in the style appreciated by "la gente decente" of both ethnic groups.[35]

At least three other cities had large orquestas during the late nineteenth and early twentieth century—Brownsville, Laredo, and San Antonio. For more than twenty years, from 1876 to the 1890s, one of the most popular musical groups in Brownsville was the Mexican Brass Band.[36] Laredo had at least one group that toured throughout South Texas—Gloria's Band. In 1883 it had seven instruments: one lead violin, one flute, one cornet, one guitar, two French horns, and one contrabass.[37] Finally, at least one orquesta played at the annual ball organized by the Mexican Social Club of San Antonio during the 1880s and 1890s—Pablo Persio's.[38] Although very little is known about these orquestas and their repertoires, the limited evidence suggests that they contained nationalistic elements and appealed primarily to the class-based aesthetic sensibilities of the urban Mexican-origin elite.

Orquestas de cuerda were generally smaller and included mostly string instruments, such as violins and guitars of various sizes. At least two specific types have historically been present in the Tejano community: *jarocho* groups and mariachis. The former used the harp with other string instruments and originated in Vera Cruz in the nineteenth century. The latter, prior to the 1920s, was usually composed of Hawaiian guitars, mandolins, and violins. Trumpets were added to the mix in the 1920s. Many people think of mariachi music as the most typical of all Mexican regional styles. In fact, its origin lies with the French occupation of Mexico in the 1860s. One author has suggested that the French obtained the services of these musicians for all their festivities, especially weddings.[39] "Mariachi" is derived from the French word for "marriage." During the late nineteenth and early twentieth centuries the term referred to any kind of orchestra performing at a wedding.[40]

On occasion, the orquestas de cuerda were quite large; in the early twentieth century there were a few female-only groups. Houston-based La Orquesta Típica Torres, directed by Albino Torres and managed by Curtis Farrington, had at least fourteen male members in 1928, most of whom played various sizes of guitars.[41] A second example is the Orquesta Típica Laredo, a twelve-member group that utilized only string instruments, such as the guitar, mandolin, violin, and *tololoche* (contrabass). This orquesta was based in Laredo, Texas, and became popular during the late 1920s and early 1930s.[42] A women's musical group from Houston, Texas, whose name is unknown, appears in a 1933 photograph sitting together with their instruments and wearing white dresses, hats, and medium-high heels. This nine-member group is shown holding a variety of string instruments, including mandolins, guitars, and banjos.[43]

Orquestas de pitos, commonly called bandas, were usually large ensembles composed of wind instruments, such as trumpets, trombones, clarinets, saxophones, French horns, flutes, and tubas. Bandas, like orquestas típicas, were popularized and supported by the elites of the Porfirio Díaz regime during the 1880s. They were initially used for ceremonial purposes, especially parades, patriotic festivities, and international concerts. This began to change by the end of the nineteenth century due to the increasing demand for social dance music by working-class communities on both sides of the border. One of the most popular Mexican bandas in the late 1800s was the Eighth Cavalry Mexican Band. Consisting of over sixty musicians and under the direction of Encarnación Payen, this group played at the World's Industrial and Cotton Centennial Exposition that opened in New Orleans, Louisiana, on December 16, 1884.[44]

Bandas also began to appear in South Texas during the latter part of the nineteenth century. Brownsville, for instance, was the home of the Mexican Brass Band. As early as 1876, this banda played for the city's centennial.[45] By 1891 it had at least twenty instruments—four clarinets, one alto, one tenor, and one baritone saxophone, three cornets, three euphoniums, three valve trombones, two tubas, one bass drum, and one snare drum. Another group called the Eighth Calvary Brass Band played in San Antonio in 1884.[46] The popularity of military brass bands was not limited to Mexico or South Texas. They were quite popular throughout the United States. John Philip Sousa, for instance, had one of the most popular brass bands in the United States at the turn of the century.[47]

On occasion, and probably because of increasing immigration into the state, churches and work places in Texas established their own bandas in the early part of the twentieth century. The Southern Pacific Lines, for instance, established one such group in Houston during the mid-1920s. Composed of about fifty members, the Southern Pacific Lines Band included many Mexican-origin musicians who brought their talent with them from Mexico or the rural areas of Texas. Our Lady of Guadalupe Church in Houston also established its own large banda of about twenty members in the 1920s. It played for church functions and entertained many residents during this decade.[48]

The different types of orquestas—típicas, de cuerda, and de pitos—played for a variety of social and political events. Elite-based orquestas played at "society" parties, at private social balls organized by social, literary, and other nonpolitical organizations, or in large concert halls in small, medium-sized, or large urban areas.[49] Working-class-based orquestas played at various locations where dancing was part of the celebration.[50] Before the 1870s, they played at weddings or at a variety of large, boisterous, and violence-prone celebrations that at times lasted for several days and were attended by all sectors of the community.[51] After the 1870s, these ensembles played in open-air pavilions, in the streets, and in makeshift platforms during *ferias* (fairs held in fall after the harvest season), national holidays, *fiestas patrias,* anniversaries of special events (for example, the fall of Aztecs in June), or at fandangos.[52] For example, Aurelio L. Solis's Mexican Orchestra played in San Antonio for a Cinco de Mayo celebration in 1896.[53] In most cases, however, only orquestas típicas and orquestas de cuerda were used for dancing. These orquestas thus became associated with popular dance music for almost every social strata of Mexican society on both sides of the border from the 1880s to the 1930s. Despite the existence of various types of orquestas, only those utilizing strings and a mixture of strings and pitos were represented in these historical recordings. For some unknown reason, bandas were not recorded by the major labels during this period.[54]

Típicas were the most popular orquestas, as indicated by the recordings. Most of these were meant for the elite, such as the Orquesta Colonial, El Trio Alegre, Cuarteto Monterrey, and Orquesta Fronteriza.[55] Others, such as the Orquesta Pájaro Azul and the Cuarteto Carta Blanca, appealed to the working-class Tejano population. The former recorded the well-known canción "La Cucaracha" in the mid-1930s; the latter recorded the popular song "A Mi Juana" in 1928 and consisted of the popular Mendoza family.[56]

Several mariachi groups also were represented in these recordings, including the Mariachi Coculense Rodríguez and the Mariachi Acosta. The former recorded the song "La Cuatro Milpas," the latter "Ojitos Chino y Negros."[57]

Jarocho groups rarely recorded during the early twentieth century. This is borne out in the historical recordings. Only one jarocho group is found in them: Andres Huesca y Su Trio Huracán. This group apparently was very popular in South Texas and toured this area during the late 1930s and 1940s. It recorded the popular song "El Jarabe Veracruzano."[58]

Occasionally, individuals acquired respect and popularity because of their exceptional ability to play string, wind, or percussive instruments. Historically, this was usually limited to individuals who played a variety of instruments in concert halls or in theaters. Virtuosos in piano, violin, and guitar were the most popular musicians heard at these concerts, or *concertos.* But these types of elite musicians were not represented in the historical recordings. Two working-class musicians, however, were featured. Both, apparently, were violinists from San Antonio, El Ciego Melquiades and Santiago Morales. El Ciego recorded extensively and played many dances, parties, and public arenas, such as the Alamo Plaza. Morales, known as El Ranchero on his records, played violin as well as string bass. He was a better-trained musician than El Ciego.[59]

Conjuntos

In addition to vocal singing and orquestas, early recordings also included conjunto groups. Conjuntos during these years were usually composed of one or two, or occasionally three, male individuals. The primary instrument in this ensemble was the accordion. Although several theories as to the origins of the use of the accordion have been proposed, anecdotal information from the early twentieth century suggests that the Germans introduced it to Mexicans in Central Texas.[60] The experience of Flaco Jiménez's father suggests that the German accordion was introduced to Mexicans in San Antonio at least by the first decade of the twentieth century. Two scholars, for instance, note, "Every Saturday night they [German immigrants] held dances where German families would polka to accordion bands, dressed in Tyrolean hats and lederhosen. The most famous of the German settlements was New Braunfels, near San Antonio, and as a child Santiago Senior used to creep up to the high walls around those houses and listen to the German accordionists playing polka. He knew that was the kind of music he wanted to play. When he was old enough to purchase a button accordion, it was polka music that he, and others like him, adapted into the norteño idiom."[61]

The conjunto ensemble during the late nineteenth and early twentieth centuries was flexible and its instrumentation undetermined. In addition to the accordion, it also consisted of whatever other instrument was available: a guitar of some sort, a violin, a *tambora del rancho* (a crudely made drum), or a mandolin. Throughout its early history, from the mid-1800s to the early 1900s, conjunto music was instrumental in nature. Vocal lyrics were not added until the 1940s.[62]

Conjuntos, like orquestas, played a variety of dance tunes introduced into Mexico from Europe during the eighteenth and nineteenth centuries. Some of the most popular dances were mazurkas, polkas, valses, one-steps, two-steps, huapangos, and schotises. Conjunto groups performed at community celebrations, such as fandangos, community bailes, fiestas patrias, and special events. They also played at *bailes de regalos* or *bailes de negocio*. The former acquired their name from the customary practice of requiring young men to offer their female partners gifts of candy, sweet bread, peanuts, or other treats for the privilege of dancing with them. These types of events ceased to exist by 1930. The latter were based on an exchange of money for dancing. Unaccompanied women would usually come to a cantina or bar where men would pay to dance with them. The establishment's owner usually kept a part of the money to pay the musicians. Fights, drunkenness, and prostitution were common at these events. The unsavory aspects of this exchange relationship quickly gave bailes de negocio in particular and cantinas in general a negative reputation in the Tejano community.[63]

A few conjunto groups were represented in the historical recordings. Some of the most important were R. de León and L. Villalobos, Estanislado Salazar y Hermanos Mier, Roberto Rodríguez y Clemente Mendoza, Flores y Montalvo, Narciso Martínez, Jesús Casiano, Bruno Villarreal and Santiago "Flaco" Jiménez.[64] Little information is available on the first four groups. The other four were part of a group of musicians who popularized the emerging conjunto sound. They were, as Peña notes, the forerunners of this music.[65]

From 1929 to 1941 these accordionists competed for audiences. R. de León and L. Villalobos made the first conjunto recording in 1929, a vals called "A Palerno." Unlike later recording artists, de Léon (his first name is not known) used a piano accordion. Chris Strachwitz argues that the particular sound made by the piano accordion was very popular in restaurants and in the *salones de baile* (dance halls) of that period. "His sound, however, was not to be the future sound of Norteño accordion music," he stated. "Norteño and conjunto music was almost entirely created, first on a one, then a two, and finally on a three row, button, diatonic accordion."[66]

The emerging conjunto sound was initiated by several artists. Bruno Villarreal, who by the late 1920s was known as "El Azote del Valle" (The Scourge from the Valley), was born in La Grulla, Texas, a small community in the southern part of the state, and was nearly blind. He originally played a two-row button accordion but switched to a piano accordion at some point in his career. Rodríguez began to record in the early 1930s. Jesús Casiano, professionally known as "El Gallito" (the Little Rooster), began to record in the mid-1930s.[67] Narciso Martínez began to play the one-row button accordion in 1928 but did not record until 1935. By then he used a two-row button accordion. He recorded commercially for Bluebird Records from 1935 to 1940. His first recording, a polka entitled "La Chicharronera," became an immediate success.[68] He soon recorded other songs that became regional hits. Martínez eventually came to be known as the father of conjunto because of the popularity of his songs and his influence. He laid the basis for the emerging style, as will be discussed later, and began to play in a style liked by the Tejano working class.[69] Santiago "Flaco" Jiménez was the second most popular conjunto performer in Texas. He began to record commercially in 1936 and continued recording into the early 1960s. Jiménez, unlike Martínez, was raised in the urban environment of San Antonio, Texas. He had a soft style to his accordion and was less skilled in his playing than Martínez.[70]

CHANGES IN MÚSICA TEJANA

The early recordings tell us much about the diversity of música tejana but little about how it changed over time. Evidence from several sources suggests that the Tejano community's appreciation of these musical ensembles and the styles they played varied within certain regions and across time. Changing musical tastes in combination with other social forces eventually led to the decreased popularity of orquestas, to the increased appreciation of vocal singing, and to the growing popularity of conjuntos. These developments gave Tejano music a distinct identity and a special meaning to those who experienced it.

Orquestas
Orquestas declined in popularity largely because of changing musical tastes within the population in general and the increased interest in the accordion in particular. The decline occurred most rapidly among those orquestas that sounded very European and reflected a "genteel tradition." It also occurred among the orquestas de cuerda of various sizes.[71] Among the small string quartets and trios that became less popular over time were Quarteto Carta

Blanca and El Trio Alegre. Larger orquestas, especially those using such instruments as the Hawaiian guitar, harp, violin, and mandolin, also declined
in popularity. This is especially true in the case of the Medina River Boys,
with their "earthy" style and Hawaiian guitar, or of groups that played jarocho
and mariachi music. Those that used Hawaiian guitars and mandolin or violins were rarely listened to after 1930.[72]

Ironically, mariachi music decreased in popularity even as new wind instruments were added to the ensemble. In the early decades of the twentieth
century, most mariachis were composed of almost any instruments available.
An example of this phenomenon is Mariachi Acosta, discussed above. The
majority of these groups, however, utilized mostly string instruments, especially violins. Among these were the following groups: Los Trovadores
Tamaulipecos, Los Montaneses de Alamo, and Los Cítricos de Montemorelos,
from Monterrey.[73] In the 1920s a few mariachi groups changed and began to
incorporate the flute. The following decade, others added the trumpet. This
led to a wide diversity in sound.[74] Despite these innovations, the mariachi
ensemble and the music it played became less popular in Texas during the
third decade of the twentieth century, probably because of its failure to play
the dance tunes desired by Tejanos.

The decline in the popularity of orquestas was so widespread that even
individual string musicians, such as the violinists El Ciego Melquiades and
Santiago Morales (El Ranchero), were affected. They did not record any songs
after World War II.[75] A major factor responsible for the decline of the orquestas
was the fascination with the accordion. Armando Marroquín, founder of Ideal
Records, a Tejano recording company located in South Texas, best stated the
reason for their decline when he said, "Vino el acordeón y tumbo a todos esos
grupos" (The accordion came and toppled all those groups).[76]

Vocal Singing

Vocal singing, the dominant musical tradition in the Tejano community,
maintained and possibly enhanced its position during the 1920s and 1930s.
Much of this was due probably to the ascendency of the canción típica and
the corrido and to the incorporation of the accordion in its accompaniment.[77]
As noted earlier, the vast majority of the songs recorded during this period
were canciones, especially corridos. Together, canciones and corridos composed over half of all recorded music.

Not all forms of vocal singing increased in popularity during these years.
This was true especially of religious singing. This type of singing was not
represented in the early recordings, probably as a result of the increasing

secularization of American life and the decline of the elite within the Mexican-origin population. Popular among religious elites were musical styles associated with the church and its activities, including organ music, liturgical singing, and religious dramas. These declined over the years.

Conjuntos

Conjunto music, although present in the Tejano community since the mid-1800s, appealed to an increasing number of the population during the early decades of the twentieth century. By the 1930s, as indicated in the proportion of recordings done by conjuntos, it became a preferred musical style among working-class Mexicanos. This music, more so than all the other types, was a product and reflection of the working class. Conjunto musicians came from the working class and developed a distinct form of entertainment that appealed to those who worked with their hands. Theirs was music rooted in the experiences of agricultural workers in rural areas and of unskilled laborers in urban areas of South and Central Texas.

The increasing popularity of conjunto music during these years can also be attributed to several other factors. Some of these are the increased role of recording companies, the availability of cheaply made records, record players, and jukeboxes, the demand for dance music, the emergence of dance promoters in various parts of the state, the emergence of Spanish-language radio, and an increasing working-class population. The recording industry and Spanish-language radio popularized a variety of musical styles and ensembles during the 1920s. Canciones típicas, corridos, schotises, and huapangos were some of the most popular styles heard on the radio and on records; duets, trios, mariachis, conjuntos, and string and wind ensembles were also recorded and heard on radio during these years.[78] Despite this diversity, commercialization eventually narrowed the stylistic variation of Mexican music found in Texas and contributed to the rise of the conjunto sound.

Immigration was also an important factor in this rise. Immigrants brought many of their traditional forms of Mexican music to the United States and reenergized forms already here. This, as Steven Loza has argued, led to the decline and resurgence of some musical styles among the Mexican-origin population residing north of the border.[79] Among the styles introduced or revived were vocal singing and conjunto music. Immigrants also brought their love of corridos and rancheras to this country.

Immigrant workers were not the only ones who brought Mexican musical traditions to the United States. So did entrepreneurs and traveling minstrels. Entrepreneurs, for instance, brought the music and styles popular in the salons and social clubs of the urban areas to the United States. These were essentially for the elite, but they were accepted by the working classes and transformed in the process.[80]

Touring groups of musicians and artists were additional sources of imported Mexican musical traditions.[81] Many came with traveling shows and were part of an emerging popular theater that developed during the eighteenth century. These traveling shows were a common sight in Spain, Mexico, and most of Spanish America well into the early part of the twentieth century.[82]

A final factor in the increased popularity of conjunto music was internal change. The conjunto acquired a basic form and style during these years. At the turn of the century, the conjunto style was in its rudimentary stages—that is, it had not yet acquired its basic form. Musicians were still experimenting with the instruments, the songs, and the dance forms.[83] The heart of the conjunto ensemble, as noted earlier, was either a one-row or two-row button accordion. But the instruments that accompanied it were not yet fixed. Some conjunto groups used an accordion and a tambora del rancho. Villarreal, Rodríguez, and Casiano, for instance, used the tambora de rancho until the early 1930s. Most groups abandoned this instrument by the beginning of the decade because it was too loud and drowned out the other instruments.[84]

Others, such as Flaco Jiménez and Narciso Martínez, used an accordion and a string instrument of some sort. Jiménez turned to the tololoche and Martínez to the bajo sexto, a twelve-string Mexican guitar. Jiménez's distinct sounds and his use of the accordion in combination with the tololoche had no impact on other groups at that time. Martínez's mix of instruments, however, by the end of the 1930s, became the most popular type of ensemble in the Tejano community.[85] He was thus responsible for establishing the accordion and the bajo sexto as the most basic components of the unfolding conjunto style of music.

The style of playing also changed during this decade and began to appeal to larger audiences. Martínez was instrumental in this process. In the early part of the 1930s, conjunto players such as Bruno Villarreal used the left-hand bass and right-hand treble chord elements of the accordion. By mid-decade, many of them were deemphasizing the bass part of the accordion, primarily using the treble end. This allowed them to better articulate the melody in a song.[86] Both Narciso Martínez and Flaco Jiménez practically abandoned the use of the left-hand buttons to concentrate more on the melodic, treble-clef side, which gave the accordionists more time to concentrate on their melodies. Martínez played with a *marcato* style (a more marked or agressive style), Jiménez with a softer mode of articulation.

The emphasis on the right-hand, treble-clef side of the accordion led to the search for an instrument that would replace the lost bass sound in conjunto music. Martínez chose the bajo sexto, whereas Jiménez chose the tololoche. Both of these instruments served their purpose.[87] But the combined instrumental mix of the accordion and the bajo sexto began to have a greater impact on the musical sensibilities of the Tejano population.

Changes also occurred in the types of dances recorded and performed by conjuntos. In the early twentieth century, their repertoire was diverse and included polkas, redowas *(vals bajitos)*, schotises, waltzes *(vals alto)*, huapangos, and even a few mazurkas.[88] But by the 1930s, the polkas were becoming the "hallmark of the unfolding conjunto style of music."[89] Martínez played an influential role in narrowing the conjunto repertoire, recording a variety of songs and dance pieces for Bluebird between 1935 and 1940. By the latter part of the decade, the most popular of his compositions were polkas.[90]

CONCLUSION

The initial recordings of Tejano music were extremely important because they reflected the diversity of styles present in the early twentieth century. Several types of musical groups and individuals utilized a wide range of instruments to record a variety of songs and dances during these years. Despite this diversity, only three fundamental types of musical groups were present: orquestas, vocal singing with guitar accompaniment, and rudimentary conjunto groups. The early recordings, in conjunction with other pieces of historical evidence, also allow scholars an opportunity to gauge the extent of change that occurred in this music over time. As noted above, these musical styles were present, but they were not all equally popular at any one time. Varying musical tastes in the population, among other things, led to perceptible changes in the three types of musical groupings responsible for playing música tejana. During this period, orquestas of all types declined, vocal singing increased in popularity, and conjuntos became more widely accepted in the community. Although this music changed over time, one can appreciate the variety of groups, instruments, and songs recorded by the musicians of that era.

Chapter 3

Post—World War II Developments, 1946—64

During the war years, from 1941 to 1946, all types of Texas-Mexican music recordings were halted, due in large part to the shortage of materials for the making of records and to the abandonment of regional music by major record companies. These companies abandoned regional music to concentrate on popular national music in both the United States and Mexico.[1] After the war, however, and for the next two decades, local companies emerged and began to record música tejana. The recording industry's involvement, as well as the impact of American culture, increased socioeconomic opportunities, and other factors, led to significant changes in this music. Among the most important developments were the emergence of two different musical styles—the female-based duet and the orquesta Tejana—and the reemergence and eventual dominance of conjunto music. This chapter traces some of these developments and the forces responsible for them.

THE ESTABLISHMENT OF IDEAL RECORDS, 1947

The increased popularity of música tejana during the post–World War II era was due in large part to the establishment of local recording companies owned by Mexican-origin entrepreneurs. The first and most influential of these independent companies, or "indies," was Discos Ideal. Two enterprising businessmen—Armando Marroquín and Paco Betancourt—established the company in 1947.

Marroquín was born on September 12, 1912, and went to college in Kingsville, Texas, during the late 1920s. Several years later, he married Carmen Hernández, a local woman he met while in college, and settled in Kingsville. Soon thereafter, Marroquín went into the lucrative jukebox business in nearby Alice.[2] Jukeboxes were found in cantinas, restaurants, and other businesses throughout the area.

Betancourt was born on January 15, 1903, in the Lower Rio Grande Valley. In the 1920s he built and operated the Queen Theater on Main Street in Brownsville, the first theater in the Valley to show talking movies. Sometime in the 1930s he sold it and went into the record business. He owned and operated the Rio Grande Music Company in San Benito, Texas, a retail record shop. In addition to selling records, he also serviced over a hundred jukeboxes and pinball machines.[3]

During the 1930s, records by the known local artists such as Narciso Martínez, Gaitan y Cantú, and Lydia Mendoza were readily available from the major labels like Bluebird, Vocalion, Okeh, and Decca. In the early 1940s, these major labels quit recording "regional and ethnic" music for social and economic reasons. The demand for regionally popular artists and music, however, increased after the war. Chris Strachwitz has argued that a major reason for this had to do with the increased purchasing power of the Tejano population. "With the end of World War II in 1945," he notes, "millions of workers all over the country, especially those of rural background who had found work in the lucrative war industries, were making good wages and were willing and able to support their favorite regional music, musicians, and singers."[4]

There was no lack of Mexican and Mexican American music. Recorded Mexican music was available across the border or from Los Angeles, but a great deal of red tape and too much frustration was involved in obtaining it.[5] The available Mexican music also was not geared toward the Tejano musical sensitivities. It comprised primarily vocal singing with guitar or mariachi accompaniment. This type of musical style had been popular in Texas prior to World War II, but Tejanos had acquired different musical tastes over the years and wanted to hear accordion-based music.[6]

Determined to supply his jukeboxes with the music loved by Tejanos, Marroquín bought some recording equipment in 1945 and began to record local artists. Afterward he contracted with a company in California to press and distribute his recordings. He used these "home-grown" records in his own jukeboxes or sold them directly to other regional jukebox operators in South Texas.[7]

Marroquín soon encouraged his friend Betancourt, an individual familiar with the distribution of records along the border, to join him in forming a record company. Betancourt agreed, and in 1947 the two men established Discos Ideal. During the next two decades, Ideal became the leading producer of Tejano music in the state and "the most representative of the artists and musical culture of the Lower Rio Grande Valley."[8] In a period of under two decades, it recorded hundreds of songs by a variety of local artists from South and Central Texas, many of whom became local, state, or regional hits. A host of popular Tejano artists of the 1950s, such as Valerio Longoria, Tony de la Rosa, Paulino Bernal, and Beto Villa, the "father" of orquesta music in Texas, recorded for this label.

Ideal also played a significant role in shaping música tejana by incorporating women into the Tejano recording industry and by launching two musical trends then taking place in Texas—the orquesta Tejana and the conjunto. Its most significant influence, however, was in "helping to establish the dominance of conjunto and orquesta over all other types of music in Texas."[9] This dominance of styles was reflected in the recorded songs of the female duets. The overwhelming majority of the female duets recorded only with conjunto or orquesta accompaniment.[10]

LAS MUJERES EN MÚSICA TEJANA

The initial recordings took place in Marroquín's home and were sung by his wife and sister-in-law, Carmen and Laura Hernández. Professionally, they were known as Carmen y Laura. Carmen was born in Kingsville, Texas, in 1921 and came from a talented family who had sung at family gatherings for years. Carmen met her husband, Armando, while he was in college in Kingsville. They married and settled down in Alice, Texas. Her sister, Laura, who attended school in Mexico, was also born in Kingsville, in 1926.[11]

The first song Carmen y Laura recorded was called "Se Me Fue Mi Amor." This song laments the absence of a woman's loved one overseas in the armed forces: "Se me fue mi amor . . . Se me fue a la guerra . . ." (My love has gone . . . He left to go to war . . .). The song discusses her desire to be with him: "Quisiera por él volar, hacia adonde está mi bien, volar por las aves, cruzar esos mares, llegar a morir con él" (I wish I could fly for him to wherever he may be, fly like the birds across the sea, to die along with him.) She asks God

Lydia Mendoza, 1950s. *Courtesy Chris Strachwitz,*
Arhoolie Records, www.arhoolie.com

that "si no vuelvo a verlo que me dé la muerte, que es mejor morir" (If I don't
see him again grant me death, for death would be a better fate).[12] This song
was important for several reasons. First, it presented a woman's point of view.
The song dealt with the feelings of a woman longing for her lover. The female
perspective in this love song was highly unusual, given the limited role that
women had in the highly patriarchal Mexican culture and their relative absence from the recording industry.

Although women played a variety of creative roles in society in general,
within the traditional confines of Mexican culture, women were expected to
be virgins or housewives and mothers, not singers, composers, or performers.[13] Despite the limited roles assigned to women, some were involved in the

entertainment industry in the early decades of the twentieth century. Most of their participation, however, was limited to the vaudeville theater stage, where women assumed roles as singers, comediennes, dancers, and chorus girls. In the late 1920s the role of women expanded with the rise of recorded music. Many of them became singers beyond the stage and recorded songs as solistas or as part of a duet.[14] Female duets, such as the Herrera, Posada, and Padilla sisters', either recorded locally in Los Angeles during the 1920s and 1930s or else visited the United States from Mexico City.[15] Tejanas, for the most part, were relatively absent from the recording industry during these years.[16] The only exception to this pattern of exclusion was Lydia Mendoza.[17] As early as 1928, she recorded with her parents and a sister in the Cuarteto Carta Blanca. In the 1930s she went out on her own and recorded songs with guitar accompaniment.[18]

Because of the relative absence of women from the recording industry, almost the entire range of Mexican and Tejano music came from a man's point of view. In some cases, when women sang in public, the lyrics were not changed to reflect their experiences. This led to absurd situations, such as when Las Abajenas, two sisters by the names of Catalina and Victoria, sang a song with the following lyrics: "tú carino me hace falta mujer, ya no puedo vivir lejos de tí, ni pensar que tus caricias perdí" (I've missed your loving, woman; I can't live far from you now, nor recall I had lost your affection). The lack of a female perspective, as noted by Strachwitz, "did not limit the depth of heart-felt emotions that these women expressed in their singing, and it is to their credit that they could turn many of these songs around."[19]

A second reason for the importance of "Se Me Fue Mi Amor" was that it gave rise to the "Tejano" sound, a style unique to Texas and different from traditional Mexican music. Female singers, whether from Mexico or the U.S. Southwest, usually were accompanied by a variety of ensembles or instruments, but none utilized accordions during the pre–World War II years.[20] Carmen y Laura broke with this female musical tradition and featured the accordion in their recordings.[21] This new Tejano sound gained quick acceptance, as indicated by record sales.[22]

Most of the songs performed by mujeres Tejanas initially were recorded with the accompaniment of accordionists, such as Narciso Martínez or Paulino Bernal, and with the assistance of bajo sexto players, such as Santiago Almeida and others. Marroquín, however, was quite aware of the disdain that the growing Tejano middle class had toward accordion music. Many of these individuals associated this music with the lower classes. So as not to offend them, he recorded his wife and her sister, as well as other singers, with the new orquesta sound of the saxophone and other wind instruments.[23] Among the most popular orquesta musicians to accompany Carmen y Laura were Beto Villa and Eugenio Gutiérrez.[24] The repertoire of the female duets was diverse and included both traditional Tejano tunes, like rancheras and valses, and new ones, such as boleros, porros, mambos, and fox-trots. Although the fox-trots performed were American, the lyrics were usually in Spanish.[25]

The musical style and grouping of Carmen y Laura began a new trend in música tejana. In the next decade and a half, countless other duets formed and recorded this type of music with conjuntos or orquestas Tejanas. Among the most popular during these years were the following: Las Abajenas (Catalina and Victoria), Hermanas Fraga, Hermanas Segovia, Delia y Laura, Rosita y Laura (Rosita Fernández and Laura Cantú), Hermanas Cantú (Nori and Ninfa), Hermanas Guerrero (Maria Luisa and Felipa), Las Rancheritas, and Hermanas Mendoza (Maria and Juanita).[26] Occasionally, a few vocal duets recorded with the traditional trumpet and horn sounds of the mariachi style.[27] The majority, however, were accompanied by either a conjunto or an orquesta Tejana. In public appearances the women would sing in front of the bands for hours at a time.[28] The female duets toured extensively throughout the Southwest and Midwest. However, they did not tour by themselves, nor were they part of *caravanas* (caravans) like so many recording artists from Mexico. They were always accompanied by their husbands on the road and toured with established conjuntos or orquestas.

Individual female artists also recorded during this period. The two best-known Tejana singers during the post–World War II era were Lydia Mendoza and Chelo Silva. As previously mentioned, Mendoza began her career in 1928 with her parents and sister as the Cuarteto Carta Blanca. In the 1930s she embarked on a solo career and eventually became the number-one pioneer Tejana recording artist. Unlike other females, she recorded with conjuntos, orquestas, and guitar accompaniment and sang boleros, rancheras, and valses. In the early 1940s Mendoza quit recording. She came out of this semiretirement at mid-decade and renewed her career as a living legend. She toured exten-sively throughout the Southwest, Midwest, and Mexico during the 1950s. The following decade she participated in a variety of festivals and tributes in her honor.[29]

Chelo Silva was born in 1922 in Brownsville, Texas. She began her career at the Continental Club in Brownsville and made her first recording for Discos Falcon in 1954. Falcon, formed by Arnaldo Ramírez in the early 1950s, also promoted música tejana and became Ideal's main competitor in this decade.[30] Silva's career was quite distinct from Lydia Mendoza's. Both performed in the

Hermanas Guerrero, 1950s. *Courtesy Chris Strachwitz, Arhoolie Records,*
www.arhoolie.com

United States, but Silva was more popular in Mexico and South America. She
was principally known as a bolero singer. Usually she was accompanied by a
large orchestra, although occasionally she recorded with a variety of musical
instruments, including the accordion.[31] Mendoza, on the other hand, included
boleros in her musical repertoire but did not concentrate on this type of music.
She also sang rancheras, valses, and other tunes and was backed-up by either
a twelve-string guitar or a variety of conjuntos and orquestas Tejanas.[32]

Chelo Silva, 1950s. *Courtesy Chris Strachwitz, Arhoolie Records,*
www.arhoolie.com

Several other female artists achieved a modicum of success during these
years—Rosita Fernández, Ventura Alonzo, Delia Gutiérrez, Juanita García,
and Beatriz Llamaz. Fernández, the daughter of a captain in the Mexican
army, was born in Monterrey, Nuevo Léon. Her family moved to San Antonio when she was a young girl. At the age of nine she began singing with her
uncles in a group called El Trio San Miguel. "They thought maybe a little girl
would be an attraction to the public," she said.[33] She toured South Texas in
the 1920s and 1930s with the trio. In 1932 she won a radio singing contest.
This led to a long career in radio and later television. Fernández, known
simply as Rosita, made four motions pictures and many sound recordings
from the 1940s to the early 1960s.[34] Like Chelo Silva, Rosita was primarily a

bolero singer. Unlike Silva, Rosita performed both in Spanish and English for a mixed audience. One of her most accessible songs, "Mi Fracaso," was recorded in 1950 with a conjunto group.[35]

Ventura Alonzo, like Fernández, was primarily a local phenomenon and had a limited impact on Tejano music. However, she was one of the few pioneering female artists in a male-dominated recording and dance industry. For this reason alone she deserves to be recognized and acknowledged. Alonzo (her maiden name was Martínez) was born in Matamoros in 1905. Her family immigrated to Brownsville in 1910 and later moved to Houston, where she married her husband Frank and assumed his last name.[36] Alonzo learned to play the piano at an early age. When her husband, a self-taught guitar player, discovered his wife's piano-playing ability, he immediately thought about forming a band. Needing something more portable, she began playing a piano accordion. Within a couple of months, they acquired two additional musicians and formed the core of what would eventually become Alonzo y Sus Rancheros. Ventura played the accordion for the group. Because of her ability, she was known as the queen of the accordion. Unlike other singers, she did not tour the South Texas circuit, nor did she record many songs. She was primarily a local artist performing for a Houston audience. In 1956 the Alonzos opened La Terraza, a ballroom located in east Houston. Alonzo y Sus Rancheros was the house band and opened for other acts. The couple retired from music in 1969.[37]

Very little information is known about Delia Gutiérrez, Juanita García, and Beatriz Llamaz. Gutiérrez was born in Weslaco and began singing at eight years old with the orquesta headed by her father, Eugenio Gutiérrez. She also collaborated with Laura Hernández Cantú of Carmen y Laura on numerous recordings. Gutiérrez recorded mostly during the late 1940s and early 1950s. García and Llamaz, on the other hand, launched their recording careers in the 1950s and 1960s, respectively. Unfortunately, no further information is available on their lives or their music.[38]

The female artists were an extremely important force in the emerging Tejano music industry. They initiated a completely new style and helped to establish the dominance of conjuntos and orquestas over all other types of music in Texas. They also increased the social base of Tejano music by appealing to immigrant, working-class, middle-class, and acculturated groups of Tejanos. At times, they even provided their own perspective on Tejano social relationships. Their presence added significantly to the shape and content of música tejana during the post–World War II years.

LAS ORQUESTAS TEJANAS

Origins and Emergence

A second major development in Tejano music during these years was the emergence of a new type of musical ensemble that came to be known as the orquesta Tejana. It acquired other names in later years, including Tex-Mex in the 1950s and La Onda Chicana (the Chicano Wave) in the 1960s. Orquestas Tejanas were forged in the midst of a society undergoing rapid economic and ideological transformations. They played a prominent role in reflecting and shaping the musical and cultural tastes of a group of highly urbanized and acculturated Texas Mexicans. A small number of these individuals also were part of the growing middle-class sector within the Mexican-origin population.[39]

Orquesta musicians found the culture of the less-assimilated and working-class Mexican population too limiting, since it did not reflect their diverse experiences based on increased rates of acculturation, urbanization, and economic mobility.[40] For the most part, they were willing to play what one scholar referred to as "popular folk dances of the region," but they also wanted a more sophisticated and "polished" sound.[41] Likewise, they wanted to play other types of dance music popular in the United States and Mexico, including danzones, mambos, boleros, fox-trots, swing, and rock and roll. The orquesta Tejana allowed them the opportunity to be ethnic and American simultaneously. Orquestas Tejanas legitimated the musical tastes of this group and communicated a middle-class, acculturated, and urbanized alternative to the rural-based conjunto and working-class culture in general.[42]

The orquestas Tejanas that existed in the years prior to World War II were quite distinct from those that emerged in the 1940s. Generally speaking, there were three types of orquestas before the Second World War—orquestas típicas, orquestas de cuerda, and orquestas de pitos. The most popular were the first two.[43] During and after the war, the different types of orquestas underwent significant changes. Orquestas de cuerda and bandas generally declined as viable traditions within música tejana. Orquestas típicas, on the other hand, were transformed and replaced by the modern orquesta Tejana. Orquesta musicians, it must be noted, created the modern ensemble through a process of appropriation and creative blending. At times, they took existing models popular in the United States and appropriated them for their own musical purposes. In most cases, however, they took elements from both the old Mexican orquestas and the new American and Latin American ones and blended them to forge a more modern orquesta Tejana.

Generally speaking, the musicians of the post–World War II era eliminated the violins and mandolins common in the old orquestas and added saxophones and trumpets. Of particular importance was the incorporation of the saxophone into this musical ensemble. The two indisputable kings of orquesta Tejana, Beto Villa and Isidro López, for instance, emphasized the new sound of the saxophone in the orquesta.[44] Occasionally a small piano or an accordion was used as the key melody instrument.

Beto Villa, the son of a prosperous tailor, established the first orquesta Tejana in Falfurrias, Texas. Villa organized his first band, the Sonny Boys, as a high-school student, in 1932. It played no Texas-Mexican music—polkas, valses, or huapango—and instead specialized in American big band tunes. The name of the group as well as the songs it played reflected the impact of American life on Mexican youth in Texas in a period of constant change along the border, in the state, and throughout the nation.[45] Sometime between 1932 and the Second World War Beto Villa lost interest in playing only American-type music and began to appreciate the musical traditions of the border. By the 1940s the latter was known as *música ranchera* (country music), a particular type of music historically associated with the mariachi in Mexico and the conjunto in the U.S. Southwest. It included the songs and dances popularized by Tejano musicians during the first decades of the twentieth century, especially polkas, valses, schotises, huapangos, and baladas.[46] Non–ranchero type music eventually came to be called *jaitón* by many of the conjunto fans, but, because of this term's negative connotations, I will refer to it as *música moderna,* a particular form of music associated with the orquesta, with American modern music, and with the occupationally mobile, acculturated, and urban Tejano population.[47]

By the mid-1940s, Villa wanted to play música ranchera, but in a more sophisticated way. He felt that this could be done by using instruments associated with the modern American and Latin American big bands. In other words, he wanted to play música tejana but with saxophones and trumpets. In 1947 Villa approached Armando Marroquín of Discos Ideal about recording a couple of Tejano songs in the orquesta style. Betancourt was skeptical about its potential success, given the community's preference for accordion-based dance music. After some prodding, he agreed to the recording session, but only if Villa had an accordionist in the group.[48] In October 1947 Villa recorded his first two sides for Ideal. Side A was a polka entitled "Las Delicias" (Sweet Delights) and side B contained a waltz called "Porqué Te Ries?" (Why Do You Laugh?).[49]

The combined use of instruments associated with the orquesta and the conjunto led to a totally new sound in música tejana, something that was quite different from what Villa had envisioned. His vision was one based on the combination of Mexican rhythms with American instruments but what emerged was a more complex development that blended the unique sounds of two distinct ensembles—the conjunto and the orquesta—within traditional Mexican music. Some scholars have referred to this new sound as "bimusicality" or as music hybridity. Villa was the creator of this musical development.

Villa's records sold "by the bunches" in the South Texas area. Paco Betancourt, responsible for distributing the records made by Discos Ideal, called Marroquín from San Benito, Texas, and said, "Tell him to record some more."[50] For the next decade or so, Villa recorded a variety of hit songs in this new style. These hits assured his position in música tejana and made him one of the most popular musicians in the industry. "His name and music," notes Manuel Peña, "quickly became legendary." Wherever he performed during the 1940s and 1950s, Villa drew large numbers of fans and continually packed the public dance halls that became extremely popular throughout Texas after the Second World War.[51]

By combining *lo ranchero* with *lo moderno*—that is, the accordion with the saxophone, the conjunto with the orquesta, the rural with the urban, and the Mexican with the American—Villa created a distinct sound that was rapidly replicated throughout the state and nation. In the 1950s, his continuing popularity led to the establishment of other orquestas by individuals such as Mike Ornelas (1951), Balde González (1952), Eugenio Gutiérrez (1952), Pedro Bugarin (1953), Isidro López (1954), Chris Sandoval (1956), and Dario Perez (1957).[52] Each of these orquestas followed, to some extent, the lead set by Villa. For about a dozen years, Villa reigned as *el rey de las orquestas* (the king of the modern orquestas Tejana).

Evolution of Orquestas

Orquestas Tejanas, like most other musical ensembles, were not constant; they changed over time. In the beginning orquestas were small, and the music they played was instrumental, typically utilizing the accordion.[53] Beto Villa's early recordings reflected these developments. Within the next several years, at least three major changes were made to orquestas and their music.

From 1946 to 1949, Villa maintained a balance between the ranchero and the moderno sound; he used the accordion in combination with the saxophone and trumpet. After 1949, however, he quit using the accordion. He did not abandon the ranchero songs and dances, only the ranchero sound made by this instrument. He also increased the size of the band from around eight to eleven members. "Beto made the orquesta real big," noted Reymundo Treviño, a piano accordionist who had been with Villa for years, "and those of us who couldn't read music, we were fired."[54] The reasons for these changes are unclear, but most likely he wanted a different type of sound that corresponded more with the orquesta style of American and Latin American big bands such as Glenn Miller's, Tommy Dorsey's, and Xavier Cugat's.[55]

Some groups followed Villa and abandoned the ranchero sound made by the accordion but not the ranchero songs. Among the most important orquestas with a non-ranchero sound were Balde González, Eugenio Gutiérrez, Chris Sandoval, Mike Ornelas, Dario Perez, and Pedro Begarin from Arizona.

One of the most interesting singers of this group was Balde González, a blind pianist, singer, and composer from Victoria, Texas. Unlike Villa or other orquesta musicians, González abandoned both the ranchero sound and the ranchero songs and dances. He, in other words, did not record Texas-Mexican music. He recorded mostly boleros from Cuba and Latin America and American fox-trots or blues, the latter two in Spanish. Although González represented the most moderno of all the orquesta musicians of the 1940s and 1950s, he remained rooted in his culture by singing in Spanish and by recording styles popular in the Caribbean and in Latin America. He became known

Eugenio Gutiérrez y Su Orquesta con Delia Gutiérrez y Minerva Rodríguez, late 1940s. *Courtesy Chris Strachwitz, Arhoolie Records, www.arhoolie.com*

for a smooth, crooner style in his performances, reminiscent of Agustín Lara, and he constantly used the piano in his recordings.[56]

Other orquestas retained the ranchero sound and continued using the accordion in their recordings. Among these were Isidro López, Eugenio Gutiérrez,[57] and Ventura Alonso y Sus Rancheros. These orquestas were fond of the "squeezebox" and continued using it for many years. The latter group, in fact, used it until the end of the 1960s, when its members retired from the music scene.[58]

Isidro López's was among the most influential of these groups with a ranchero sound. López, from Corpus Christi, learned to play the saxophone and clarinet in high school. Although he graduated from high school and managed to attend college for a year, López strongly identified with the less-educated working-class population in the barrios of "Corpitos" and with conjunto music. Nonetheless, he was strongly influenced by the urbanized, acculturated, and middle-class ideology of his orquesta peers. The music he played reflected these twin influences. López began to record for Ideal in 1954. Like Beto Villa, he played popular folk dances of the region but with orquesta instruments or with a combination of accordion and orquesta instruments. Similar to Villa, López recorded highly sophisticated polkas and rancheras in this style. Some of his most important hits during the 1950s and 1960s were "Desilución," "Diganle," "Sufriendo y Penando," "Emoción," "Pasajera," and many others. He also expanded the traditional repertoire of Tejano musical groups and specialized in the recording of boleros. López recorded over sixty singles and eight LPs under the Ideal label during these two decades.[59]

The second major innovation to orquesta music was the incorporation of lyrics, in the mid-1950s. Prior to this year all the dance tunes played by the orquestas were instrumental. In 1954 Isidro López changed all this. López was influenced by the canción ranchera, a lyrical song popularized in Mexico by artists such as Jorge Negrete and Pedro Infante.[60] This vocal singing tradition had been popularized by the Tejana duets in the mid-1940s and incorporated into conjunto music by Valerio Longoria in 1948. The increased popularity of this tradition probably encouraged López to incorporate lyrics into the orquesta ensemble. In 1954 he added lyrics to two of the most popular dance tunes he played—the polka and the vals. This innovation brought him tremendous and immediate success. By the late 1950s, practically all of the orquestas included lyrics in their musical tunes.[61]

A third major innovation was the broadening of the musical repertory to include not only songs and dance styles from Mexico but also from Latin America, the Caribbean, and the United States. The orquestas, as noted earlier,

Isidro Lopez y Su Orquesta, 1950s. Lopez is third from left.
Courtesy Mary Gutierrez

played the popular folk dances of the region. The "bread and butter" for
many of these groups, in many cases, were the polka and the ranchera."[62]
Over the years, however, orquestas Tejanas added some of the more-popular
Latin American and Caribbean musical styles into their repertoire, including
the mambo, bolero, rumba, and danzon. One of Beto Villa's biggest hits, for
instance, was "Mambo #7," recorded in 1948. In the 1950s, Eugenio Gutiérrez
recorded an extremely popular porro (a Latin American dance tune), entitled
"Mi Marianita," while Isidro López recorded "La Hiedra," a danzon. Balde
González and Lydia Mendoza recorded several boleros that became hits.[63]

Orquesta leaders likewise added some American tunes such as swing, rhythm
and blues, and rock and roll to their repertoire. This suggested an increasing
impact of American culture on Texas-Mexican music. Beto Villa, for instance,
recorded a boogie-woogie song by the name of "Pachuca Blues" in January
1950. Isidro López recorded a rock and roll song, "Mala Cara," in the early
1950s, and Balde González recorded a blues song called "No Esperar Más De
Mí" during the same period.[64] Although orquestas Tejanas incorporated
American tunes into their repertoire, they did not record in English, nor did

they play primarily these types of songs. Unlike Mexican Americans in other parts of the Southwest, they remained true to their roots and either sang in Spanish only or continued playing polkas and rancheras.[65]

Not all the existing orquestas recorded during these years. Despite the lack of record deals, many of them were well received by the public. In Houston, for instance, at least four extremely popular orquestas Tejanas existed between 1946 and 1960: The Tommy Flores Orchestra, Eloy Pérez and the Latinaires, Gaston Ponce, and Alonzo y Sus Rancheros Orquesta.[66] Other cities, such as Corpus Christi, Brownsville, and San Antonio, also had a number of orquestas Tejanas that recorded only occasionally or not at all but were extremely popular.[67] Because of the diverse developments in the orquestas Tejanas and their increased size and influence, they quickly began to compete with conjuntos for audiences.

THE REEMERGENCE OF CONJUNTO MUSIC

Another major development that occurred after the Second World War was the reemergence of conjunto music. The establishment of local recording companies was instrumental in the style's reintroduction into the Tejano community. Post–World War II recordings of conjunto music began in 1946. In this year, Marroquín at Discos Ideal recorded music played by none other than Narciso Martínez. Born in Reynosa, Tamaulipas, Mexico, in 1911, Martínez began to play the accordion when he was still very young. He started recording in 1936 after a music store owner from South Texas, Enrique Valentine, introduced him to Eli Oberstein, the "roving record director" for the Bluebird label. Oberstein was in San Antonio to record all kinds of regional music for his label.[68] That initial recording, in a San Antonio hotel room, soon led to many others; audience reception of his music was excellent.[69] All of his recordings during the 1930s were instrumental. So were those he did in the post–World War II years. Two important hits recorded in 1946 by Narciso Martínez were the polka "La Cuquita" and the vals "Ausencia."[70]

Martínez initiated a resurgence in conjunto music during the postwar years. Within a decade large numbers of conjuntos were formed throughout the state; many got record deals with Discos Ideal or other local recording companies. Among the most popular conjuntos during the 1940s and 1950s were the following: Valerio Longoria, Tony de la Rosa, Juan López, Rubén Vela, Flaco Jiménez, Conjunto Trio San Antonio, Los Pinquinos del Norte, Los Donnenos, and Conjunto Bernal.[71] Tejano companies also recorded conjunto groups from Mexico, usually norteño groups.

INNOVATIONS IN CONJUNTO MUSIC

Conjunto music did not remain static. From the mid-1940s to the early 1960s, it changed significantly and acquired both a stable form and a particular identity. This evolution occurred as a result of several innovations introduced at different periods during the 1940s and 1950s.

At least one major innovation was made to conjunto music during the 1940s. The first occurred in 1948, when Valerio Longoria introduced vocal singing.[72] Longoria was born in Kenedy, Texas, a small community about sixty-five miles north-northwest of Corpus Christi. He came from a migrant family and rarely attended school. "Fui poco a la escuela. Era muy duro para mi padre; mejor me llevaba a trabajar" (I had very little school. It was hard on my father; he would rather take me to work with him).[73]

Despite the lack of formal education, Longoria was a talented child. He learned to play the guitar at six and the accordion at seven. His first paid performance was when he was eight. He continued playing conjunto music until he was drafted into the army at the beginning of World War II. Upon his discharge from the army, he resumed his playing. Longoria recorded his first pieces in 1947 under the Corona Records label from San Antonio.[74] Two years later, he switched record labels and went to Discos Ideal, where he stayed for about eight years.[75] It was at Ideal, noted Peña, "that Longoria left his mark as the most innovative conjunto musician until that time."[76]

The addition of lyrics to conjunto music, as noted above, was a selective process. They were added to only two dance forms: the polka and the vals.[77] This development, in turn, led to the creation of the ranchera Tejana and the vals ranchera. The incorporation of lyrics into conjunto music had a significant impact on the female duets and orquestas Tejanas. With respect to the former, it decreased their popularity by encouraging the merging of the vocal singing tradition with the male-only conjunto. This development also had the effect of excluding women from the music industry, since most of the conjuntos, and later the orquestas, were male-based. The addition of lyrics to conjunto music likewise had a significant impact on the evolution of the orquesta Tejana and served to increase its popularity. The rise of Isidro López in the mid-1950s and other groups such as Balde González and Eugenio Gutiérrez was, in large part, due to the incorporation of lyrics and the vocal singing tradition into this type of music.

In the 1950s several additional innovations came to the conjunto. First, there were instrumental changes. Most groups added a modern, American drum, substituted an electric bass guitar for the stand-up bass or tololoche, and introduced amplification—speakers and microphones.[78] Longoria was the first to add the drum, but it was Tony de la Rosa who popularized it in the late 1950s. De la Rosa was born in 1931 in Sarita, near Corpus Christi. He learned to play the accordion as a teenager by listening to Narciso Martínez on the radio. At sixteen years of age he went to nearby Kingsville to play his accordion in the cantinas. He played in cantinas until 1949, when he made his first recording under the short-lived label of Arco, a company from Alice, Texas.[79] The following year, he switched over to Discos Ideal and began to turn out a series of hits that lasted for decades and that made his group the most popular conjunto in Texas during the 1950s.[80]

The American drum was quite different from the *tambora de rancho* used by conjuntos prior to the 1930s. The latter was a noisy contraption and had little, if any, impact on the emerging conjunto. The former, however, "created an entirely new dimension in that it altered the function of all the other instruments in the conjunto." Manuel Peña best describes this impact: "The drum 'settled down' the tempo, especially for polkas, and freed the bajo sexto and the accordion from the constant necessity of attending simultaneously to melody, harmony, and tempo. With the drums taking over the primary function of rhythm and 'keeping time,' both the accordion and the bajo were left to explore new modes of articulation."[81] Although introduced in the early 1950s, the drums did not become a standard feature of the conjunto until the latter part of the decade because many people felt that they were too overpowering. "People laughed at us, because no one used drums," Tony de la Rosa said in an interview in 1978. "People thought it was like a circus. Even the recording companies didn't want drums," he added.[82] De la Rosa likewise was responsible for initiating a new style of playing the accordion that had significant impact on Tejano dancing. An official publication of the Guadalupe Cultural Arts Center in San Antonio noted the impact of Tony de la Rosa's manner of playing the accordion on Tejano dance styles: "[It was] his stylized staccato accordion playing, with its unique combination of mechanical precision and harmonicalike wailing, that were of special significance because it slowed down the tempo of the music which had come to be played extremely fast. This new, slower sound directly created a dancing style known as [el] tacuachito."[83] These changes catapulted Tony de la Rosa to the top of the Tejano music industry by the end of the decade and led to the consolidation of a basic form to this ensemble.

A second major change occurred in the musical repertoire of conjunto groups during the 1950s. Conjuntos generally played a diverse selection of polkas, valses, redowas, schotises, and mazurkas.[84] Sometime during the 1950s, different groups added rancheras and boleros to their repertoire. By the end of the decade, the ranchera, in conjunction with the polka and the occasional bolero, became the core of conjunto music. Other musical selections, such as the redowa, schotis, and mazurka, continued to be played, but less frequently.

During this period a few conjuntos also began to specialize in certain types of dance tunes. Tony de la Rosa was one of them. He specialized in polkas and acquired the name "King of the Polkas."[85] Although he played other dance tunes, especially boleros and rancheras, Tony de la Rosa was most known primarily for his lively polkas, such as "El Circo" (The Circus [his first big hit]), "Sylvia," "Los Frijoles Bailan," (The Beans Dance), "La Grulla," (The Crane), and "Atotonilco."[86]

A final set of innovations was introduced by Conjunto Bernal in the late 1950s. Paulino Bernal, the founder of the group, was born in 1939 in Raymondville, Texas. He grew up listening to the two most important accordion giants of the conjunto genre—Narciso Martínez and Valerio Longoria. While still young, Bernal's family moved to Kingsville. In 1952 he and his brother Eloy started a group called Los Hermanitos Bernal. Paulino played the accordion, Eloy the bajo sexto. Even by this early age, both brothers were becoming virtuosos. Armando Marroquín soon discovered this conjunto and began to use it to back up such artists as Carmen y Laura. The group, now known as Conjunto Bernal, recorded its first record in 1955. Side A of this record was called "Mujer Pasada." The flip side was "Desprecio." In 1955 Conjunto Bernal recorded "Mi Unico Camino," a beautiful song with two- and three-part vocal harmony. This was the first time harmonies were used in conjunto music. Two- and three-part harmony, in fact, would be one of its most important innovations.[87] Bernal also came to be known for two other innovations in conjunto music: the full use of the accordion and the virtuosity of accordion and bajo sexto. These made this group the leading conjunto by the early 1960s.[88]

Despite it's popularity, Conjunto Bernal had little impact on other conjuntos during this period, due to several possible reasons. First, most of these groups were not interested in adding more voices or instruments to the traditional conjunto. Second, most were satisfied with either one or two singers or with playing the accordion in less complex ways. Third, the Tejano dancing population made few demands for complexity in the music or for virtuosity in its musicians. They were satisfied with the basic conjunto ensemble—composed of an accordion, a bajo sexto, an electric guitar, and an American drum—and playing dance music for their own pleasure.

TRENDS IN CONJUNTO MUSIC

Several significant trends also became apparent during this period. First, conjunto music went from being played mostly in the cantinas to also being played in private and public dance halls. Prior to the 1940s, conjuntos played in the streets, at house parties, or in a few selective community dances. Sometime after the Second World War, they began to play in cantinas, that is, "beer joints" with a predominantly Tejano drinking and dancing clientele. The number of cantinas in large cities such as Houston and San Antonio or in small towns like Kingsville, Alice, or Corpus Christi steadily increased during the post–World War II era.[89] Although cantinas were viewed negatively by many in the Tejano community, conjunto musicians such as Tony de la Rosa or Rubén Vela found a receptive audience in them. These places provided a source of income for them and an avenue for their particular type of music.[90]

In the latter part of the 1950s, a few conjunto groups began to play in public or paid admission dances. Many of these dances were originally held in existing private or public facilities such as exposition halls, coliseums, or civic centers in various cities or towns. Others were held in lodges or privately constructed dance halls. Public-paid admission dances emerged in 1948 and grew after that period.

TABLE 2

SELECTED DANCE HALLS, 1948–64

City	Dance Halls
Houston	Pan American Nite Club
	The Carousel
	La Terraza
Alice	La Villita
	The VFW Hall
Corpus Christi	Coliseum
	The Exposition Hall
	La Terraza
	Galvan Ballroom

Source: Author's personal knowledge (based on twenty years of attending Tejano dances).

Emergence of Conjunto Norteño

A second major trend in this music was the emergence of the norteño conjuntos. These types of conjuntos were accordion-based but their instrumentation, their repertoire, their style of playing or singing Mexican music, and the number of vocalists varied somewhat from Tejano conjuntos. Norteño groups generally sang more corridos than their Tejano versions, had a more nasalized form of singing, two vocalists, a faster beat, and additional instruments besides the accordian and the bajo sexto.

Tejano recording companies were directly responsible for the creation and promotion of norteño conjunto music. Two of the first norteño conjuntos recorded by regional companies were Los Alegres de Terán and Los Hermanos Torres-García (later they became Los Pavos Reales). The former group, called the "father" of norteño conjunto by Chris Strachwitz, began to record in 1948; the latter in 1949.[91] Los Alegres de Terán comprised two brothers, Egenio Abrego and Tomás Ortiz. Both of them came from the little village of General Terán just southeast of Monterrey in the state of Nuevo Leon but, in the mid-1950s, they moved to McAllen Texas.[92] Los Alegres de Terán was probably the most widely known and respected of the norteño conjuntos during these years.[93] It was the first group to incorporate duet singing into the conjunto ensemble.

Norteño groups, for the most part, did not incorporate many of the innovations that Tejano conjuntos did during the 1950s.[94] They maintained their own identity and continued to play in a style that was unique to them.

Similar to Tejano conjuntos, norteño groups became extremely popular in the Mexican-origin community, primarily because of the large numbers of immigrants residing north of the border. National recording companies in Mexico, like those in the United States, ignored these regional groups but independent record companies picked up the slack and promoted norteño music in South and Central Texas. More research on norteño groups in Texas, however, needs to be conducted in order to get a better sense of their popularity in the community.

The Growing Dominance of Conjunto Music

A final trend that occurred in conjunto music is that by the late 1950s conjuntos became the dominant form of music in the Tejano community. Peña's comment about the dominance of conjunto music in Weslaco, a border town in South Texas, is probably applicable to the rest of the state. "At this time [1950s] conjunto music reigned supreme at la placita [town plaza], and performers like Rubén Vela, who were very much in demand, were regularly featured." Delia Gutiérrez Pineda, who had been a featured singer in her father's orquesta in the 1940s and 1950s, also agreed that conjuntos were more popular than orquestas by the 1950s.[95]

The dominance of conjunto music was due to at least five major reasons. First, it was due to the role played by local independent Tejano companies committed to recording this type of music after the Second World War. As mentioned earlier, major recording companies abandoned the field of regional music during the war years to concentrate on popular national music in the United States and Mexico. This led to a void in the recording of all forms of regional Mexican music in the United States. Beginning in 1946, small, independent recording companies founded by Mexican-origin individuals were established in various parts of the state. Among the largest and most prolific was Discos Ideal, but there were others. Between 1946 and 1956, at least eight other companies throughout South Texas and Mexico recorded Tejano groups, including Rio (San Antonio), Arco (Alice), Del Valle-Oro (McAllen), El Toro (Mexico), Rovi (Mexico), DLV (Monterrey, Mexico), Corona (San Antonio), and Falcon (McAllen).[96] Although these record companies supported different musical styles, they all concentrated on conjunto music. Because of the increasing interest in conjunto, some musical ensembles and traditions began to disappear from the public arena. One of these was the string band. It died down and became an insignificant part of the community's musical tastes.[97] As noted above, vocal singing also experienced a significant decline.

A second reason for the emerging dominance of conjunto music was the growth of the number of cantinas and paid admission dances during the 1940s and 1950s. These new venues provided important means for the dissemination of conjunto music and for the growing popularity conjunto musicians such as Tony de la Rosa, Valerio Longoria, and Conjunto Bernal.

A third reason for the dominance of the conjunto was the appearance of the new dance style popularly known as el taquachito, a slower and more expressive way of dancing polkas and rancheras. Before it was danced with a quick loop in the manner of Polish or German polka dancing. Afterwards, a swaying motion replaced the hop and the skip.[98]

A final reason for the emerging dominance of conjunto music was the rapid increase in the number of working class individuals within the Mexican origin population. The *bracero* program, undocumented immigration, as well as high birth rates among the Mexican origin population led to a phenomenal growth of working-class individuals who loved this music.[99] Urbanization also played a role. Agricultural workers and those living in South Texas moved in large numbers to cities and urban areas. They brought their love of conjunto music to the cities and other parts of the United States. The increase in the number of cantinas and public dance halls, and of conjunto music in general, was largely a direct result of workers' migration to the cities.

CONCLUSION

During the postwar years, there were significant developments in música tejana in general and in conjunto and orquesta music in particular. Between 1946 and 1964, the music scene changed dramatically as a result of the impact of American culture, Tejano-owned recording companies, increased socioeconomic opportunities, and other factors. During the 1940s two new types of musical ensemble emerged and competed with conjuntos for audiences. Both female duets and orquestas lost out to the growing dominance of accordion-based music, which was on the way to becoming the most-listened-to music in the Tejano community. However, the emergence of rock and roll in the Anglo-American community during the late 1950s, as well as other changes in the Tejano community, quickly led to the development of new musical forms that again challenged the dominance of conjunto music and led to significant changes in the existing orquestas. The emergence of these new forms and their impact on conjunto music is the topic of the next chapter.

Chapter 4

Before the Arrival of the
Major Record Labels, 1964—89

From 1964 to 1989, música tejana evolved in new directions and expanded beyond South Texas. The conjuntos and orquestas continued to be an integral part of the community's musical heritage but significant changes occurred in them. Furthermore, three new distinct types of musical ensembles—the progressive conjunto, the Chicano country bands, and the grupo Tejano—emerged and competed with each other, with the conjunto and orquesta, and with other non-Tejano styles for fans. Despite the changes in música tejana, it continued to be rooted in traditional Mexican music, in the Spanish language, and in the experiences of the Mexican-origin population. In many respects, then, both change and continuity characterized música tejana during this period. This chapter provides a history of its evolution and expansion during these important years before the arrival of the major record labels.

CONTINUITY AND CHANGE IN
TRADITIONAL CONJUNTO MUSIC

Although conjunto music was an integral aspect of Tejano culture, its popularity fluctuated from the 1960s to the 1980s. In the 1960s it was the dominant form of music in the community, but its influence waned in the 1970s and 1980s, in part because of the emergence of new types of musical ensembles.

Dominance of Conjunto Music in the 1960s

During the 1960s, conjunto was the dominant musical form in the Tejano community. This was due largely to the emergence of Spanish-language radio, the rapid growth of the working-class Mexican-origin population, its increased migration to the urban areas, and the innovative thrust of Conjunto Bernal. It was most popular among adults and some working-class youth, especially *pachucos*.[1]

Tejanos and Mexicanos both played conjunto music. The music played by the former, as noted in earlier chapters, was called simply "conjunto," the latter "música norteña." Although there were some differences between the Tejano and Mexican conjuntos, most of these groups conformed to the instrumentation and musical repertoire established in the 1950s. The vast majority included four men and featured the accordion and bajo sexto as key

Conjunto Bernal with two accordions, McAllen, Texas, 1968.
Top, left to right: Joe Moscorro, Eloy Bernal, Chacha Jimenez, Juan Sifuentes, and Manuel Solis. *Bottom, left to right:* Oscar Hernandez and Paulino Bernal.
Courtesy Juan Sifuentes, Jr. and Tejano R.O.O.T.S.
(Recognizing Our Own Tejano Stars) Museum, Alice, Texas

instruments. Although many of these groups occasionally played a few baladas and cumbias, the majority continued to play primarily polkas and rancheras. With a few exceptions, the majority of conjunto groups had one primary vocalist.

Tejano conjuntos increased in popularity during the 1960s, as indicated by attendance at dance halls, album sales, radio airplay, and longevity of the groups. Some of the most popular conjuntos during this decade were Tony de la Rosa's, Conjunto Bernal, Los Donnenos, Rubén Vela, El Trio San Antonio, Flaco Jiménez y Los Caporales, Henry Zimmerle y Conjunto San Antonio, and Los Caminantes (with Mingo Saldívar and others).[2] Each of these groups recorded countless albums, played in a variety of settings, and contributed to enriching the cultural life and practices of Tejanos throughout the state.

Norteño groups were also popular among Tejanos. Among the most popular were older groups such as Los Alegres de Terán, Los Pavos Reales, Los Tremendos Gavilanes, Los Cadetes de Linares, Los Hermanos Prado, Los Norteños de Nuevo Laredo, and Los Pinquinos del Norte. In the 1960s new norteño groups, such as Los Relámpagos del Norte, Los Tigres del Norte, Los Cuatitos Cantú, and Carlos y José, gained a following in the Tejano community, especially in South Texas.[3]

The only major exception to the pattern of conservatism in conjunto music during the 1960s was Conjunto Bernal. Unlike other groups, Bernal experimented and expanded the traditional conjunto ensemble by adding two accordions, utilizing a new type of accordion (with five buttons), and incorporating both two- and three-part harmony into the music. His conjunto expanded the repertoire and played diverse songs, including polkas, rancheras, cumbias, valses, schotises, and even rock and roll.[4] The group's exploration of the limits of conjunto music made it the dominant conjunto during the 1960s.

These innovations attracted large numbers of new fans to conjunto music, including those living in the cities, the acculturated Mexican-origin youth, and some members of the middle classes. Conjunto Bernal thus played a key role in expanding the social base of conjunto music since it appealed to all sectors of the Mexican community, not simply those that belonged to the rural working classes.

Decline of Conjunto Music in the 1970s and 1980s
During the 1970s and 1980s, conjunto music declined in popularity among many Tejanos. Although it was far from extinct, conjunto music lost its appeal. One indicator of this decline was the absence of recordings by youth-

Tony de la Rosa, 1978. *Courtesy Freddie Records*

based conjunto groups. A few new conjuntos were founded during this period, including Los Dos Gilbertos, Rubén Narango y Sus Gamblers, and Steve
Jordan, but the vast majority of recordings were by older conjunto groups.[5]
Tony de La Rosa, for instance, remained a strong force in the late 1970s,
though his conjunto was formed in the 1950s. Rubén Vela and Henry Zimmerle
from San Antonio also were important conjunto artists during these decades,
though they had been around for many years. Few albums, indeed, were recorded by young Tejano artists. Another indicator of the loss of appeal was
the lack of conjunto groups in the top-ten lists of hits throughout the state.[6]
Few observers of música tejana wrote articles on conjunto groups. Most of
them focused on the rising stars of the orquestas or grupos Tejanos rather
than on conjuntos.[7]

The decline of conjunto music was due to the lack of interest in or rejection of accordion-based music by large segments of the Tejano population, especially the more acculturated, urbanized, and younger members of the Mexican-origin community. Their rejection was based, in many cases, on the perceived negative associations of this music. The accordion in particular and conjunto music in general was associated with the more unsavory aspects of *barrio* life: cantinas, alcoholism, violence, and low-life individuals like *cantineras* (prostitutes) and *pachucos*.[8] For many individuals, then, the accordion was an instrument of shame, not pride.[9]

Others lost interest in conjunto music because of its failure to incorporate the new sounds and songs of the 1970s and 1980s. Most conjuntos, for instance, did not play any contemporary soul, funk, or rock songs. As noted earlier, in some cases, conjunto groups expanded their musical repertoire to include an occasional cumbia, but, for the most part, they stuck mostly to polkas and rancheras.

The Exceptions to Conservatism: Jordan and Chavela

These groups also played or sang in a very traditional style. There was little innovation in playing the accordion and few changes in the vocal singing tradition of conjuntos. The only exception to this traditionalism in conjunto music was Steve Jordan y El Rio Jordan and Chavela y Brown Express. Steve Jordan was a "musician's musician" and played over thirty-five instruments. He was one of fifteen children born into a family of migrant farm workers in the tiny community of Elsa in the Rio Grande Valley of Texas. When he was born, in 1939, a midwife mistakenly dropped contaminated eye solution into his eyes. This left him blind in one eye and partially blind in the other. Because he began to use a patch, Jordan was given the nickname "El Parche" (The Eye Patch). Although partially blind and poor, Jordan had a talent for music. At age seven he learned to play the guitar. A year later, he picked up the accordion. He soon began to play in a variety of conjuntos and developed a unique style.[10]

Steve Jordan y El Rio Jordan was different from all other conjuntos in several distinct ways. First, he played a variety of English and Mexican dance tunes. His repertoire was grounded in the traditional polkas, rancheras, and boleros, but he expanded it to include other styles, including cumbias, corridos, rock, country, and even zydeco. As the accordion player in his group, Jordan also incorporated jazz and rhythm and blues into many of these songs. Second, he wrote songs with political lyrics and transformed English-language songs into Tejano music.[11] Third and most importantly, Jordan played the

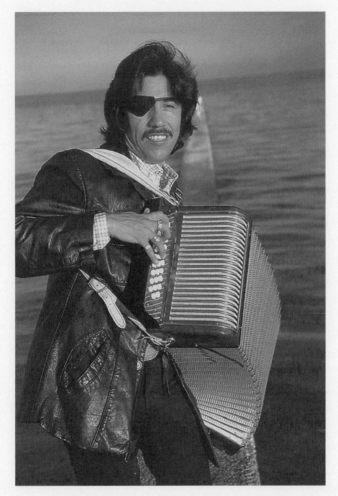

Steve Jordan, 2000. *Courtesy Freddie Records*

accordion in such a creative manner that no conjunto artist could match his virtuosity. Because of his energy and intensity, Jordan was often called "The Jimmy Hendrix of the Accordion." Despite his creativity, his fans wanted him to play traditional conjunto music without the frills.[12]

Chavela was born in Fresno, California around 1952 but was raised in East San Jose. Her Christian name was Isabela Salaiza Ortiz. She learned to play the accordion at a very early age. She joined her first group, Las Incomparables Hermanas Ortiz, by the time she was nine years old. This conjunto included her mother on bajo sexto, her grandfather on electric base, and her sister

Stella on drums. Although the group disbanded in 1968, Chavela continued to play with area bands. She joined the group Brown Express in 1976 but four years later left it to form her own group.[13] Not only was she from California, a rarity in the Tejano music industry, but she also was the lead singer and accordionist for the group. Chavela y Brown Express was the first and only female-based group to record conjunto music during this entire period. While females were not absent from the music industry, most recorded as solistas or in duets. None led a conjunto group or played the accordion and served as lead singer. Chavela successfully broke this gender barrier.

Despite the innovations of Jordan and Chavela, the majority of conjunto groups failed to change. Three decades after its establishment, the conjunto ensemble was still composed mostly of one male vocalist and four basic instruments: the accordion, the bajo sexto, the bass guitar, and the drum. Failure to change led to a declining interest in this type of music in the 1970s and early 1980s. It is important to note that there was not a blanket rejection of Tejano music, only the traditional conjunto style of playing it. Tejano musicians continued to play rancheras, polkas, and other traditional Mexican musical genres, but they updated these songs and used different instruments. For many of these individuals, the keyboard, pitos, and rhythm guitar, rather than the accordion and bajo sexto, became the instruments of cultural pride and choice among them. While the youth, middle class, and acculturated U.S. residents rejected or lost interest in conjuntos and conjunto music, Chicano activists embraced it as "the best-known and most clearly identifiable expression of Texas Chicano culture."[14] These individuals praised this music and began to find ways of preserving and promoting it. One of the most important events associated with this effort was the establishment of the annual Tejano Conjunto Festival in San Antonio in 1982. This festival, organized by the Guadalupe Cultural Arts Center in San Antonio, initially occurred over a few days but it was later expanded to a full week. During the 1980s it became one of the most important means for celebrating this type of music.[15] This renewed interest in the symbolic value of accordion-based music did not have a significant impact on its declining popularity during these years but it did influence the modern orquesta.

The Growth of Conjuntos Norteños

The declining interest in conjunto music occurred primarily among Tejanos, not norteños. This development provided norteño groups an opportunity to advance their particular style of music. Beginning in the early 1970s, they began to compete seriously for dominance of the conjunto market in Texas.

Norteño groups, especially the newer ones, such as Los Relámpagos del Norte, Ramón Ayala y Los Bravos del Norte, and Los Tigres del Norte, increased their promotions, recordings, and sales in Texas during these years. These Mexican norteño groups played the same type of music as Tejano conjuntos but with some minor differences, such as a faster beat, more corridos, and different singing styles.[16] Like Tejano groups, they used the accordion, bajo sexto, bass, and drums. Occasionally, a saxophone or a stand-up bass, instead of a bajo sexto, was used.

By the mid-1970s, the popularity of norteño music increased, as indicated by the greater number of records sold and the large number of individuals attending public dances featuring these groups. The popularity of norteño music increased for several important reasons. One was the absence of a dominant Tejano conjunto group. In the 1960s Conjunto Bernal was considered the most important group in the Tejano music industry. This conjunto, however, disbanded in the early 1970s. Cha Cha Jiménez, one of his former singers, formed Los Chachos and tried to follow in the tradition of Bernal. The group recorded several albums but did not retain the popularity of its predecessors.[17] The lack of any dominant Tejano conjunto group thus left the market open to competition. Norteño groups took advantage of this opening.

Los Relámpagos del Norte at the recording studio, early 1960s. Guitar player and drummer unknown, Cornelio Reyna (bajo sexto), and Ramón Ayala (accordion). *Courtesy Juan Sifuentes, Jr. and Tejano R.O.O.T.S. (Recognizing Our Own Tejano Stars) Museum, Alice, Texas*

Ramón Ayala at Hullabaloos, Houston, Texas, 1999. *Courtesy Annette Cruz*

Aggressive marketing by non-Tejano and Tejano recording studios, especially Bego Records from South Texas, and the influx of Mexican immigrants to the state during these years also gave norteño groups an edge in the conjunto market. Among the groups having a significant impact in Texas were none other than Los Relámpagos del Norte and Ramón Ayala y Los Bravos del Norte. Los Relámpagos, composed originally of Ramón Ayala and Cornelio Reyna, was formed in Mexico in the mid-1960s and recorded several hit albums.[18] In the early 1970s, the group broke up. Reyna headed into the Mexican movie industry, whereas Ayala continued with music and formed his own group, Los Bravos del Norte. Ayala's group continued to record hit after hit under several different labels. By the late 1970s he became known as the king of norteño music.[19] He has retained this title ever since, and, in the year 2000, his was one of the most popular conjuntos in Texas and Mexico.[20]

RISE AND FALL OF THE MODERN ORQUESTAS TEJANAS

During the years from the 1960s to the 1980s, the orquestas also were an integral part of the community's musical heritage. Unlike the conjuntos, they experienced significant changes over time in their instrumentation, their repertoire, and their popularity. Orquesta musicians of the 1960s modified the instrumental mix of the older ones and added the organ to the ensemble. They also deleted many of the Caribbean and American based rhythms of the older groups and substituted the songs and dances popular in the U. S. during the 1960s and 1970s.

Because of these and other changes, the orquestas Tejanas became the dominant style of ensemble in the 1970s. It appealed primarily to the younger, more assimilated, and more urbanized Mexican American youth. Their dominance was not merely a middle-class phenomenon, as Peña argues, but a broad social one. Orquestas, in other words, were not popular because they appealed only to the middle classes but because they also appealed to the more urbanized and acculturated sectors of the working-class Mexican-origin community. Despite their dominance, by the early 1980s the orquestas faded from view and were replaced by the grupos Tejanos.[21]

The Rock and Roll Foundation of Orquestas, 1957–64
The modern orquesta and its distinctive sounds, known as "Tex-Mex" or "La Onda Chicana," originated in 1964, when Sunny Ozuna and his Sunglows began to record Mexican music in Spanish. In this year he recorded "Carino Nuevo." Unlike existing conjunto groups, Sunny did not use an accordion.

Also unlike existing orquestas, he incorporated the "modern" sounds of the organ and the electric guitar into his music. "Carino Nuevo" became an instant hit. Soon other Spanish-language hits followed.[22]

Sunny, however, did not begin his recording career playing this type of music. He, as well as many other members of his generation, dismissed or rejected Mexican music in general and conjunto music in particular. Their failure to embrace this music was based, in some respects, on its negative associations and on its perceived irrelevance.[23] The youth viewed Mexican music as part of their parent's cultural heritage, not theirs. For this reason, many young Tejano musicians viewed Mexican music as old-fashioned or else as irrelevant to their lives in the United States.

Instead of their parents' music, Sunny's generation sought the styles and songs reflective of its own interests and tastes. The various forms of popular American music, including rock and roll, doo-wop, and soul, met the youth's new musical tastes. Its inspiration initially came not from Tejano or Mexicano performers but from musicians that were popular with U.S. youth, such as Chuck Berry, Little Richard, Bill Haley, the Clovers, Joe Turner, and the Beatles.[24]

According to several scholars, two distinct strands of American popular music—rhythm and blues and rock and roll—influenced Mexican American teens throughout the country.[25] In the late 1940s and early 1950s, rhythm and blues musicians such as Chuck Higgins, Big Jay McNeeley, and Richard Berry encouraged Mexican Americans to play jazz, swing, and rhythm and blues. Among the first Mexican Americans to record this type of music was the Don Tosti Band from Los Angeles. Its first hit, "The Pachuco Boogie," recorded in 1948, was a mixture of English, Mexican American, and African American rhythms and languages. It sold more than two million copies. L'il Julian Herrera, from the Los Angeles area, also recorded regional hits that mixed Mexican American and African American vocal styles. One of his most important hits was the 1956 song "Lonely, Lonely Nights."[26]

Rock and roll artists and groups such as Bill Haley and the Comets and Dion and the Belmonts likewise influenced Mexican American musicians. The most important and early Mexican American rock star of the late 1950s was Ritchie Valens. Valens, born Richard Valenzuela, began his recording career while in high school. He recorded several top-ten hits, including the popular Mexican folk song "La Bamba," before his untimely death in an airplane crash. According to several scholars, Valens was the most talented and confident Mexican American rock and roll performer of all time.[27] "Valens and his group the Silhouettes," note the historians Arnoldo de Leon and

Richard Griswold del Castillo, "mixed traditional Mexican folk songs, hill-billy ballads, and black rhythm-and-blues to produce a Mestizo rock-and-roll sound."[28]

These two particular strands of contemporary American musical forms also influenced Mexican American youth in Texas.[29] Their impact, however, was not as great as on Mexican-origin youth in other parts of the country. Only two Tejano groups, for instance, recorded rhythm and blues–oriented tunes in the 1950s: The Beto Villa Orquesta and the Orquesta of Balde González, both recording artists for Ideal. The Beto Villa Orquesta recorded "Pachuca Blues" in 1950; Balde González, a lesser-known orquesta musician, recorded the "canción blues" song "No Esperar Más de Mí," (Don't Wait Anymore for Me) in the early 1950s.[30]

A larger number of Tejanos played and recorded rock and roll in the late 1950s, but unlike Mexican Americans in California, they initially sang the lyrics in Spanish. As early as 1957, for instance, Conjunto Bernal recorded a rock and roll song in Spanish called "La Novia Antonia."[31]

In the early 1960s, the most prolific Tejano rock and roll artist was Balderama Huerta, from South Texas. Huerta was known by several names during his early professional years. In the 1950s and early 1960s he was known as the Be-bop Kid. Later he assumed the name Freddy Fender. Two of his most important hits in the early 1960s were "Que Mala" and "Corinna, Corinna." Fender recorded the former song in 1961 with a group called Eddie Con Los Shades; the latter was recorded in 1963 under his own name. Both of these songs were recorded in Spanish.[32] However, Freddie Fender and other Tejano musicians soon switched to English, effectively ending the "rock and roll en español" movement.

In many cases, the new crop of Tejano musicians wanted to make it in the mainstream of American music, but because of stiff competition from national recording companies, limited resources, and discrimination, the primary listeners to these rock and roll songs were members of the Mexican American community.[33] One of the first Tejano groups to record in English during this period was Los Dinos from Corpus Christi. This group was composed of three vocalists—Seff Perales, Bobby Lira, and Abraham Quintanilla.[34] They recorded their first song, "So Hard to Tell," in 1959 under the J. W. Fox label, and during the next three years they issued approximately nine additional singles in English.

Countless other groups like Los Dinos emerged in the late 1950s and early 1960s. A tentative list of some of the more popular groups would include the following: Rudy and the Reno Bops from San Antonio, David Coronado and

Los Dinos, 1964. *Clockwise from left:* Ray Villareal, Johnny Cadena (guitar), Seferino Perales, Bobby Lira, Abraham Quintanilla, Manuel Hernandez (bass), Danny Contreras (guitar), and George Martinez (middle).
Courtesy Abraham Quintanilla and Q Productions

the Latinaires, Little Joe and the Latinaires, Sunny and the Sunglows, George Jay and the Rocking Ravens, René and René, and Sam the Sham and the Pharoahs.[35] Undoubtedly, the most successful of this new generation of musicians was Sunny and the Sunglows. The Sunglows played what musicians called Latin soul. Sunny and his group scored several top-ten hits in the early 1960s.[36] His first hit was "Talk to Me," recorded in 1962. Sunny also appeared in the popular TV show American Bandstand. It was one of the highlights of his career and one of the proudest moments of the Tejano community. In the next year Sunny recorded several other hits, including "Just a Dream" and "I'm a Fool to Care."[37] Because of his success in the early 1960s, Sunny Ozuna and the Sunglows became the role model and pride of most Tejano groups.

The Switch to Música Tejana

Despite Sunny's success in the English-speaking musical mainstream, in 1964 he began to record in Spanish. Continued discrimination in the English-language market, increased community pressures for Spanish music, and the need to try new things encouraged Sunny to switch to Spanish-language tunes.[38] As noted earlier, the first Spanish song he recorded in 1964, "Carino Nuevo," became an instant hit. This was the first of many other hits in the 1960s. Because of his popularity and tremendous success, when Sunny switched to Spanish-language music in 1964, it brought a halt to the fledgling Tejano English-language recording industry and initiated a trend toward the development of a new sound in Tejano music, the modern orquesta Tejana.

The modern orquestas were different in at least three respects from those established in the 1940s. First, they had a smaller horn section. Whereas the orquestas of the past used anywhere from six to twelve brass and wind instruments, including saxophones, trumpets, and clarinets, this new generation of musicians limited the number of horns to four or fewer. Most groups had either two trumpets and a tenor or alto saxophone or a different combination of these types of instruments. Second, they were organ-driven—that is, the organ became an important and, at times, significant part of the new orquestas. Third, these new groups used electric guitars. They rejected the traditional bajo sexto used by conjuntos and replaced it with the electric guitar used by many rock and roll groups. The small number and particular mix of pitos, as well as the use of electric guitars and the organ, made the modern orquesta a unique musical ensemble and gave it its distinctive sound.

Changes also were made to the musical repertoire of established orquestas. Like others before them, they played a variety of polkas, rancheras, and baladas. Unlike the orquestas of the post–World War II era, those in the 1960s changed the type of English- and Spanish-language tunes that they played. In keeping with contemporary American musical influences, for instance, they played rock and roll, soul, and even country. Probably because of their Americanization, they abandoned the variety of Caribbean and Latin American tunes played by orquestas of the 1940s and 1950s, such as danzones, cha-cha-chas, porros, guarachas, and paso dobles. However, they did incorporate the cumbia into their repertoire. It is unclear who began to play cumbias initially or when it became part of the Tejano music repertoire, but by the latter part of the 1960s, most groups included them in their musical repertoires.[39]

All these differences suggest that while the orquestas Tejanas emerged out of the orquesta tradition within the community, they were not organically linked to the orquestas of the past. Few musicians, for instance, turned to the orquestas of Isidro López or other well-known groups for advice or for assistance. There seems to have been a break in communication between the orquestas of the past and the new modern orquestas Tejanas. More research needs to be conducted regarding the relationship between the old and the new orquestas and the extent to which there was continuity and change between them.

Rise and Dominance of Orquestas Tejanas, 1964–77

The orquesta style of música tejana increased in popularity after Sunny began to record in Spanish. Other established groups quickly made the big switch to Texas-Mexican music in the mid- and late 1960s. Among the most influential of these groups initially were Little Joe and the Latinaires and Los Dinos. Little Joe recorded his first Tejano album, *Por Un Amor,* in 1964. Several years later he recorded *Arriba,* an album containing several traditional rancheras and polkas. One of his rancheras, "A La Guerra Ya Me Llevan" ("They Are Sending Me to War"), contained an anti-war theme. This politically inspired song soon established him as an important musician, especially with the emerging Chicano movement of the 1960s.[40]

Los Dinos also made an easy transition to Spanish-language Tejano music in the mid-1960s. Their first Tejano album, *Con Esta Copa,* recorded in 1964, established them as a first-rate orquesta.[41] From 1964 to 1974, they recorded more than six LPs and about a dozen singles. Many of their songs became regional hits and received a significant amount of airplay. The group broke up in 1974 and did not record or play anymore after this year. For over a decade, however, Los Dinos were at the forefront of both the English- and the Spanish-language music played by orquestas Tejanas.[42]

Los Dinos played an influential role in popularizing the orquesta sound in the Gulf Coast region and introducing it to audiences in the Lower Rio Grande Valley. Los Dinos performed in the latter region and toured the country with the caravan of conjunto artists organized by Falcon and other recording com-

Los Dinos and the Caravanas Tejanas in Bakersfield, California, 1965.
Front, left to right: Leonel Sanchez, Abraham Quintanilla, Ramon Ayala, Senor
Guerrero (dance promoter), Cornelio Reyna, and George Rodriguez.
Back, left to right: Seff Perales, unknown, and Bobby Lira.
Courtesy Abraham Quintanilla and Q Productions

panies during the 1960s. As part of these popular traveling shows, they performed with such conjunto greats as Conjunto Bernal, Los Relámpagos del
Norte, and Carlos Guzman y su Conjunto. "Los Dinos introduced the orquesta
sound to South Texas, not Little Joe or Sunny," noted Abraham Quintanilla,
one of the former members of the group. "We toured with the conjunto
caravanas in the 1960s and prepared the way for this new sound," he added.[43]
Despite Los Dinos' initial popularity in South Texas, Little Joe and Sunny
Ozuna soon became the dominant groups in the orquesta Tejana tradition.
Better musical arrangements and a more aggressive management probably
accounted for their dominance in the Tejano music industry.

The orquesta sound indeed increased in popularity during the late 1960s
and the 1970s. Indicative of this popularity was the number of new orquestas
formed in this period. In just over two decades, at least twenty new groups
formed and recorded a variety of albums for different labels. Among the

better-known groups that emerged in the 1970s were the Royal Jesters, Latin Breed, Freddie Martínez, and Agustín Ramírez (see table 3).[44] The increased acceptance of this new sound is also reflected in the number of orquesta-based songs that made the top-ten list throughout the state. Countless of these songs consistently stayed on the top-ten lists of major radio stations in Corpus Christi, Kingsville, San Antonio, Houston, and McAllen during these two decades.[45]

TABLE 3

SELECTED ORQUESTAS TEJANAS,
1950S–70S, BY YEAR ESTABLISHED

Name of Group	Year Established[a]
Alfonso Ramos y Su Orquesta	1950s
George Jay and the Rocking Ravens	1950s
Rudy and the Reno Bops	1950s
David Coronado and the Latinaires	1956
Royal Jesters	1958
Sunny Ozuna and the Sunglows	1958
Little Joe y Latinaires	1959
Carlos Guzman	1960s
Freddie Martinez y Su Orquesta	1960
Augustín Ramírez	1967
Joe Bravo y Su Orquesta	1968
Johnny Canales y Su Orquesta	1969
Latin Breed	1969[b]
Roy Montelongo	1969
Big Lu	1970s
Carlos Miranda	1970s
Diablo Band	1970s
Los Bandidos de Albert López	1970s
Los Playboys de Eddie Olivarez	1970s
Markey Lee	1970s
People	1970s
Showband USA	1970s
Tortilla Factory	1970s
Rubén Ramos and the Mexican Revolution	1970
Jimmy Edward	1975

Source: Various entries in Burr, *Billboard Guide,* and Author's personal music collection from the 1960s to the present.
[a]If a precise date is known it is included in the list. If no precise date is noted, then only the decade in which the group was established is noted.
[b]The original group disbanded within a year after its establishment, but it was reorganized in 1973.

The Decline of Orquestas in the 1980s

Despite their popularity in the 1970s, the orquestas Tejanas died down by the early 1980s. Among the few groups that remained in the 1980s were Latin Breed, Rubén Ramos and the Mexican Revolution, and Little Joe. During the 1990s, only Rubén Ramos and the Texas Revolution remained a viable orquesta.[46] For all intents and purposes, La Onda Chicana—the particular type of sound played by the orquestas of the 1960s and 1970s—was dead by the 1980s.[47]

Why did this music fade? There are two possible reasons. First, the orquestas Tejanas failed to keep up with the changing musical tastes of Tejano listeners. In the 1980s the new generation of young people lost interest in the big, brassy sounds popularized by the orquestas. For most of them, the new sounds made by the synthesizer in the 1980s were more appealing.[48] Second, the new generation of Tejano youth was more interested in different types of popular American and Latin American music than the ones initially played by orquestas. Most of these listeners were not into soul or rock; they enjoyed the new rhythms of pop, dance music, country, and rap, as well as cumbias, merengue, and música romántica. Groups willing to abandon the pitos and able to incorporate new instruments and musical styles became increasingly popular during the 1980s and 1990s.

THE EMERGENCE OF NEW ENSEMBLES

During the quarter century from the mid-1960s to the late 1980s, other Tejano groups with different musical styles emerged in the community. Key among these were the progressive conjuntos, the Chicano country bands, and the grupos. The grupos originated in the 1960s and became a significant force in the 1980s. Progressive conjuntos first formed in the 1970s, but did not become a significant part of música tejana until the 1990s. Little information is available on the Chicano country bands but they probably originated in the 1960s, if not earlier. These types of bands remained hugely popular, but mostly in the lower Rio Grande Valley. Progressive conjuntos, Chicano country bands, and grupos played música tejana but the instrumentation, repertoire, and performance differed from each other and from the conjuntos and the orquestas.

Origins of Progressive Conjuntos

As noted earlier, progressive conjuntos originated in the early part of the 1970s when Robert Pulido changed the instrumentation of the traditional four-piece ensemble and added several saxophones. Pulido was a fan of conjunto music and had learned to love the music at an early age. He also enjoyed the "brassy" sound of the orquestas tejanas popular in this decade. In the early 1970s, he decided to merge these two distinct sounds. The addition of *pitos* or horns to the conjunto, while not new among norteño groups, was a novel idea in Texas.[49] These, as well as other changes to be described below, eventually led to the creation of a new musical ensemble in the Tejano community—the progressive conjunto.

Pulido was born in Edinburgh, Texas in 1950 and learned to play the guitar at the age of twelve. In his first year of high school, he joined a conjunto group called Los Hermanos Layton from Elsa, Texas. Two years later he learned to play the saxophone, and upon graduation he received several music scholarships. He enrolled at Pan American University in his home town to study music. In 1970 he began playing with Cecilio Garza y Los Kasinos of La Joya, Texas. After graduating from college in 1973 with a degree in music, he tried teaching for a while. He soon resigned his teaching post and formed his own group, Roberto Pulido y Los Clásicos. This group included his uncle Leonel on accordion and brothers Roel and Joel on saxophones. A series of albums produced only regional hits, but his distinct sound consistently attracted fans to the dances where he played.[50]

Pulido not only introduced new instrumentation into the conjunto to form a new type of ensemble, he also added country songs and ballads to the traditional mix of polkas and rancheras. Country music was an important aspect of Tejano culture and life, especially in South Texas. Pulido's recording of country tunes indicated an increasing appreciation for this music among Tejanos. Pulido, in some ways, was taking advantage of the trend toward country music by Chicano bands along the border. "Chicano country" bands, in most cases, did not use any instruments identified with the traditional conjuntos or orquestas. Although they did not use accordions or pitos, they sang traditional Mexican canciones, but in a "country" style. Chicano country bands, unlike other Tejano groups, also sang traditional country songs but mostly in Spanish.

Pulido played a key role in popularizing country music in the Tejano community and in developing a new musical ensemble still in its embryonic stage in this period. Many of his fans fully accepted these changes in the instrumental mix and in the repertory. They consistently bought his music and attended his dances in large numbers. Pulido's unique sound allowed him to remain true to conjunto while adding new instruments and expanding the traditional repertoire.

Los Kasinos, 1970s. *Courtesy Mel Villarreal*

In the mid- and late 1970s, at least three other groups followed in Pulido's footsteps: Cecilio Garza y Los Kasinos, Los Formales de Cali Carranza, and David Lee Garza y Los Musicales.[51] Of these three, David Lee Garza was the most influential. Garza, born in 1957 in Jourdanton, Texas, began playing the accordion at the age of eight. By eleven he was playing with his father in the band Margarito Hernández y Su Conjunto. In 1968 the band changed its name to David Lee Garza y Su Conjunto. During the mid-1970s, he added saxophones to his group and began to expand his Tejano repertoire.[52] Like Pulido, David Lee Garza experienced some success in the Tejano music market and in the dance circuit throughout the state.

During the 1980s David Lee Garza y Los Musicales began to attract increased attention by Tejano music fans. One of the reasons for this increased

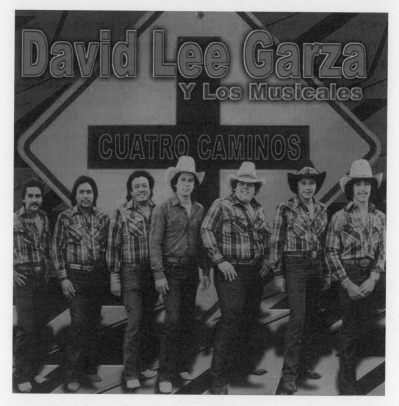

David Lee Garza y Los Musicales, 1981. Ram Herrera appears far left.
Courtesy Hacienda Records

popularity was the group's lead singer, Emilio Navaira.[53] Navaira had been preceded by Ramiro Herrera (1980–83), who had left Los Musicales to form his own group, Ram and the Montana Band. Emilio's presence increased Los Musicales' popularity, especially among the youth. With Navaira as lead singer, Los Musicales began to win numerous Tejano Music Awards, including best conjunto album for *Award-Winning Musicales* (1985) and best album for *Cuantas Veces* (1987).[54] In 1989 it won two awards, one for album of the year—conjunto *(Tour 88),* and the other for single of the year ("Me Quieres Tu").[55] It is unclear yet what was so appealing about Emilio but he definitely brought a new style to progressive conjunto music in the mid- and late 1980s.

Chicano Country Bands

Chicano country bands are a phenomenon in música tejana. No written documentation exists on their origins but most likely they emerged in the lower

Rio Grande Valley in the post–World War II era and became increasingly popular over the years. Chicano country bands, in most cases, did not use any accordions, saxophones, or trumpets. Similar to Anglo country and western bands, they initially used violins, steel guitars, and rhythm guitars. Unlike Anglo groups, Chicano country bands sang both traditional Mexican canciones and country songs. Some of these songs, especially the country tunes, were in English but most of them were sung in Spanish. These bands also played traditional Mexican dance tunes such as rancheras, corridos, polkas, baladas, and valses, as well as one-steps, two-steps, and other dances popular among country fans. Although more research needs to be done on Chicano country bands, it is very possible that they were linked to música tejana through their rural orientation, their themes, and their dance tunes, many of which were not played by Tejano groups anymore. This is especially true of the one-steps and the two-steps, dance tunes that were popular in the pre–World War II years, but abandoned by conjuntos and orquestas after 1946.

The most influential Chicano country group of the 1970s and early 1980s was the Country Roland Band. This group's popularity coincided with the expanding commercialization of country music in the United States, generally, with the greater acceptance of these rhythms by significantly larger numbers of individuals, including Tejanos, and with the growing popularity of Mexican American country singers such as Freddy Fender and Johnny Rodriguez.[56] In the early years, Country Roland consisted primarily of the Roland Garcia family, including Roland, Sr. and his four children: Roland, Jr., Gore, Judy, and Wendy. The senior Garcia provided the lead locals while the others played various instruments or sang backup vocals. Country Roland, as Mr. Garcia was commonly known, recorded for Falcon Records in McAllen, Texas, but ARV International distributed many of his albums in Mexico. He either sang traditional country songs or he converted popular Mexican tunes like "Con Cartitas," "Gabino Barrera," and "Las Margaritas" into country-flavored songs. Likewise, he performed and popularized country dance tunes, such as the Cotton Eyed Joe and the Bunny Hop.[57] Other Chicano country bands soon followed in Country Roland's footsteps. Among the best-known groups in the late 1970s and early 1980s were Patsy Torres, the Cactus Country Band, Texas Country Band, and Country Roland, Jr.[58]

The country sound reflected in the above bands was so popular that other Tejano groups began to incorporate this rhythm into música tejana. Among the most important groups that included country tunes in their repertoire during the 1970s were Rudy Tee Gonzalez and the Reno Bops, Roberto Pulido y Los Clasicos, Laura Canales, and Mazz.[59]

Country Roland, 1980s. *Courtesy Hacienda Records*

The Chicano country bands, it would be safe to state, were popular primarily in South Texas. They thus remained highly regionalized and had only a limited impact on música tejana. Their impact generally was indirect and mediated through more popular groups such as Pulido and Canales in the mid-1970s and Mazz in the latter part of the decade.

The Emergence of Grupos Tejanos
In the 1970s another type of musical ensemble known as the grupo Tejano emerged in the community. Grupos were smaller than the orquestas Tejanas and initially about the same size as the conjuntos.[60] The keyboard, rather than the accordion, became the dominant instrument in the grupos. In the early 1970s, prior to the development and popularization of the synthesizer among American and European bands, an organ was used. The synthesizer was added in the late 1970s. Shifting public taste, accompanied by increased economic and social opportunities, facilitated the emergence and popularity of this type of musical ensemble.

These keyboard-driven groups originally did not have a particular name, although they were extremely emphatic about not being labeled as either orquestas or conjuntos.[61] In the early 1990s, the Texas Talent Music Association (TTMA), the leading proponent of música tejana in the state, developed a term for this type of musical ensemble—"grupos Tejanos." Grupos, more particularly, were defined as synthesizer-driven bands that played música tejana.[62] This definition, in part, was derived from the Mexican usage of "grupos" or "onda grupera," but with some minor differences. Grupos in Mexico were synthesizer-driven bands that played primarily pop ballads or música romántica. Among the best-known grupos in Mexico during the 1960s were Los Babys and Los Freddys. In the 1970s examples of la onda grupera included Los Temerarios and Los Bukis.[63] In Texas, grupos also depended on the keyboards for their sounds, but unlike Mexican groups, they played the entire repertoire of música tejana, not simply música romántica. Despite the TTMA's labeling efforts, most commentators and music critics failed to consistently use this term. In the majority of cases, the keyboard-driven groups playing música tejana were commonly referred to as simply "Tejano." In the following pages, the term "grupos" or "grupos Tejanos" is used to identify those bands that emphasize the keyboard in their music. This term is also consistent with the TTMA's original definition of grupos Tejanos.

Grupos Tejanos emerged out of the conjunto tradition in the mid-1960s. The originators of this type of ensemble were members of Los Fabulosos Cuatro (The Fabulous Four).[64] In the early 1960s, this group was a traditional conjunto composed of four individuals and one lead vocalist, Carlos Guzman.[65] Within a period of several years, however, the conjunto began to change its image and sound. First, the members assumed the name "Los Fabulosos Cuatro." This name was inspired by the Beatles and is a Spanish translation of "Fab Four." Second, the group replaced the accordion with the organ. Initially, the group only experimented with the sounds of the accordion. Armando "Chore" Hinojosa, the accordionist, for instance, wanted to get a different sound out of his instrument. In 1964 or 1965 he decided to connect the accordion to an amplifier to see what it sounded like. The group liked the unique vibrato-like quality of the electrified accordion and began to perform and record music with this new sound. By 1965 the group switched to an organ because of its increased popularity with American bands and with the new orquestas Tejanas. Although the group continued using an accordion, it increasingly depended on the organ for its primary sound. Third, Los Fabulosos replaced the bajo sexto with an electric guitar. The bajo sexto, in fact, was used on only two songs on the first album.[66] Soon thereafter, the group decided

Los Fabulosos Cuatro, mid-1960s. *Left to right:* Armando "Chore"
Hinojosa (bass), Mel Villareal (accordion), Carlos Guzman (lead singer),
Juan Hinojosa (drums), and Ramiro "Snowball" de la Cruz
(with sunglasses). *Courtesy Omar Rivera*

to forego the bajo sexto and used the electric guitar exclusively.[67] Thus, in a
three-year period, from 1963 to 1965, Los Fabulosos had replaced the accordion and bajo sexto with an organ and an electric guitar. In doing so, it had
created a new, distinctive sound in música tejana and a new ensemble—the
grupo Tejano.[68]

During the next several decades, the influence of Los Fabulosos would be
felt by the Tejano music industry as an increasing number of new grupos
emerged and emulated its sounds. Among the most popular were Laura Canales

in the 1970s, and Mazz, Selena, and La Mafia in the 1980s. These keyboard-based grupos not only used different instruments, they also expanded the musical repertoire. In addition to playing traditional Mexican songs such as rancheras and polkas, for instance, they added an increasingly larger number of cumbias and baladas. They also played more country songs and American pop tunes such as disco and funk. Manuel Peña has recently argued that these groups promoted a non-Tejano aesthetic because they did not keep to the polka and ranchera repertoire of prior musical groups.[69] I prefer to call it a new Tejano, rather than a *non*-Tejano, aesthetic. These groups still played música tejana, but they extended its repertoire to include other dance tunes as well.

Los Fabulosos Cuatro started the trend in 1964, but not until the early 1970s did the new organ-based musical ensemble become popular. The dominance of the orquestas Tejanas and the need to become accustomed to a new sound probably stalled its popularity in the late 1960s and early 1970s. During the 1970s and early 1980s, however, this type of musical ensemble became increasingly popular. Indicative of this increased popularity was the formation of several new organ-based groups, such as Los Unicos, Snowball & Co., Mayo, Charro Band, La Movida, and Arturo Montes y Ternura (see table 4).[70]

A possible reason for the increased popularity of grupos in the 1970s was Laura Canales. Born in Kingsville, Texas, in 1954, Laura Canales, age nineteen, with a "smooth, clear voice," became the lead singer for Los Unicos.[71] With the exception of Chavela y Brown Express, Canales was the only woman recording música tejana in the 1970s. She was thus the second female to break through the traditionally male-dominated Tejano recording industry in this decade.

In 1975 Canales joined Snowball & Co.[72] By 1976 or 1977, Canales was heading her own group. Originally it was called Felicidad; later she formed Laura Canales and Encanto. She had a series of hits in the 1970s, and by the early 1980s she emerged as the "reigning queen of Tejano music," as indicated by her dominance of the female categories in the Tejano Music Awards (TMA).[73] From 1982 to 1986 and again in 1988, for instance, Canales won the female vocalist of the year award at the TMA. She also won the female entertainer of the year award from 1983 to 1986.[74]

In the 1980s the grupos Tejanos and their distinctive sound became more popular than ever before. Much of this was due to the tremendous impact of three new groups: Mazz, La Mafia, and Selena y Los Dinos. All of these groups utilized keyboards, especially the synthesizer, and promoted a new Tejano aesthetic—they expanded the musical repertoire of older Tejano groups.

TABLE 4

SELECTED ORGAN-BASED GRUPOS,
1970S–80S, BY YEAR ESTABLISHED

Name of Group	Year Established
Los Fabulosos Cuatro	1963
Los Unicos	1968/1969
Charro Band	1970s
La Movida	1970s
La Raza of Houston	early 1970s
Mel Villarreal	early 1970s
Snowball & Co.	early 1970s
La Connexion Mexicana de Joe Cisneros	mid-1970s
La Herencia	mid-1970s
TJ & Company de Emilio Guerrero	mid-1970s
La Feria de Rene Rodriguez	late 1970s
Los Bandidos de Albert Lopez	late 1970s
Los Chavos	late 1970s
Los Jokers de Joel Silva	late 1970s
Tacho Rivera & Tequila	late 1970s
Laura Canales	1973
Felicidad	1976/1977
Kanela	1978?
La Nueva Illusion	1978?
Arturo Montes and Ternura	1980s
Mayo	1980s
Encanto	1981
Romance	1981

Source: Burr, *Billboard Guide;* Guile González, "New Hit Due for Los Fabulosos," *Corpus Christi Sun,*
September 16–22, 1978, p. 7B; Guile González, "Chicano Music Scene," *Corpus Christi Sun,* May 20–
26, 1978, p. 6B, and September 1–9, 1978, p. 7B; author's recollections as a dancer during the 1970s and
1980s; selections from *Tejano Goldies,* Lago LC1006, 1995, and *Tejano Goldies II,* Lago LC2000, 1996.

In the late 1970s the synthesizer was added to the grupo ensemble. This
instrument, used by many disco and rock and roll musicians, added a fuller
sound to the traditional music played by organ-based grupos. The initiator of
this new sound in the late 1970s was the group Mazz, headed by Joe López
and Jimmy González. López was the lead vocalist and songwriter; González
played lead guitar, sang background vocals, and produced and arranged the
tunes. López and González shared more than musical talent. Both were born
on the same day, in the same year, and at the same hospital in Brownsville,
Texas. They also attended the same high school. While in school together in

1966, López and González formed their first musical group, first called Little Joe's Group, which performed under various names for more than a decade. In 1977 Cara Records asked them to come up with a short, catchy name for their first album. They came up with the name Mazz.[75]

Mazz, like most other grupos of the early 1970s, promoted an expanded repertoire in música tejana that included not only traditional Mexican polkas and rancheras, but also country, cumbias, and baladas.[76] In doing so, it popularized the new Tejano aesthetic for a new generation of listeners—an aesthetic reflected in the first album the group recorded in 1977. Out of the ten songs on this album, five are cumbias, three are country, and two are rancheras.[77] On Mazz's second album, issued in 1978 and self-titled *Mazz*, not a single ranchera or polka was included. Out of the ten songs recorded, four are baladas, four are country, and two are cumbias.[78] Mazz recorded one ranchera on its 1979 album ("Te Perdi"). The other songs are cumbias (one), country (three), baladas (three), and pop (two).[79] Over time, Mazz recorded an increasing number of rancheras but emphasized songs without a polka beat.[80]

Mazz's musical style became increasingly popular, as indicated by the number of awards that the group began to win in the 1980s. As early as 1981, the first year of the statewide Tejano Music Awards, Mazz won an award for most promising band. In 1983 Joe López won the male vocalist award. Mazz won two awards in each of the following years: 1986, 1988, and 1989.[81] In total,

Laura Canales. *Courtesy Freddie Records*

between 1980 and 1989, of the seventy awards won by male musicians or male-based groups, Mazz won a total of eight.[82] Despite the group's increasing popularity, Mazz had many problems with promoters. In some cases, the group failed to show up to contracted performances. In others, the members came late and left early. In still other cases, they simply played a short, uninspired set. Although Mazz was unpredictable, the fans loved the group and its music.

The second group to have an impact on música tejana in the 1980s was La Mafia, from Houston, Texas. Three individuals founded this group in 1978—Oscar and Leonard Gonzales and Mando Lichtenberger. La Mafia considered itself a norteño outfit because it used the accordion and bajo sexto combination and it recorded mostly polkas and rancheras. But, similar to progressive conjuntos and grupos Tejanos, the group also used pitos (a saxophone and trumpet) and a synthesizer. La Mafia, in many ways, was neither a conjunto, a progressive conjunto, nor a grupo, but a transitional musical group in search of a distinct identity. Lacking one, the group assumed different identities in its recordings and performances. For several years La Mafia played música tejana with three distinct ensemble styles. On some of its songs, it used only the conjunto instruments: accordion, bajo sexto, drums, and electric bass.[83] On other songs, it added the pitos to make the progressive-conjunto sound popularized by Roberto Pulido y Los Clásicos and David Lee Garza.[84] At times, La Mafia played in the grupo style and anchored its music in the keyboards.[85] Although it recorded in all three styles, resulting in a mixture of sounds, these were not fused or blended into a new form. The accordion, for instance, was used by itself or in combination with the pitos, but not in combination with keyboards. The synthesizer-driven songs, in many cases, would include some pitos but no accordion.

Over time, however, La Mafia assumed the trappings of a grupo—they depended more on the sounds generated by the synthesizer and used the horns and accordion less frequently and more selectively.[86] Toward the latter part of the decade, many commentators and observers labeled Tejano music that used synthesizers as "techno-music." In many ways, then, La Mafia served as a transitional group until it decided to join the ranks of the grupos Tejanos.[87]

La Mafia made a significant contribution to música tejana during the 1980s. It introduced showmanship and "high-tech" sound to the industry. Showmanship initially was based on what one commentator derisively referred to as "silly high jinks on stage." "The band would dress up like Sha Na Na and do an oldies-rock routine or put on cowboy clothes and sing Hank Williams songs."[88] They soon outgrew these "silly high jinks" and by the middle of the decade developed a more polished form of showmanship, with flashy costumes and fancy dance routines accompanying traditional rancheras, polkas, and baladas.

An important ingredient in this transformation, along with the flashy outfits, was the utilization of sophisticated lighting and high-tech sound systems, fog and explosions on stage. By the late 1980s La Mafia's stage presence was unique in Tejano music.[89] Heavily inspired by the visceral power of MTV, it earned a reputation as a top show band with an inspiring stage performance. This "MTV effect" increased their popularity and served to "re-ignite an interest in Tejano music among young, bilingual listeners who otherwise might have abandoned their Mexican American heritage for English language pop, rock, and country."[90]

Increased album sales and awards reflected La Mafia's growing popularity. Although it was a Tejano group, La Mafia's first statewide hit, ironically, was an English-language song done by the group the Chi-Lites, "Oh Girl." In 1982 it became the only English-language song to win single of the year at the annual Tejano Music Awards. During the next several years, the group had at least one hit song on every new album. Between 1989 and 1991, three albums recorded by the group—*Xplosive, Enter the Future, Con Tanto Amor*—were certified gold by CBS's Latin division. In the Tejano market, sales of 50,000 were considered gold; 100,000 were platinum.[91]

La Mafia also garnered a variety of music awards.[92] In 1985 the group dominated the Tejano Music Awards by wining five out of eleven categories.[93] In total, between 1980 and 1989, La Mafia won seventeen out of a total seventy Tejano Music Awards given to male musicians or male-based Tejano groups. As indicated by these awards, by the end of the decade La Mafia had conquered the regional Tejano market and was ready to venture into the international arena. It would accomplish this feat in the next decade.

The third and final group to have a strong impact on this industry during the 1980s was Selena y Los Dinos. Most individuals, including artists and record industry officials, remember Selena as a beautiful, cheerful, and wonderful person. Her fans generally viewed her as a role model and a positive influence on youth. She was brown, beautiful, and proud of her Tejano roots. Selena, however, was more than simply a beautiful person and wonderful role model. She was an innovative, engaging, and influential artist who shaped música tejana in general and grupo music in particular.

Selena was born in 1971 and began to sing in 1979. She formed her band, Los Dinos, in 1981 and began to record professionally in 1985. Between 1985 and 1989 Selena became the queen of Tejano music. By the end of the decade, she, like La Mafia, was ready to conquer other frontiers and to cross borders in her quest for fame and fortune.[94] Selena made several important contributions to música tejana during the 1980s. Similar to Mazz and La Mafia, she promoted a new Tejano aesthetic by focusing on cumbias and baladas.[95] She also added choreography and a feminist touch to macho-oriented Tejano songs.

From the beginning of her recording career, her repertoire was diverse. On her first album, for instance, she recorded rancheras, baladas, cumbias, and one dance song. Over the years, she recorded an increasing number of cumbias and actually helped to popularize this dance type within Tejano music. On her first album, *Mis Primeras Grabaciones,* only 20 percent of the songs were cumbias.[96] This increased to 30 percent on the following two albums and to 50 percent a few years later.[97] The trend toward cumbias increased in the following decade.[98] In addition to popularizing cumbias, Selena also introduced pop, rap, and rock influences into Tejano music. She later added dance, hip-hop, and mariachi to her songs. On her first album, for instance, she recorded a guitar-inspired rock song and a soft English-language ballad.[99]

Selena's contributions were not limited to song selection; she was also innovative in her performance on stage. She was probably the first female to introduce charisma and choreography into Texas-Mexican music.[100] On stage, she twisted, turned, and twirled to the dynamic rhythms of cumbias, rancheras, and dance beats provided by Los Dinos. Selena not only made this music fun to dance to, she also make it enjoyable to watch. Likewise she provided a much-needed female perspective on love, which had been missing since the 1940s. Through her lyrics she projected an evolving image of a Chicana who was willing to let go of a failed relationship and start over, of an assertive individual who criticized men for mistreating her and who sought independence from them.[101]

Selena's increased popularity was reflected in album sales, in concert attendance, and in music awards. Her innocent voice and dynamic performance on stage quickly earned her the Tejano Music Awards' female vocalist prize in 1987 and its female entertainer prize in 1988. Throughout the second half of the 1980s, Selena's popularity increased as more and more individuals began to buy her records and attend her dances. By the end of the decade, she had conquered the female market of the Tejano music industry and was on her way to becoming a more influential force in música tejana. Selena was not yet a dominant force in the industry, nor was she an international artist, but she had taken the first steps toward becoming both.[102]

Selena, in combination with La Mafia and Mazz, were the dominant influences in the grupo tradition during the 1980s. Because of their popularity, the grupo Tejano began to supplant all other musical ensembles in the Tejano community, taking música tejana in new directions and expanding its social base. By the end of the decade, they were ready for new challenges that only corporate America could provide, and in the 1990s major record labels helped to fuel the rapid explosion of Tejano music throughout the western hemisphere.

CONCLUSION

Música tejana experienced significant changes in the years 1964 to 1989. Conjunto music did not disappear but faced increased competition from several new types of musical ensemble—progressive conjuntos, orquestas, Chicano country bands, and grupos. Each of these ensembles, with the exception of Chicano country bands, became dominant in different decades and then declined in popularity or faded from view. Conjuntos achieved this status in the 1960s, orquestas in the 1970s, and grupos in the 1980s. The progressive conjunto, in turn, was an emergent form during these decades but would soon supplant all the other ensembles.

Despite the competition and changes in musical ensembles, música tejana continued to be rooted in the ranchera and polka dance tradition and sung in Spanish. The grupos, however, challenged the dominance of this Tejano aesthetic and began to promote new dance tunes, especially country, cumbias, and baladas. These trends would be strengthened in the 1990s primarily as a result of changing musical tastes among the Tejano population and the involvement of corporate America. The entry of the major record labels and their impact on música tejana will be discussed in the following chapter.

Chapter 5

The Era of
Corporate Involvement, 1989—99

During the 1990s, música tejana experienced significant changes in its ensembles, musical repertoire, and artists. In the last decade of the twentieth century, grupos continued their growing dominance of the music industry, but progressive conjuntos challenged them for ascendancy. Traditional conjuntos, on the other hand, reemerged as a creative musical force during these years. The core of música tejana continued to expand so that by the end of the century it was composed of five basic song types: the ranchera, polka, cumbia, balada, and country tune.

The changes in this music were due to several factors, including the growing influence of multinational corporations, which acquired ownership of the Tejano music industry; the rapid growth and mobility of the Mexican-origin population in the United States; and the impact of American, Caribbean, and Latin American musical forms on Tejano musicians. The following chapter provides a history of these changes from 1989 to the end of the century.

EMILIO AND PROGRESSIVE CONJUNTOS

During the 1990s progressive conjuntos became extremely popular in música tejana. The primary differences between these types of conjuntos and grupos were the instrumentation and repertoire. Grupos, in most cases, used the keyboards as their primary instrument and rarely, if ever, used an accordion. Progressive conjuntos, on the other hand, used the accordion in combination with either the pitos or the synthesizer as the primary instruments in their songs.[1] In some cases, they used all of these instruments. The "progressive" in this ensemble referred to the particular mix of instruments, not, as some authors have suggested, in how they played this music.[2] Progressive conjuntos also maintained, to a large extent, the older Tejano aesthetic in their repertoire and played primarily rancheras and polkas. Grupos Tejanos, on the other hand, significantly deviated from this aesthetic and increasingly played relatively fewer rancheras and more cumbias, baladas, country tunes and other types of tunes.

The progressive conjunto, as noted earlier, originated in the early 1970s when Roberto Pulido y Los Clásicos added pitos to the traditional conjunto ensemble. It was, in some ways, a synthesis of the conjunto and the orquesta ensembles popular during the late 1960s and 1970s. This particular mix of accordion and pitos, while quite popular in general, as indicated by Pulido's longevity as a musician, did not catch on with many other musicians. Only a few additional groups imitated Pulido's sound, including David Lee Garza y Los Musicales, Los Formales de Cali Carranza, and Cecilio Garza y Los Kasinos.[3]

In the 1990s progressive conjuntos became an extremely important force in música tejana. Much of this had to do with the emergence and influence of Emilio Navaira y el Grupo Río. Prior to forming his own group, Emilio was the lead singer for David Lee Garza y Los Musicales. He joined this group in 1984 while still in college. His presence increased Los Musicales' popularity, especially among young audiences. Because of Emilio, the band won several Tejano Music Awards in the latter part of the 1980s.[4] In 1989 Emilio left Los Musicales and formed his own group. He kept the conjunto ensemble but expanded it by adding the synthesizer.[5] The popularity of grupos such as Mazz and Selena probably encouraged him to add this new instrument to his conjunto ensemble. The addition of the synthesizer to the accordion-driven conjunto ensemble brought a new, modern sound to Emilio's group. This mix of instruments was, in some ways, a synthesis of the conjunto and the grupo ensemble popular during the 1980s. His new progressive conjunto sound quickly dominated the airwaves and made Emilio an immediate hit with Tejanos, especially the youth.

Emilio made additional contributions to Tejano music that greatly increased his influence and stature. First, he introduced modern vaquero and country fashions into música tejana. Prior to his arrival, a few Tejano musicians, especially those that played conjunto or Chicano country, dressed in country and western fashion, but it was an old-fashioned look. The cowboy hats were often made of straw, the shirts were dull-colored plaids with snap-on buttons, and the cowboy boots were either black or brown, pointed, and with a tall, slanting heel.[6] Emilio and el Grupo Río updated this old country and western look by donning Stetson hats, Wrangler jeans, solid-colored western shirts with button-down collars, and ropers (smaller than traditional cowboy boots, with lower heels and rounded toes) in various colors.

By modernizing and popularizing this particular look, Emilio gave added legitimacy to the community's historical presence in the state. Vaquero wear among Tejanos was not simply an imitation of popular country and western stars such as Garth Brooks, Clint Black, and George Strait, it was an integral part of their heritage. Emilio reminded the youth that Mexican Americans were the original vaqueros of Texas. They had established ranchos and the clothing, culture, and lifestyle associated with this type of living as early as the 1700s. Tejanos, especially those living in the urban areas, now had an additional reason to be proud of their music, and many of the youth began to wear this clothing with pride. His impact was so pervasive that it even affected the fashions of other Tejano groups and of their fans. Prior to Emilio's popularity, Tejano groups had no particular style of dressing. Some dressed in matching outfits, in tuxedos, or in colorful clothing. After Emilio's success, groups in the Tejano music industry increasingly began to adopt the country and western look as part of their image, as did many fans of música tejana.[7]

Second, Emilio maintained the traditional Tejano aesthetic of rancheras and polkas, but he selectively incorporated other contemporary influences. While artists such as Selena or La Mafia added an international flavor to música tejana by mixing in Latin pop ballads and tropical rhythms, Emilio brought American rock and country flavor to this music. Between 1989 and 1995, for instance, he recorded several country and rock tunes. His first country song ("South of the Border") was recorded in 1991, the second one year later, and the third in 1992. He began to record some "rock-flavored" tunes in 1992. On his album *Unsung Highways*, for instance, he included the guitar-inspired "Naciste Para Mí" (You Were Born For Me), and the acoustic ballad "Juntos" (Together).[8] In 1993 he recorded two additional "guitar-inspired" rock tunes,

Emilio at National Council de la Raza, Houston, Texas, 2000.
Courtesy Annette Cruz

"Ay Mi Dios" (Oh My Lord) and "En Que Brazos" (In Whose Arms).[9] Interest in country music eventually led him to record two country CDs, the first one in 1995, the second one in 1997.[10]

Despite his dreams of crossover success in the country market, Emilio continued to be rooted in música tejana and in the traditional Tejano aesthetic of ranchera tunes. For instance, on his first four CDs, issued between 1989 and 1992, Navaira recorded a total of forty-two songs; thirty-two of them, or 77 percent, had a polka beat. More specifically, twenty-nine of these songs were rancheras and three were polkas. The other 23 percent were either valses (5 percent), cumbias (9 percent), ballads (7 percent), or country tunes (2 percent).[11] All the other CDs, with the exception of his country ones, maintained a similar mix of mostly rancheras and polkas as well as a sprinkling of cumbias, baladas, and rock and country songs.[12]

Third, Emilio developed a unique performance style when he originated the "Emilio Shuffle," a shoulder-swiveling, hip-shaking, 360-degree-rotating dance routine. This was usually done to a rousing ranchera or polka beat. Emilio's heavy-set brother, Raul, actually came up with the dance routine. Emilio recalled the origins of this dance sensation: "He started that dance onstage back in '88 or '89. He was just excited about being alive and doing what he wanted to do. It's like seeing a big old teddy bear swinging around, man. If we don't do it, people get upset, so we do it every night."[13]

Emilio's new look, his distinct sound, and his performance style gained quick acceptance, as reflected in album sales, music awards, and concert attendance. For instance, from 1990 to 1997 he won over twenty-nine Tejano Music Awards. He received a total of six awards in 1996 alone.[14] At the same time, his albums sold quite well. His first album spun two hits, "Pienso en Tí" and "Guerita Consentida," and a Grammy nomination.[15] Between 1990 and 1996 Emilio released five albums of Tejano music for Capitol-EMI Latin. Each sold between 150,000 and 200,000 copies. His first country album, released in 1995, *Life is Good,* sold over 500,000 copies, an impressive number for a debut artist.[16]

Another indicator of Emilio's popularity was his concert appearances. In 1990, the first year in which Tejano artists performed at the annual Houston Livestock Show and Rodeo, Emilio and two other artists drew a crowd of 51,000 and set a rodeo record for a Sunday afternoon show.[17] Five years later, he and Selena broke all records for a matinee performance at the Houston Livestock Show and Rodeo. In February 1997 his performance at the show, headlining with Grupo Limite, drew a record attendance of 66,771 at the Astrodome, breaking the old Emilio/Selena record by close to 2,000. Emilio also became the first Tejano artist to headline the San Antonio Stock Show and Rodeo.[18] He toured with Alan Jackson in 1996, performing at more than seventy concerts. In 1997 he made a country and western tour with Clay Walker and again played in over seventy concerts. Wherever he went, Emilio set new records. He was definitely the most influential Tejano artist in the 1990s.

Finally, many new groups began to imitate the progressive conjunto sound created by Navaira. By the latter part of the 1990s, at least two of them—Bobby Pulido and Elida y Avante—emerged as the new superstars of the Tejano music industry.[19]

THE RESURGENCE OF TRADITIONAL CONJUNTO MUSIC

Emilio's success led to the increased popularity of the accordion as an instrument of cultural pride. For over three decades the accordion had been associated with cantina music, with backwardness, irrelevance, and low class status. Navaira helped transform the negative image of this instrument into a positive one in the 1990s. Most importantly, Navaira made the accordion an instrument of pride and respectability. The youth of the 1990s quickly accepted this instrument as part of its heritage and began to favor its use in música tejana.

Several other factors contributed to the transformation of the accordion from "cantina trash" to "cultural treasure" in the 1990s. Among the most important were the initiation of an annual conjunto festival in San Antonio, the establishment of a traditional conjunto and a progressive conjunto award category in the annual Tejana Music Awards, the rise of bilingual, Tejano FM radio stations, and the entry of the major record labels into the Tejano music industry. The increased popularity of a once-shunned instrument in particular and of a new type of ensemble in general led to an unexpected development in música tejana—the resurgence of traditional conjunto music.

Both types of conjunto music—the Tejano and the norteño variety—were revitalized in this decade. As in earlier decades, Tejano and norteño conjuntos competed for dominance and for avid fans. In the first part of the decade, Tejano conjuntos reigned supreme. Norteño conjuntos, however, became the dominant ensemble in the conjunto genre in the second half of the 1990s and even began to challenge all other types of music in the community.

Conjunto music was reenergized by a new generation of acculturated working-class and middle-class youth who provided vitality and charisma to a stagnant musical style. These new artists brought needed changes to the instrumentation, repertoire, and performance of traditional conjunto music. They also brought an increase in ethnic pride in this particular type of ensemble and its music. In the first half of the 1990s, this resurgence was led by a few conjunto groups, including Los Chamacos, Los Palominos, and the Hometown Boys.[20] These groups were originally founded in the 1980s or earlier, but they did not become popular until the following decade.

Los Chamacos, for instance, was formed in 1979 as part of a family group called Los Chamacos de Raul de Anda. Sometime in the mid-1980s, the group changed its name to Jaime y Los Chamacos. This probably occurred at the time that Jaime de Anda, the lead singer and accordionist, introduced showmanship into the act. De Anda decided to add some "flair" to the conjunto's show after watching the performance of American and European rock groups dressed in flashy costumes. While belting out Tejano songs and playing the accordion, he danced, pranced, spun, and jumped around the stage. These lively shows earned Los Chamacos a solid following in the mid-1980s and many nominations for Tejano Music Awards, including most promising band and conjunto of the year in 1984 and male entertainer of the year in 1985.[21]

The group's popularity increased in the 1990s when it signed on with Freddie Records. Between 1990 and 1994 Los Chamacos began to produce top-selling albums and to win several awards.[22] In 1992 Los Chamacos received the award for best regional conjunto of the year at the annual Pura Vida Awards. The group's *Unrivaled* won a TMA for best album of the year in 1994. The following year "Tren" was named best instrumental song of the year. The band was twice nominated for a Grammy Award in the Mexican American category for best performance: in 1996 for *No Se Cansan* and in 1997 for *En Vivo: Puro Party Live.* Undoubtedly, Los Chamacos were one of the most exciting conjuntos Tejanos in the late 1980s and 1990s, with "a combination of swirling accordion runs, sweet vocal harmonies, and lively foot-stomping polkas."[23]

Los Palominos was formed in 1985 in Uvalde, Texas, by four brothers: James (bajo sexto/vocals), Johnny (vocals/accordion/keyboard), Jess (drums), and George Arreola (bass). The group was known initially as Los Tremendos Pequeños and later as Los Tremendos de Johnny Arreola. In 1990 they were discovered by La Mafia's Armando Lichtenberger and Oscar de la Rosa. Lichtenberger and de la Rosa helped the group land a deal with Sony Discos in 1991 and came up with the name Los Palominos. Their first CD, issued in 1991 and titled *Entre La Espada y La Pared* sold fewer than 10,000 units. However, the next six CDs, issued between 1992 and 1998, produced a variety of hits and went either gold (over 50,000 units sold) or platinum (over 100,000 units sold).[24] In 1999 this group won a Grammy for their CD *Por Eso Te Amo.*[25] Their style, described by one observer as "old-time, minimalist," with a "solid rhythm section and sweet vocal harmonies," proved irresistible and popular with both adults and youth.[26]

Another conjunto of importance during the 1990s was the Hometown Boys. The group's music featured "infectious polkas and irresistible foot-stomping rhythms."[27] The band began as El Conjunto Internacional and was formed by brothers Ricky and Joe Martínez from Lubbock, Texas, in the 1980s. The group changed its name to the Hometown Boys in 1990 and soon came to be known locally as the "Homies." In 1991 the Hometown Boys were signed by Capitol-EMI Latin. After producing five albums with Capitol, in 1995 the group switched labels and went with FonoVisa. Most of their hits were produced while they were with this label. For instance, their second CD with FonoVisa, *Mire Amigo,* went gold in the first week after its release. Several other CDs also went gold. Between 1995 and 1998 the Hometown Boys received two TMAs, one for *Tres Ramitas* (best album, 1995) and one for "Joe's Special No. 10" (best instrumental song, 1997).[28]

These three groups were the leaders of Tejano conjunto music during the early and mid-1990s. By the middle of the decade, however, norteño groups began to challenge their dominance. Key among these new conjuntos were Michael Salgado, Intocable, and Limite.

Intocable was formed in 1993 in Zapata, Texas, by several friends who had known each other since junior high school. Ricardo "Ricky" Muñoz (lead vocals), Rene Martínez (drums), and Sergio Serna (percussion) became the key members of this conjunto. Intocable originally signed on with Freddie Records, but after a year it switched to Capitol-EMI. In 1994 it issued *Fuego Eterno* and began to produce some hits. The next CD, *Otro Mundo,* yielded several additional chart toppers, including "Besos Sin Condición" and "La Mentira," a bluesy bolero. By 1998 the group had sold a combined total of one million albums in the United States and Mexico, a feat unheard of in the Tejano music industry, especially for conjuntos.[29]

Intocable, although a Tejano conjunto, played in the norteño style. It was influenced by the norteño groups Los Relámpagos del Norte and Ramón Ayala y Sus Bravos del Norte. Some critics labeled Intocable as a Ramón Ayala clone. Ramiro Burr, however, argued that the young members of Intocable were making music relevant for their own generation. Although Ricky Muñoz, the lead singer, sounded like Ramon Ayala, he brought a mixture of "norteño/soul/blues-drenched vocals" and engaging accordion runs that made his sound unique in the 1990s. The group's thumping bass lines and almost tropical percussions also added something different to their music.[30] The group's popularity on both sides of the border indicated Intocable's uniqueness. "We say that Intocable's music has no boundaries," said Robin Flores, the program director for KQQK, the most popular Tejano station in Houston during the 1990s. "In the past, Tejano music was not well-accepted in Mexico, and Mexican music was not well-accepted in the Tejano market. They transcend both markets."[31]

Intocable at the Hard Rock Cafe, Houston, Texas, 1998.
Left to right: unknown, unknown, Sergio Serna, Ricky Muñoz (lead singer),
Rene Martinez, and Daniel Sanchez. *Courtesy Annette Cruz*

The second conjunto that contributed to the shift toward the supremacy of the norteño style in música tejana was Michael Salgado. Born in 1971 in Big Spring, Texas, Michael began to play with a family conjunto called Los Salgados del Norte when he was fifteen.[32] Los Salgados recorded four albums with Joey International in the early 1990s but did not become successful until 1994, when Michael took the lead and recorded the CD with the title track "Cruz de Madera," an old norteño classic. The single shot to number one at Tejano and regional Mexican stations all over the U.S. Southwest and Mexico. This song was one of the hottest hits of the summer of 1995 and eventually won song of the year at the 1996 Pura Vida Awards.[33]

In 1995 Salgado released *En Concierto,* an album that included his second major hit, "Sin Ella." According to *Billboard,* this song stayed on the Latin top-ten hit list for thirty-three consecutive weeks.[34] Salgado's popularity was also reflected in the music awards he began to win. In 1996, for instance, he won the TMA for best conjunto (norteño). Two years later Salgado again won a TMA for best conjunto traditional album of the year with *Un Recuerdo Especial.*[35]

Michael Salgado had a sound similar to Los Relámpagos del Norte's. Salgado acknowledged their influence and unabashedly paid tribute to them by re-cording the group's old hits. For instance, his second album, *En Concierto,* contained a tribute medley of Los Relámpagos hits called "Recordando Los Relámpagos." Many of his own songs were reminiscent of Los Relámpagos.[36] Despite this sound, or probably because of it, Salgado became one of the most important conjuntos of this decade.

Although both Intocable and Michael Salgado were extremely popular on both sides of the border, none could match the success achieved by Grupo Limite. Limite, from northern Mexico, was formed in the early 1990s. Six individuals originally composed the group: Alicia Villareal (vocalist), Sergio Ponce (guitarist), Gerado Padilla (accordionist), Jesus Cantú (bassist), Carlos Ramírez (percussionist), and Luis Mario (drummer).[37] The group's first CD, *Por Un Amor,* spawned four top-ten singles, including "Solo Contigo," "Te Aprovechas," and "Con la Misma Piedra." The CD stayed in the top twenty of *Billboard*'s Hot Latin Tracks for over thirty-seven weeks.[38] In less than a year, it sold more than 600,000 units in Mexico and more than 200,000 in the United States. The next two CDs—*Partiendome el Alma,* issued in 1996, and *Sentimientos,* issued in 1997—also spawned several top-ten singles, in-cluding "El Principe" and "Jugete," among others. By 1998 Limite had sold over 2 million albums in Mexico and over 1 million in the United States.[39]

Michael Salgado in Port Lavaca, Texas, 1998. *Courtesy Annette Cruz*

Alicia Villareal's trademark look was that of a charming country girl dressed up in blue jeans, boots, cowboy hat, with long, braided, light brown hair. This country charm, however, was accompanied by an urban sophistication and a voice of great emotional depth and range. "Her gift," comments Ramiro Burr, "is her ability to inject a range of emotional needs, wants, and fears into her songs. That, and her band's superb playing, is what creates this magical music."[40]

Without a doubt, by the end of the 1990s Grupo Limite had became the leader of the emerging norteño style of music in Texas and in Mexico. Why was it that the new norteño groups became such a dominant force in such a short span of time? Ramiro Burr argues several reasons. First, música tejana in general was suffering from a dearth of creative superstars. The truly creative stars of the early 1990s—Emilio, Selena, La Mafia, and Mazz—had run out of creative juices, moved beyond Tejano music and entered new markets, or, as in the case of Selena, were silenced forever. No additional groups with a creative sound emerged. Instead, the market was flooded with "boring has-beens, one-hit wonders, copycat clowns and career backbenchers."[41] Second, the new norteño groups had original tunes, fresh approaches to traditional music, and fabulous rhythms. They, in other words, had "cool grooves" and music that connected with the new and old generations of Tejanos and Mexicanos.[42]

THE TRANSFORMATION AND DOMINANCE
OF GRUPOS TEJANOS

Grupos Tejanos were already a dominant force in the Tejano music industry by the end of the 1980s; they extended their dominance during the following decade. The establishment of new grupos throughout the decade indicates the ensemble's growing popularity and increased dominance.

As indicated in table 5, only a handful of grupos were around in the 1980s. Beginning in 1990 and continuing through 1998, new ones formed and recorded, many of them with major labels, such as Capitol-EMI, Sony Discos, and FonoVisa. This increase was due, among other things, to the greater acceptance of "Mexican" music among youth and the entry of major recording labels into this particular industry.[43]

Grupo musicians made at least two significant changes to their ensembles during the 1990s. First, they added the accordion to the existing instrumental arrangements of the grupo. This, again, was due to Emilio's influence.[44] Mazz led this movement in the early 1990s, but others soon followed. In most cases, the accordion was used sparingly and in only a few songs on an album. Between

TABLE 5

SELECTED GRUPOS TEJANOS, 1980S–90S

Name of Group	Year of Established or Initial Recording
David Marez	1980s
Elsa García	1980s
Gary Hobbs	1980s
Joe Posada	1980s
Oscar G. y Quinto Sol	1980s
La Mafia	1980
Ram Herrera y Montana Band	1984
Shelly Lares Band	1985
Selena y Los Dinos	1986
Xelencia	1989
Annette y Axxion	1990s
Connexxion	1990s
Esmi (Talamantes)	1990s
Inocencia	1990s
Joel Nava and the Border	1990s
Linda V. and the Boys	1990s
New Variety Band	1990s
Fama	1990
La Fiebre	1990
La Sombra	1990
Esmeralda (Jaime Guzman)	1991
Stephanie Lynn	1991
Tierra Tejana	1991
Delia González y Culturas	1992
Eddie González y Grupo Vida	1992
Jay Perez	1992
La Diferenzia	1994
Pete Astudillo	1994
Stefanie	1994
Jennifer y Los Jetz	1995
Noemy (Torres Esparza)	1996
Ruth	1996
Amber Rose	1997
Becky Lee Meza	1997
Elizabeth Gutierrez y Texas Fire	1997
Grupo Vida	1997
Margarita	1998

Source: Author's personal notes.

1986 and 1991, for instance, Selena did not record a single song with an accordion. In 1992 she introduced the accordion in "Terco Corazón." Soon thereafter, she selectively used the accordion on some of her recordings.[45] Other grupos Tejanos, such as Elsa García, Laura Canales, and David Marez, among others, also introduced the accordion into their music in the early 1990s.[46]

Second, they continued to promote a new Tejano aesthetic in their recordings. Although the trend away from the older Tejano aesthetic of rancheras and polkas was initiated by the Big Three of La Onda Tejana in the 1980s—La Mafia, Mazz, and Selena—corporate America's entry into this industry encouraged further development. Corporate involvement in música tejana began in the late 1980s and early 1990s, when major music labels such as Capitol-EMI, Sony Discos, and others began to look for Tejano groups that could cross over to the English-language market. Their desire for profits and for selling to a mainstream audience quickly led to the internationalization of música tejana. By "internationalization" I mean that major recording companies sought to make Tejano music appealing first to an international Spanish-speaking market and then to the English-speaking one.[47] For this reason, they encouraged the selective recording of two distinct types of tunes within the Tejano repertoire that were popular in places such as Mexico and Latin America—cumbias and baladas. Some of these companies also encouraged the recording of mariachi songs and other types of music not generally played in the Tejano community.[48]

Grupos Tejanos in general welcomed these new opportunities to move beyond the repertorial and stylistic limits of música tejana. Three groups in particular led the internationalization efforts during the 1990s: La Mafia, Mazz, and Selena. They established the standards and provided the leadership for venturing into new markets and for modifying the traditional repertoire played by Tejano groups. Each contributed something special to música tejana and helped forge its distinct sounds.

The leader among these grupos was La Mafia. In the 1990s the group made several strategic and stylistic changes that expanded the appeal of música tejana to areas beyond the U.S. Southwest. First, it began to tour in Mexico. Their first gig was in 1989 at the Nuevo León Casino in Monterrey, Mexico, about 150 miles inside the border. Armando Lichtenberger, one of the original founders of the group, recalls this first performance: "We worked hard on our set for that one. The fans didn't know any of our music. It was a big challenge. So we picked the most emotional ballads we had, songs that would reach an audience. We gave it all kinds of energy, threw in everything we had. People loved it."[49] After this positive experience, the group found a good booking agency and "started going in deeper." By 1993, La Mafia was touring Mexico with headliner status.[50] The group also toured the East and West Coasts of the United States. Many groups before La Mafia had toured the Midwest and West Coast, but La Mafia expanded this circuit and added locations such as Miami, Florida, and New York City.

Second, La Mafia made three stylistic changes to Tejano music. It slowed the tempo, began to play more cumbias and ballads, and became more "techno"—used more synthesizer and heavy bass lines. With respect to the tempo, Lichtenberger explained, "We wanted to do Tejano [i.e., polka], but we were tired of the same stuff . . . so we slowed the tempo." He also commented on the new sound: "We used keyboard sounds not heard in Tejano, sort of a techno Tejano."[51] This musical shift began in 1990 with the album *Enter the Future,* which had a slowed-down tempo on its rancheras and polkas.[52]

La Mafia also began to record more cumbias and baladas. For instance, the 1991 album, *Estás Tocando Fuego,* featured four cumbias and one balada. In 1994 the group took an unusual step and recorded *Vida,* an album containing only cumbias and baladas.[53] The lack of rancheras on this album in particular led to complaints among many fans that La Mafia had abandoned its Tejano roots. But according to its members, this was far from the truth. "Our new songs," noted Mando Lichtenberger, "are more like 'Tejano international.' We still play norteño because that is our roots, but we also play ballads and rhythm and blues with a touch of Caribbean."[54]

Despite these criticisms, the pioneering new sound initiated by La Mafia attracted a wider following, including audiences in Mexico, Latin America, and Puerto Rico, as well as in New York, Chicago, Miami, and Los Angeles. Their increased popularity was reflected in the group's huge album sales, in concert appearances, and in the awards the group won. The 1991 album, *Estás Tocando Fuego,* for instance, sold more than 1 million units. *Ahora y Siempre* sold more than 250,000 units in the first two weeks after its issue in 1992. The last four albums, issued from 1994 to 1997, were nominated for Grammy Awards; two of those, *Un Million de Rosas* (1996) and *En Tus Manos* (1997), won.[55] La Mafia broke concert attendance records in the United States and Mexico. In 1990 more than 60,000 individuals attended their Monterrey, Mexico, concert. La Mafia broke all records at the annual Houston Rodeo in 1991, with over 55,000 in attendance. The band broke attendance records into the late 1990s, regardless of where it played.[56]

Mazz quickly followed La Mafia's initiatives in Mexico. However, the group was not as successful as it had hoped. Still, Mazz played on both sides of the border and began to attract fans from Mexico. Mazz also promoted the new

Tejano aesthetic. Mazz's repertoire was slightly more diverse than either La Mafia's or Selena's. Despite its diverse recordings, Mazz's bigger hits were mostly baladas. In 1990, for instance, Mazz recorded "Canciones del Corazón," a string of classic mariachi-style baladas, including one by the late Javier Solis. The following year, the group recorded "Canciones de Amor," a medley of well-known trio standards. In 1992 it recorded another medley of boleros on its album *Lo Hare Por Tí*. All these songs became hits for the group. Mazz also successfully recorded other types of songs that became hits, including rancheras, cumbias, two-steps, and even banda tunes (see table 6).[57]

The diversity of tunes, among other things, made Mazz extremely popular among Tejanos in the 1990s. In the early part of the decade the group dominated the Tejano Music Awards.[58] In 1991 and 1992 Mazz swept the Tejano Music Awards by winning in six different categories: male vocalist, vocal duo, song of the year, songwriter, single, and album of the year. The group also received two nominations for prestigious awards in 1991 and 1993. In the former year, it was nominated for a Grammy for the song "No Te Olvidare." Two years later Mazz was nominated for a Billboard Award in the regional category Mexican group of the year. Four albums released between 1989 and 1992—*No Te Olvidare, Para Nuestra Gente, Lo Hare Por Tí,* and *Mazz-Juntos Live*—all went platinum, with more than 200,000 units sold.[59]

Despite the group's popularity, Mazz continued to have problems with promoters, including canceled or late shows and short, uninspired sets at contracted dances. This, however, did not discourage fans from buying Mazz's recordings or attending its dances, even if they knew that the band might not show up.[60]

Selena, although relatively new to the music industry, followed La Mafia's leadership and ventured into Mexico. Unlike Mazz, Selena quickly conquered the hearts of Mexicans across the border as well as in other parts of the United States, especially in Los Angeles. By the early 1990s, she was readily performing on both sides of the border in areas not traditionally visited by Tejano musicians.

Selena also promoted the new, expanded Tejano aesthetic.[61] In 1991 she took the lead in this effort and produced an album that contained half cumbias and half rancheras.[62] Until her untimely death in 1995, she recorded a variety of cumbias that became regional and international hits. Her biggest hits were cumbias, such as "Techno-Cumbia," "Como La Flor," and "La Carcacha." The most popular, as indicated by record sales, was "Amor Prohibido."[63] Despite the promotion of cumbias and baladas on her albums, Selena did not abandon rancheras. At least half, if not more, of all her recordings were songs with a polka beat.[64]

TABLE 6

TYPES OF SONGS RECORDED BY MAZZ, 1977–98, BY YEARS

Year	Ran	Cum	Country	Balada	Polka	Huap	Banda	Other	Total
1977	2	5	3	0	0	0	0	0	10
1978	0	2	4	4	0	0	0	0	10
1979	1	1	3	3	0	0	0	2	10
1980a	2	2	3	3	0	0	0	0	10
1980b	3	2	0	2	0	0	0	2	9
1980c	2	3	1	3	0	0	0	1	10
1981	3	1	4	2	0	0	0	0	10
1983	4	1	2	2	0	0	0	1	10
1984a	5	2	1	1	0	0	0	1	10
1984b	4	1	0	3	0	0	0	2	10
1985	4	2	0	2	1	0	0	1	10
1986a	5	1	1	1	0	0	0	2	10
1986b	4	1	1	3	0	0	0	1	10
1987	4	1	1*	2	0	0	0	2	10
1988	3	2	3*	1	1	0	0	0	10
1989	3	1	1	1	1	0	0	3[a]	10
1990	5	1	0	4	0	0	0	0	10
1992a	4	1	0	3	0	0	0	2	10
1992	4	3	0	4	1	0	0	0	12
1993a	5	2	0	3	0	0	0	0	10
1993b	0	2	1	4	0	0	3	0	10
1995	4	1	4	1	0	0	0	1	11
1997	5	4	0	2	0	0	0	1	12
1998	6	1	0	0	1	0	0	2*b*	10
Total	82	43	33	54	5	0	3	24	244
Percent	34	18	13	22	2	0	1	10	100

Ran = ranchera; Cum = cumbia; Huap = huapango
1980a = *1980;* 1980b = *Class;* 1980c = *Perfect 10, Volume 2;* 1984a = *It's Bad;* 1984b = *Standing Ovation;* 1986a = *Number 16;* 1986b = *La Continuacion;* 1992a = *Beyond;* 1992b = *Lo Hare Por Ti;* 1993a = *Que Esperabas;* 1993b = *Mazz Románticos Que Nunca.*

[a]One of these was a mariachi song.
[b]Both of these are valses.
*Song is sung in Spanish or bilingually.

The promotion of a new Tejano aesthetic, as well as dynamic performances and excellent songs, made Selena the queen of Tejano music. By the late 1980s, Selena was no longer a maturing singing sensation. She was a beautiful and sensuous Tejana performer and recording artist. She skillfully and successfully used her new sensuality to promote herself and her recording career in

TABLE 7

SELECTED DISCOGRAPHY OF MAZZ, 1977–99

Perfect 10, Cara CA-10B, 1977.
Mazz, Cara Santos4000, 1978.
Album of the Year, Cara CA-012, 1979.
1980, Cara CA-17, 1980.
Class, Cara CA-23, 1980.
Perfect 10, Volume 2, Cara M10-2, 1980.
Look of Mazz, Cara CA-028, 1981.
The Force, Cara CA-051, 1983.
It's Bad, Cara CA-054, 1984.
Standing Ovation, Cara CA-062, 1984.
Bad Boys, Cara CA-067, 1985.
Number 16, Cara CA-077, 1986.
La Continuacion, CBS CRL-84333, 1986.
Beyond, CBS DRL-10495, 1987.
Straight from the Heart, CBS DRL-80010, 1988.
No Te Olvidare, EMI H1E42136, 1989.
Para Nuestra Gente, EMI H2H42367, 1990.
Una Noche Juntos: Live, EMI H2Y42549, 1991.
Lo Hare Por Tí, EMI H2077774259323, 1992.
Beyond, Sony CDB-80808, 1992.
Que Esperabas, EMI H2724383091324, 1993.
Mazz Románticos Que Nunca, EMI H2542833, 1993.
Solo Para Tí, EMI H2724383091324, 1995.
Al Frente de Todos, EMI H2724382880424, 1997.
Cuantas Veces, EMI H2724349410121, 1998.

the early 1990s. By 1994 she had taken the Tejano music industry by storm and was on the verge of becoming an international artist when she was killed by one of her fans. Since then, Selena has become an idol to millions.[65]

Selena made several additional contributions to Tejano music in the 1990s. First, as noted above, she recorded an increasing number of cumbias and actually helped to popularize this dance style in Tejano music. Second, Selena introduced pop, rap, rock, dance, and mariachi influences into Tejano music. On her first album, for instance, she recorded a guitar-inspired rock song and a soft English-language ballad.[66] In 1991 she recorded a rap-flavored Tejano song called "Enamorado de Tí."[67] In 1993 and 1994 she recorded a host of Spanish rock and Spanish-English hip-hop-flavored songs.[68] Selena also popularized mariachi music.[69] Every type of music she performed or recorded seemed to turn to gold.

Selena's contributions were not limited to song selection. She was probably

Selena y los Dinos, 1992. *Left to right:* Chris Perez, Joe Ojeda,
Suzette Quintanilla, Selena Quintanilla, Ricky Vela, Pete Astudillo, and
A. B. Quintanilla. *Courtesy Abraham Quintanilla and Q Productions*

the first female to introduce dynamism and choreography into the performance
of música tejana. She had a vivacious personality that came through on stage.
Selena could charm men into submission and thrill an audience of women.
She performed a variety of energetic and sensuous dance routines to the cumbias,
rancheras, and dance tunes played by Los Dinos. Selena was a joy to watch.

Finally, Selena refined the neofeminist perspective that she had introduced in the late 1980s. Through her lyrics she projected an evolving image of a sensitive, caring, and assertive young Chicana; of an individual willing to let go of a failed relationship and to start over; of someone not afraid to criticize men for mistreating her; of a confident woman who sought independence; and of a faithful, loving person with dreams and lofty ideals.[70]

Selena's increased popularity was reflected in album sales, in concert attendance, and in music awards. At the annual Tejano Music Awards in 1987, the first year in which she was nominated, she won female vocalist; the next year she won female entertainer of the year. From 1989 to 1994 Selena won both categories—female vocalist and female entertainer—at the TMAs. Her biggest year was 1995, when she won in seven categories: female vocalist, female entertainer, song of the year ("Bidi Bidi Bom Bom"), songwriter ("Amor Prohibido"), album of the year (orquesta) (*Amor Prohibido*), album of the year (conjunto) (*Amor Prohibido*), and Tejano crossover ("Techno-cumbia"). In 1994 she also won a best female vocalist (regional/Mexican) award at the Latin Music Awards sponsored by *Billboard* and Univision in Miami, Florida.[71] In January 1994 *Selena Live* won a Grammy for best Mexican American album. Her next LP, *Amor Prohibido,* also received a Grammy nomination.

Selena's album sales were phenomenal and increased over time. Her 1992 LP *Entre a Mi Mundo,* for instance, sold more than 100,000 units. This was the first time that a female artist within the Tejano music industry had sold that many albums. This album also reached the number-one spot in *Billboard's* regional Mexican charts, edging out La Mafia, who had been there for almost three months.[72] In April 1994 *Amor Prohibido* reached quadruple platinum status, selling more than 400,000 units. The title track, "Amor Prohibido," reached number one on *Billboard's* Latin chart to become the biggest hit of her career. The album remained at number one or two on *Billboard's* Latin top fifty for 1994.[73] *Dreaming of You* was the top-selling Latin pop CD of 1996.[74]

Selena also broke attendance records. The best-known concerts were at the Houston Livestock Show and Rodeo at the Astrodome. In February 1993 she performed with David Lee Garza before a Sunday matinee for a record audience of 66,994. The following year, the attendance, while still high, decreased slightly to 66,842. In 1995, a month before her death, she performed a triumphant concert for another large Sunday crowd of 64,831. On that day, she appeared with Emilio Navaira, the Tejano Music Awards' male vocalist of the year. The extremely high attendance figures indicated that by 1995 Selena "was la onda [Chicana]. La onda was Selena."[75] Selena helped shape Tejano music and influenced its style and its direction. Although gone, she continues to influence this music, as indicated by her continuing popularity and the public's unending thirst for her music.[76]

The Big Three of música tejana—Selena, La Mafia, and Mazz—in many ways provided much of the creativity and energy of the grupo phenomenon in the state, and in música tejana in general, during the 1990s. The death of Selena at mid-decade, as well as the breakup of Mazz and the dissolution of La Mafia in the late 1990s, has left the industry without any significant musical leaders. What impact other grupos or ensembles will have on música tejana and the Tejano music industry is difficult to gauge, but one fact is certain— others will replace the Big Three and continue to make the music enjoyed by Tejanos and non-Tejanos alike.

CONCLUSION

Tejano music experienced significant changes in the 1990s. Emilio emerged on the scene and quickly achieved an influence previously unheard of in música tejana. He created a new type of musical ensemble, promoted a more positive image of the accordion, incorporated country and rock influences into the Tejano aesthetic, popularized a "modern" vaquero look within the industry, and developed a unique performance style.

Emilio's impact led to the resurgence of traditional conjunto music in the early part of the decade and to the dominance of the norteño style in música tejana by the end of the 1990s. The conjunto groups of the 1990s were different from those of the past in several distinct ways. First, they expanded the ensemble and added new instruments to the traditional conjunto. Many Tejano conjuntos, for instance, added the keyboards to the traditional ensemble. Norteño conjuntos, on the other hand, added a percussion instrument, usually a conga, to the ensemble.

Second, they modified the traditional conjunto repertoire and expanded it somewhat to include more cumbias and fewer rancheras. In certain respects, then, these groups, like the popular grupos of the 1980s, promoted a new Tejano aesthetic during this decade.

Grupos Tejanos also increased in number and influence, especially in the first half of the decade. Because of Emilio's success and the growing popularity of the accordion, most of them added this instrument to their ensemble. Unlike progressive or traditional conjuntos, however, the grupos used the accordion selectively—that is, they used it on only a handful of songs. Progressive or traditional conjuntos, on the other hand, used it on most, if not all, of their songs. The grupos of the 1990s, like those of earlier years, also continued to promote a new Tejano aesthetic during this decade. In the 1960s and 1970s, the polka beat was the core of música tejana. Several decades later, the repertoire expanded to include not only polkas and rancheras, but also cumbias, baladas, and country tunes.

These new directions and developments, in many cases, were encouraged by corporate America and readily accepted by Tejanos, especially Tejano youth. Several other changes and trends were apparent in the 1990s. The most important will be discussed in the following chapter.

Chapter 6

Trends in Música Tejana during the 1990s

During the past decade, música tejana, or "Tejano," as it came to be known, has been accepted by hundreds of thousands of individuals throughout Texas, the country, and the western hemisphere. Selena's popularity and unfortunate murder probably had much to do with this phenomenon, but so have other factors, such as corporate involvement, increased immigration from Mexico, Latin America, and the Caribbean, and changing tastes among the Mexican-origin population in the United States. These diverse factors have contributed to the shaping and reshaping of música tejana and the development of several additional trends in the music industry. The most important include the mainstreaming of Tejano singers, the emergence of female singers, and the explosive growth of música tejana in general.

THE MAINSTREAMING PHENOMENON

One of the most important trends during the 1990s was mainstreaming—that is, making it in the national English-language market. Mainstreaming is not a new phenomenon in the Tejano community. In the 1950s and 1960s, for instance, Tejano groups such as Los Dinos, Little Joe, and others recorded music in English. Most of them were unsuccessful in this market, largely because of discrimination in the recording industry, among other things. A few artists, however, did produce hit records, including Sam Saucedo (Sam the Sham and the Pharoahs), Rene Victor Ornelas and Rene Herrera (Réne and Réne), and Sunny Ozuna. In most cases, these individuals did not have an "ethnic" sound and played music that appealed to a mostly Anglo and English-speaking audience. The band who came closest to the Tejano sound was Réne and Réne. This group sang bilingually, in both English and Spanish, but they did not play any polkas, nor did they record any rancheras or cumbias. Most, if not all, of their songs were ballads.[1]

The Tejano dream of crossing over and making it in the Anglo market has continued into the present. In many respects, crossover dreams have been reinforced by the increased interest in this music by major record labels. The majors began to look for crossover acts in the mid-1980s. Little Joe became the first Tejano act to be signed by a major recording company—CBS-Sony Discos—in 1986. Although he recorded several hit albums in Spanish, including *25th Silver Anniversary,* a live recording; *Timeless,* an album that was on the *Billboard* charts for fifty-seven consecutive weeks; and *16 de Septiembre,* which won a Grammy for best Mexican American performance—he was less successful in the English-language market.[2]

Soon the major labels signed the four top Tejano acts in the industry: La Mafia, Mazz, Selena, and Emilio. Selena had plans for making a pop album in English before she was killed in 1995. Her crossover dream was realized later that year with the release of *Dreaming of You.* It became one of the hottest-selling albums of all time in the American music industry and stayed on the charts for several weeks.[3]

Emilio's crossover dream was to make it in the country music industry. He recorded several country songs on his first three Tejano albums and in 1992 signed a booking contract with a Nashville-based company—the Refugee Management Agency. It promised to promote the group within the country music industry and to book it into rodeos and bigger concerts and as an opening act for other country stars.[4] Two years later Emilio got his wish when he signed with Capitol Nashville.[5] In 1995 he released his first country album, *Life is Good.* It sold more than 500,000 units, a decent number in the country music industry. In 1997 Emilio issued his second country CD, *It's on the House,* which sold fewer units than the first. That same year, he began to search for a new team to help him put together a hit album, but he was not very optimistic.[6] In 1999 he acknowledged his lack of success in the English-language market. "In this business," he added, "there are good times and bad times."[7]

He apparently had hit the bad times in the country mainstream. Life in this market was not so good after all.[8]

Mazz and La Mafia, unlike the others, did not have immediate plans for crossing over to the Anglo market. Their first priority was to make it in the Spanish-speaking market, especially outside the United States. CBS Discos initially signed La Mafia in 1990 with this in mind. Officials with the company said they planned to enhance La Mafia's image in the "Latin" markets in order to "generate enough interest in the English market to help them cross over the way Miami Sound Machine [also on CBS] did a few years ago."[9] Their dreams, however, soured by the end of the decade. Although La Mafia did achieve significant success in the Spanish market, neither it nor Mazz recorded an English album, and by the late 1990s, it was highly unlikely that either would accomplish this goal. In 1998 Mazz split up and faded from the Tejano music scene. The following year, La Mafia decided to break up because of exhaustion and disappointment. The group had grown weary of endless touring and performing, and it was disappointed with the way Sony Discos, its longtime label, handled the group's promotion in Mexico.[10]

The lack of success with Tejano artists has not stopped major recording companies from looking for additional groups with crossover potential. The phenomenal success of Ricky Martin, Enrique Iglesias, and a few other Latino artists in the English market during the late 1990s has kept alive the hope of finding one or more Tejano artists who can cross over to other markets.[11]

Despite the press given to the above artists, not all Tejano musicians had crossover dreams. For various reasons, some, like Jay Pérez, David Mérez, and Ram Herrera, simply enjoy playing music for Tejanos. They are Tejano recording artists playing the diverse types of songs, both English and Spanish, loved by Tejanos. This type of music is, culturally speaking, música tejana because it is intended for the listening pleasure of Tejanos. Tony de la Rosa's comment about conjunto music can be applied more generally to all forms of música tejana: "It is not what you play that counts but who you play it for."[12]

INCREASED PARTICIPATION AND INFLUENCE
OF LAS MUJERES

A second major trend in the Tejano music industry during the 1990s was the growing number of women artists signed by the major labels and the indies (independent labels). This phenomenon was not limited to música tejana; it was an international phenomenon that had an impact on all types of Latino and non-Latino music. Still, the increased representation of Tejanas in the industry was a refreshing departure from the recent past. In the period from the 1960s to the 1980s, for instance, Tejanas were excluded or discouraged from becoming recording or performing artists. Sexism in the Tejano music industry, as well as patriarchal ideals in the Tejano community, limited their participation.[13] Despite these barriers, at least seven Tejanas became recording artists—Chavela Ortíz y Brown Express, Lisa López, Patsy Torres, Laura Canales, Shelly Lares, Elsa García, and Selena. These women were cultural pioneers and innovators. Collectively, they represented four distinct ensembles and styles.

Chavela Ortíz represented the conjunto style of music. Born in 1952 in Fresno, California, she began to play accordion with Las Incomparables Hermanas Ortíz when she was nine years old. Although the group was disbanded in 1968, Ortiz continued to play with area bands. In 1976 she joined the group Brown Express and became the accordionist and lead singer. In 1980 she went on her own and formed Chavela y Su Grupo Express. Ortiz was the first successful female accordionist in conjunto music and was extremely popular during the 1970s and 1980s. In 1987 she was nominated for a Grammy for her album *El Rey del Barrio*. The following year she was invited to play at the 1988 Tejano Conjunto Festival in San Antonio. Ortiz died in 1992 from an accident that occurred during a photo shoot for an album.[14]

Lisa López, unlike Ortiz, was a solista—she recorded as a solo artist. López was the niece of the orquesta singer Isidro López, from Corpus Christi. Although a Tejana, she targeted her music to Mexican audiences and, in certain respects, followed the path of other Tejana artists, such as Lydia Mendoza and Chelo Silva. Her biggest hit, "Si Quieres Verme Llorar," reached number one on the *Billboard* Latin Tracks chart and earned her the female entertainer, song, and single of the year honors at the 1982 Tejano Music Awards. According to Ramiro Burr, she became the first Tejana artist to debut on the *Billboard* Latin top-fifty chart when the charts were initiated in October 1986. In the early 1990s López was signed to the Sony Discos label but did not produce any additional hits.[15]

Patsy Torres played both top-forty hits and Tejano country, a mixture of rancheras, polkas, and bilingual country and western songs.[16] Torres was extremely popular in South Texas during the 1970s and early 1980s. She won her first and only TMA in 1987 for best female entertainer. Although she continued recording in the 1990s, at first under WEA Latina and later under Joey International, she managed to produce only local hits.[17]

Lares, García, Canales, and Selena played in the grupo style. In most cases, the primary instrument used by their groups was the keyboard, and they played mainly rancheras and polkas. All were extremely talented and creative and, in some cases, began to sing at an early age.

Shelly Lares began singing with a group before she was ten. In 1985, when she was fourteen, she and her cousin Tony Lares formed the New Generation Band. Several years later it became the Shelly Lares Band. Lares's musical career ran parallel to that of Selena's. Both were managed by their fathers and recorded in the mid-1980s for small indie labels with minor success. From 1989 to 1994 Lares had several hit albums with Manny Music, including *Tú Solo Tú* (1989), *Dynamite* (1990), and *Apaga La Luz* (1993). Despite constant recording and touring, Lares's career did not take off; she was always in Selena's shadow. Although she was nominated for an award every year from 1984 to 1996 at the annual Tejano Music Awards, Lares constantly lost to Selena. She finally won an award in 1998.[18] Lares did not get a major recording contract until 1996. Despite high hopes of crossing over into country, Lares's career stalled by the end of the decade.[19]

Elsa García, born in 1956 in Monterrey, Mexico, began singing at the age of four, but she did not record until the mid-1980s. Her first six albums with different labels produced no significant hits. She began to be noticed in 1993 after she recorded a regional hit called "Ya Te Vi." She followed up with several more hits in as many albums, but by the late 1990s García faded from the music scene.[20]

Laura Canales was the lead singer for various groups, including Felicidad in the 1970s and Encanto in the early 1980s. She began her career in 1973 with Los Unicos and by the early 1980s was known as "La Reina de la Onda Chicana."[21] Her popularity was reflected in the Tejano Music Awards she received during the 1980s. Canales won the female vocalist of the year award from 1982 to 1986 and again in 1988. Canales also won the female entertainer of the year award from 1983 to 1986.[22] Canales's popularity declined in the latter part of the 1980s, in large part because of Selena's rise to stardom.[23]

Selena Quintanilla was only a teenager when she became the lead singer for Los Dinos in the early 1980s. Despite her youth, between 1983 and 1989 she became the dominant female vocalist in a predominantly male industry and brought a certain charm, innovative spirit, and new perspective to música tejana. In the early 1990s she dominated Tejano with her pop-influenced rancheras and catchy cumbia beats. At the time of her death in April 1995, Selena had been expanding Tejano music into other parts of Mexico and Latin America and had intentions of doing an English-language album.[24]

Selena was not only the most popular Tejana musician of the contemporary period; she also helped to open the door to other women singers and groups. Because of her popularity and influence, women singers emerged as a significant group in Tejano music in the 1990s. "We're seeing more women today because of Selena's success. Women saw that it could be done and that changed the thinking that [Tejano] music was mostly a male-dominated market," noted Bill Angelini, a booking agent from San Antonio.[25]

Because of Selena's influence and other factors, major recording companies began to increase their female representation in the 1990s. Sony Discos, for instance, had three new Tejana artists by 1996: Stefani, Connexxion's Mary Lee Ochoa, and Shelly Lares. "Shelly has that crossover potential," said Ray Martínez, Sony Discos Midwest office sales director. "She may be the first country female artist crossover act in a long time. She has the voice, the style and the look." EMI Latin, on the other hand, had five relatively new female acts: Stephanie Lynn, Elsa García, Lynda V. and the Boys, Agnes Torres of the New Variety Band, and Delia y Culturas. All, with the exception of García, were new acts that had been "discovered" in the early 1990s. FonoVisa, the dominant label in regional Mexican music, had four artists, all but one of whom were newcomers: Laura Canales, Annette y Axxion, Esmi Talamantes, and Noemy Esparza y Metal from Dallas. Finally, Polygram Latino had the new queen of norteño music, Alicia Villareal, vocalist for Grupo Limite (see table 8).[26]

The trend toward increasing the representation of women in Tejano and regional Mexican music continued through the end of the decade. Las mujeres were becoming a significant part of the entire music industry. With increased participation, they not only contributed to the unique sounds of this music at the end of the millennium, but they also had the potential for influencing it into the next one.

EXPLOSIVE GROWTH OF MÚSICA TEJANA

In certain respects, the explosive growth of música tejana was part of a larger trend toward the greater acceptance of Latin music in the United States, which began in the mid-1980s. Immigration from Mexico, Central America, and the Spanish-speaking countries of the Caribbean, as well as the emergence of a more educated, prosperous, and bilingual Latino middle class in the United States, fueled this explosion in the growth of Tejano and other forms of Latino music.[27] There were several indicators of this growth.

First, record sales of música tejana increased significantly in the early 1990s. Prior to 1990, the total sales of Tejano was only a few million dollars.

TABLE 8

SELECTED LIST OF WOMEN IN MÚSICA TEJANA, 1970–99

Name	Date of First Recording or Group Formation
Linda Escobar	1970s
Laura Canales	1973
Chavela y Brown Express	1976
Patsy Torres	1979
Elsa Garcia	mid-1980s
Janie C. Ramirez	1980
Lisa Lopez	1981
Shelly Lares	1985
Selena y Los Dinos	1986
Connexxion	1990s
Esmi (Talamantes)	1990s
Jaci Velasquez	1990s
Linda V. and the Boys	1990s
New Variety Band	1990s
Esmeralda (Jaime Guzman)	1991
Stephanie Lynn	1991
Delia Gonzalez y Culturas	1992
Elida y Avante	1992
Stefanie	1994[a]
Grupo Limite	1995
Jennifer y Los Jets	1995
Letty Guval	1996
Noemy (Torres Esparza)	1996
Nydia Rojas	1996
Amber Rose	1997
Becky Lee Meza	1997
Elizabeth Gutierrez y Texas Fire	1997
Ruth	1997

Sources: Burr, *Billboard Guide* (various selections); various newspaper clippings in author's possesion.
[a]She issued two singles in 1990 but did not record her first CD until 1994.

In 1992 sales increased to $9 million. Two years later Tejano album sales again increased, to over $20 million. The total number of albums sold by successful Tejano groups in 1990 also increased. In 1990 the measure of success for a Tejano group was the ability to sell at least 50,000 albums or CDs. By the end of the decade, however, this had gone up to 100,000 or more. La Mafia and Selena, two of the most successful artists, easily surpassed this number and sold several hundred thousand albums.[28]

A second indicator of growth was the increase in the number and size of venues where Tejano groups played. Traditionally, música tejana was heard at patriotic festivals such as Cinco de Mayo or 16 de Septiembre, at private celebrations, and at public dances. During the 1990s, more individuals throughout the state started organizing and participating in the patriotic festivals. Illustrative of this growth was Houston in 1999, when more than fifty thousand people attended the Cinco de Mayo parade. Thousands of others also attended the musical concerts scheduled for this day in celebration of *fiestas patrias*.[29]

In large cities, new and upgraded Tejano dance halls were opened during this decade. In the first half of the 1990s, Houston had several top Tejano nightclubs, including Tequila's, the Island Club, Hollywood Nights, Zazz, and El Dorado Ranch. San Antonio had Tejano Rose, Corpus Christi had La Bamba and Hollywood Nights, and the Dallas–Ft. Worth area had Dezperados. Most of these clubs had live music and a dance-club atmosphere, usually with multi-level seating, sophisticated dance-floor lighting, and, as one observer noted, "party-ready DJs ready to play the top pop and dance music between live sets."[30]

Not only were new and modern dance halls opened, the dances themselves became huge, concertlike events. They were not simply *bailes* (dances) anymore, they were *gran bailes* (super dances). The earliest documented super dance was in Houston. On December 31, 1991, more than 18,000 fans attended the first annual New Year's Eve Super Dance at the George R. Brown Convention Center. Mazz, La Mafia, and Roberto Pulido y Los Clásicos were the three top performers that evening.[31] On May 30, 1993, Mazz, Selena, Bronco, and several others played at the same convention center in Houston for more than 24,000 dance enthusiasts. The following month, a larger dance, featuring Ram Herrera, Selena, Mazz, Emilio, Little Joe, and La Sombra, was held at the Alamodome in San Antonio; more than 33,000 people attended.[32] These gran bailes soon thereafter became part of the community's cultural traditions as thousands attended them for special events such as New Year's Eve, Memorial Day, and other important holidays.

Additionally, new venues were opened to Tejano groups. In this decade, they played at mainstream rodeos, at county fairs, and at special festivals such as the San Antonio conjunto festival, Freddie Fest in Corpus Christi, and the Festival Chicano, the Accordion Kings, and the East End festivals in Houston. Among the largest venues were the rodeos and the San Antonio conjunto festival. The latter originated in 1981 in celebration of conjunto music. Sponsored by the Guadalupe Cultural Arts Center in San Antonio, the festival was a mammoth four-day celebration of food, drink, educational activities, and conjunto music.[33] In the first decade, the show attracted as many as 38,000 people per year. In the 1990s the show attracted more than 40,000 people each year. Traditional conjuntos dominated during the early years, but progressive conjuntos were showcased in the latter part of the 1990s.[34]

The largest of these new venues, however, were the rodeos, especially the Houston Livestock Show and Rodeo. Although the Houston Rodeo had been held since World War II, it was not until 1990 that it added a Tejano day to its roster and invited Tejano groups to play. From 1990 to 1999 the number of people attending this annual one-day event at the Astrodome in Houston increased from 51,000 to over 66,000 (see table 9).

Tejano groups also played at large public concerts in Mexico. In February 1992, for instance, La Mafia played at the Expo Guadalupe Fairgrounds in Monterrey, Mexico, for a crowd estimated at between 35,000 and 50,000 individuals. Two months later, the group played at the same fairgrounds with Los Tigres del Norte for an estimated 80,000 fans. On the same day that La Mafia played at the Expo Guadalupe, Mazz played at the Parque Fundadora, another facility in Monterrey, Mexico. An estimated crowd of 45,000 attended this event.[35] Both La Mafia and Mazz continued playing in large Mexican venues during the middle and latter part of the 1990s. Other groups, such as Selena and Intocable, soon followed in their footsteps.

TABLE 9

ATTENDANCE AT THE GO TEJANO RODEO,
HOUSTON, TEXAS, 1990–2000

Year	Attendance	Performers
1990	51,072	Roberto Pulido, Emilio, Vicki Carr
1991	n/a	n/a
1992	55,590	La Mafia, Texas Tornados
1993	66,994	Selena, David Lee Garza
1994	66,842	Selena, Ram Herrera
1995	64,831	Selena, Emilio
1996	61,719	La Mafia, La Diferenzia
1997	66,771	Emilio, Grupo Limite
1998	65,705	La Mafia, Intocable
1999	62,280	David Lee Garza with lead singers Ram Hererra, Emilio, Oscar G., Jay Perez, and Marco Orozco
2000	64,880	Los Tucanes de Tijuana, A. B. Quintanilla y Los Kumbia Kings

Source: Houston Livestock Show and Rodeo website, *www.hlsr.com.* See attendance records and facts and figures.

A third indicator of the increased popularity of música tejana was the growth of bilingual Tejano radio, TV programming, and print media. In the early 1990s Tejano radio stations became extremely popular throughout Texas and in other parts of the country. In 1992 San Antonio made history when KXTN 107 FM, a Tejano radio station, reached the top of the city's ratings. That same year, KQQK FM, the Tejano radio station in Houston, became the most popular Latino station in that city. Soon, other cities, such as Corpus Christi, El Paso, and MacAllen-Harlingen, had high-ranking Tejano radio stations in their areas. Changes in radio programming contributed to this phenomenon. Most Tejano stations, for instance, initiated a top-forty approach, engaged in heavy promotions, developed informative community outreach, and hired charismatic DJs who spoke bilingually on the radio.[36] The "modern" approaches to radio programming increased the stations' appeal to Tejanos of all ages and social classes.

Because of its popularity, by mid-decade música tejana was heard on the radio in twenty-three states, from California to Rhode Island. Its growth eventually led to the creation of *Tejano Gold*, a bilingual radio show that combined a top-singles countdown, trivia, artist interviews, and other insider information. *Tejano Gold* was hosted by Rudy Treviño, a public-school teacher from San Antonio, and heard in many cities throughout the United States and Mexico.[37]

Television programming also became an important factor in the rapid growth of Tejano music. Several programs geared toward its promotion became extremely popular during this decade, including the *Johnny Canales Show, Tejano Country,* and *Tejano Music Video,* a twenty-four-hour video channel in Corpus Christi. Other programs, such as *Ritmo Latino,* occasionally played Tejano videos.[38] Much of the information on música tejana was reported through new bilingual and Spanish-language publications such as *Furia* and *Que Onda*.

A final indicator of the explosive growth of música tejana is the number of awards received by Tejano musicians. Prior to 1986, only three Tejano award programs existed: the Mike Chavez Awards in Kingsville, the Houston Tejano Music Awards (HTMA), and the statewide Tejano Music Awards. Mike Chavez, a local DJ from the Corpus Christi area, hosted one of these programs in the spring of every year during the mid- and late 1970s. The program had eleven categories of awards, including band of the year, conjunto of the year, male vocalist of the year, and female vocalist of the year. The first awards show was held in 1974, and the program continued until at least 1980. In 1978 the annual Mike Chavez awards drew about five thousand music fans and industry executives.[39]

The HTMA was sponsored by several local musicians and industry employ-ees. Little is known about the sponsors or the organization, but James Torres of KYST and Mario Alberto Campos of KFRD, as well as Dr. Antonio González, a local writer of Tejano music, were members of the organization. The first HTMA ceremony was in 1985. For at least five years the Tejano Music Associa-tion held this annual ceremony, which attracted hundreds of supporters.[40]

The Tejano Music Awards, unlike the other two, is a statewide ceremony. It began as a relatively small event but soon became a huge awards show watched by millions. The TMA was the brainchild of Rudy Treviño. Treviño was a commercial arts teacher; he realized that at the cultural events he at-tended, musicians were never recognized. In order to rectify this, he set out to form the Texas Talent Musician's Association (TTMA), an organization whose primary purpose was to promote excellence in the Tejano music industry and to recognize musicians for their contributions to the cultural life of the com-munity. In 1981 the TTMA sponsored the first Tejano Music Awards, a pro-gram patterned after the Grammy Awards. The show had two official spon-sors that year—Coca-Cola USA and Budweiser—eleven categories of awards, and an attendance of about 1,500.[41]

Every year, the Tejano Music Awards got larger. By 1987 more than thirty-two radio stations and twenty-five television stations in Texas and surround-ing states broadcast coverage of the event. An estimated 12.5 million people heard or watched broadcasts of the TMA in this year alone.[42] Attendance at the TMA also increased from 1,500 in its first year to 15,000 in 1993, and to over 30,000 a year later.[43] By 1988 the TMA had grown beyond Texas and into the rest of the United States; Treviño soon looked to a Mexico City station to begin broadcasting the program internationally.[44]

The Tejano Music Awards continued to grow in stature into the 1990s, despite the protests and boycott by several Latin record labels, including Sony Discos, FonoVisa, Freddie Records, and TH-Roven, as well as glitches and a lack of professionalism. By the late 1990s, the protests by the "renegade" record labels ended after the TMA agreed to three changes in its format. First, it would develop new guidelines for conducting the program. Second, it would modify the awards categories to reflect changes in the music industry. Third, it would give more say to industry representatives.[45] Because of these changes, the public played a lesser role in the selection of nominees and in the selec-tion of winners. The TMA officials also introduced lip-synching to the awards show. Ramiro Burr criticized these changes and argued that the TMA was sacrificing quality for quantity. The show was bigger than ever before, but not necessarily better.[46]

Música tejana was recognized as a legitimate musical style in an increasing number of new state, national, and international awards ceremonies established during the latter part of the 1980s and the 1990s (see table 10).

In a few cases, Tejano categories were added to existing awards ceremonies. The National Academy of Recording Arts and Sciences, the official sponsors of the Grammy Awards, for instance, added a new category—regional/Mexican—in the mid-1980s. In 1986 the award went to Flaco Jiménez for his album *Ay Te Dejo en San Antonio.* Little Joe, Selena, and La Mafia were awarded Grammies in the 1990s.[47] In 1998, in response to political pressure from Tejano music advocates, the Grammy officials added an exclusive Tejano category to this ceremony.[48] Flaco Jiménez and Los Palominos were the recipients of this award in 1999 and 2000, respectively.[49]

During the 1990s Tejano groups also began to receive other awards, such as the Premio Lo Nuestro, Radio y Música, and Pura Vida Awards. These awards indicated that by the middle of the decade this music had gained national and international acceptance. Música tejana, in other words, was not simply regional anymore; it was an integral part of both American and international music. Música tejana's growing popularity was due to several important reasons, including its increased association with ethnic pride among youth, its Americanization and internationalization, and corporate involvement.

TABLE 10

MUSIC AWARDS PROGRAMS, 1974–99

Year Established	Awards Program	Focus
1974	Mike Chavez Awards	Local
1980	Tejano Music Awards	State
1985	Houston Tejano Music Awards	Local
1986	Grammy Awards	National
1989	Premio Lo Nuestro	International
1990	Radio y Música	International
1991	Pura Vida Awards	National
1991	Mid-West Tejano Music Awards	National
1994	Que Onda Awards	International
1990s?	Alma Awards (NCLR)	National
1999	Latin Academy of Recording Arts and Sciences (LARAS)	International
1999	Tejano Entertainers and Music Association (TEMA) Awards	State

Source: Various newspaper clippings in author's possession.

The entire spectrum of música tejana and its instrumentation, especially the accordion and keyboards, became popular among youth because it was associated with ethnic pride. Unlike the youth of the past, the young people of the 1990s were not ashamed of the accordion or of conjunto music; they embraced and celebrated it. Additionally, youth identified with the music's modern vaquero image and its diverse, Mexican-based repertoire. This music thus became an important mechanism for asserting ethnic distinctiveness in a society that historically had sought Tejanos' cultural erasure.

Música tejana also became popular because of its ability to incorporate many of the most popular musical styles found in the United States and Latin America. Selena, La Sombra, Emilio, and others creatively incorporated pop, rap, disco, and country influences into Tejano. Others successfully incorporated the Mexican norteño style and diverse musical forms such as cumbias or mariachi into this music without much difficulty. The incorporation of these influences and styles into música tejana, the Americanization and internationalization of this sound, made it appealing to a variety of people within the community.

A final reason for its increased popularity was corporate involvement. In the late 1980s, major recording labels such as Capitol-EMI, Sony Discos, FonoVisa, and others, signed Tejano artists and began to record, promote, and distribute their recordings domestically and in international markets, especially in Mexico. The involvement of major recording labels in música tejana is reminiscent of what occurred in the late 1920s. In that period, the major labels began to record the various types of music commonly found in the Tejano community. They recorded music played by solistas, duetos, trios, and larger ensembles, including conjuntos, orquestas de cuerda, and orquestas típicas.[50] By the beginning of World War II, however, they abandoned the recording of this type of music; in the late 1980s, they returned.

CBS International began this period of major-label involvement in música tejana in 1986 when it signed a distribution deal with Cara Records from San Antonio. Cara Records, owned by Bob Grever, was considered the "Motown of Tejano." It rose to prominence in the 1980s by producing such top artists as Mazz, La Mafia, Ram Herrera, Selena, Roberto Pulido, and others.[51] The deal with CBS was quite profitable and contributed to increased album sales and concert attendance for these artists during the latter part of the 1980s.

In 1989 Capitol-EMI became the most important player in the Tejano music industry when it signed top bands like Mazz and Selena for national recording contracts. The following year, it announced the purchase of Cara Records. The acquisition of top bands, such as Emilio, Selena, La Mafia, and others, gave the label major market presence. Its domination of the Tejano Music Awards during the 1990s indicated its impact on música tejana.[52]

Other major record labels also saw the possibility for profit in the growing Tejano music market. Between 1990 and 1995 more major and regional labels signed Tejano acts. Among the most influential were FonoVisa (1990), TH-Roven (1990), WEA Latina (1990), Sony Discos (1990), BMG (1992), Arista/Latin (1993), Miami-based Vedisco (1995), Mexico-based DISA (1995), and San Antonio-based AFG Sigma (1995).[53] The entry of the major record labels served to popularize this music beyond the borders of Texas and to increase its acceptance among a national and international audience.

Corporate sponsorships of Tejano groups also played an important role in the popularization of música tejana. As early as 1987, for instance, Coors Beer sponsored a free ten-concert series at the Museum of Fine Arts in Houston. This concert series showcased Tejano performers such as Ram Herrera, Saints and Sinners, Phantacy, and Lucero Villanueva y Mariachi and allowed the public to see and hear, at no cost, some of the diverse forms of music played by Tejano groups in those years.[54] During the following decade, major multinational corporations sponsored a variety of Tejano and Tejana artists at various public celebrations throughout the country. Coca-Cola, for instance, sponsored Selena, Wrangler sponsored Shelly Lares, and Bud Lite sponsored Emilio, Mazz, and other Tejano groups. Bud Lite also sponsored Festival Musical, a twenty-one-city summer concert series with Ana Gabriel and Tejano groups in the Southwest; the Tejano Party in the Plaza, a free Tuesday-evening concert in downtown Houston; and the Annual Memorial Weekend Conjunto Fest in Fort Bend County.[55] Miller Lite sponsored the annual Tejano Fest and the Conjunto Festival at Guadalupe Park in Houston, as well as many other festivals throughout the state. Corporate sponsorship of Tejano artists allowed them to play in a variety of new and old venues without charge to the public. Although it is unclear how many individuals attended these free concerts, the number is probably in the hundreds of thousands.

Although música Tejana grew significantly in the early and mid-1990s, by the latter part of the decade growth slowed. The slump in CD sales, the loss of several Tejano radio stations throughout the state, the change in format of former Tejano radio stations to regional Mexican music, and the closure of some of the larger Tejano nightclubs in several cities indicated this slowdown. A few individuals interpreted this as an indicator of the death or near death of música tejana.[56] Nothing of the sort, argued Ramiro Burr: "Whether you call it a downturn, a correction, or right-sizing, the late '90s slowdown, no matter how serious it would play out, would not cause

Jennifer Peña, 2001. *Courtesy Abraham Quintanilla
and Q Productions*

the end of a unique, original American genre," he said. This music, over the
span of the entire twentieth century, survived several wars, a major economic
depression, protest movements, and vicious political maneuverings within
and outside of the music industry, he added. It would survive this most recent downturn.[57]

All indications, in fact, showed that even after the slowdown, música Tejana was still doing better than it had done in earlier decades. "The market still had major record labels, FM stations, major clubs, and healthy representation on the charts; none of which had existed prior to 1990," stated Burr. Música tejana thus was far from dead. If anything, it would probably return stronger that ever. It would be a matter of time, however, before Tejano would again rise to make national headlines, as it did in the 1990s.[58]

CONCLUSION

Música tejana experienced significant new developments in the 1990s. First, some of its artists pursued a crossover dream. The expectation of making it in the mainstream market was not new. This was a much-cherished ambition going back many decades. The new crossover dreams, moreover, were reinforced by the major record labels and by the determination and talent of some key individuals, including Selena and Emilio. Although no Tejano crossover stars emerged during the 1990s, the major recording labels did not abandon their hopes of finding one soon.

Second, female singers became an extremely important influence on the music. In the past, Tejanas played only a small, albeit important, role in música tejana. From the late 1920s to the 1980s, their participation was limited to a few solistas, duetas, or lead singers of larger bands. This changed significantly in the 1990s as Tejana artists and groups began to record for the major record labels and for the indies as well. Selena, in many ways, opened the door to other Tejanas and encouraged the male-dominated music industry to give women an opportunity to excel and to make hit records. Females such as Shelly Lares, Jennifer Peña, and Elida Reyna have proven that they can make music as innovative and popular as males can.

Finally, música tejana experienced an explosive growth caused by the entry of corporate America, the tremendous explosion of the Latino population, and the incorporation of new instruments and rhythms to this music. During the 1990s the Tejano music industry became big business, expanding beyond the confines of Texas. Although it was still border music, the Rio Grande was not the only border música tejana crossed.

Conclusion

ejano Proud has focused on a phenomenon much talked about but little understood by the general public—música tejana. It explored the origins of recorded Texas-Mexican music and chronicled its evolution over a seventy-year period, from the early part of the twentieth century to the year 2000. Three major points were revealed in this book. First, música tejana is not a specific style of music but a complex array of evolving musical forms and styles based on traditional Mexican music but continually updated and modernized over time. Second, it has been played by a variety of musical ensembles or groups: the conjunto, vocal groups, progressive conjuntos, orquestas, grupos, and Chicano country bands. Finally, música tejana was a form of border music reflective of the historical experiences, internal differences, and ethnic identity of the Mexican-origin community in Texas.

MORE THAN CONJUNTOS AND ORQUESTAS

Manuel Peña has argued that música tejana is composed of two major types of musical ensemble and their respective styles, conjunto and orquesta.[1] These are not the only styles in the community, however. Others have formed and become dominant at different historical periods in the twentieth century. The only ensemble that has thrived up to the end of this century, however, is the conjunto.

The conjunto originated on both sides of the border in the 1920s and began as a two-person ensemble; one played the accordion and the other played a string instrument. Its repertoire, initially, was quite broad, including a host of traditional dances and songs popular throughout Mexico. The conjunto expanded to four persons and four instruments in the post–World War II period. Two distinct styles also emerged during the period after the 1940s: the norteño and the Tejano. By the late 1950s the conjunto was composed of the accordion, bajo sexto, bass guitar, and drums.

From midcentury until 1973, the standard instrumentation did not change significantly. In 1973 Roberto Pulido y Los Clásicos added two saxophones, introducing los pitos (the horns) to the ensemble and creating what later would be known as the progressive conjunto. This type of conjunto, however, was not very popular until 1990, when Emilio added a synthesizer. This innovative addition initiated a new phase of popularity for the "modernized" progressive conjunto.

The increased popularity of Emilio led to the resurgence of the traditional conjunto, but with some minor changes in its instrumentation and repertoire. Both types of conjunto styles, the norteño and the Tejano, were revived. Three Tejano conjuntos—Los Palominos, Jaime y Los Chamacos, and the Hometown Boys—led the revival in the first part of the 1990s. Michael Salgado, Intocable, and Grupo Limite initiated the second and more popular wave of conjunto music during the latter part of the decade. These groups, unlike the first three mentioned above, played in the norteño style. Most of the new conjunto groups were different in two distinct ways from those of the past. First, they increased the number of instruments in the traditional conjunto ensemble. Tejano groups generally added keyboards, whereas norteño conjuntos incorporated a percussive instrument, such as a conga or timbales. These new instruments, in most cases, were used only for special types of songs, usually cumbias.[2] Second, Tejano and norteño conjuntos changed the traditional core of this music and increased the percentage of cumbias and baladas in their repertoire.

Although the conjunto's popularity fluctuated during the decades—it was extremely high in the 1920s through the 1960s, quite low in the 1970s and 1980s, and on the increase in the 1990s—the ensemble has not faded from public view. Since its emergence in the Tejano community, the conjunto has been, and continues to be, an integral and dynamic aspect of the community's cultural life.

In addition to the traditional and progressive conjunto, there have been at least four other types of ensemble with varying degrees of popularity over the years—the vocal tradition of the solistas and the duets; the orquestas; the grupos; and the Chicano country bands.

The vocal singing tradition, unlike the others, was sit-down music. Those who recorded in this tradition, for the most part, did not play dance music. One, two, or, on occasion, three singers were backed up initially by a string instrument and then by an accordion. The vast majority of vocal singers sang corridos, canciones Mexicanas, and a host of other songs. During the 1920s and 1930s, all the vocalists, with one minor exception, were males; Lydia Mendoza was the exception. In the post–World War II era, females became an important force in this type of ensemble and set the template for the emergence and growth of orquestas and conjuntos throughout the state. Other changes in addition to the increased role of women were made to the vocal singing tradition during this era. Solistas and duets went beyond the traditional guitar accompaniment and were now accompanied in most cases by a conjunto or an orquesta. In a few cases, a mariachi ensemble provided backup. The vocal tradition was the most popular form of music in the Tejano community prior to World War II. During the 1950s, it declined in popularity because of its incorporation into instrumental dance music. Although a few individuals continued singing as solistas or in duetas, vocal singing disappeared as a viable musical tradition after the 1950s. The repertoire of these vocalists continued to be varied but most of them sang traditional baladas and rancheras Tejanas.

The ensemble most in competition with conjuntos after the Second World War was the orquesta. In the early part of the twentieth century, three types of orquestas existed—the orquestas típicas, the orquestas de cuerda, and the orquestas de pitos (bandas). The first two were extremely popular; bandas, on the other hand, were not enthusiastically embraced. Orquestas típicas were usually larger than orquestas de cuerda. The former used a large number of folk and/or classical string instruments, such as mandolins, tololoches, harps, guitars, violins, cellos, and contrabass. Some also used flutes, oboes, and perhaps a cornet or two. They performed a remarkable variety of dance music for all social classes and for all occasions. Paso dobles, danzas, one-steps, waltzes, mazurkas, huapangos, polkas, and schotises were among the most popular dances they performed.[3] Orquestas de cuerda performed similar types of songs and dances, but they usually, though not always, used fewer instruments.

The orquestas típicas and de cuerda eventually declined in popularity and were replaced by the orquesta moderna, which had new instruments and a changed repertoire. Many of the string instruments, such as violins, man-dolins, and Hawaiian guitars, were replaced by wind-based instruments, especially saxophones, trumpets, and trombones. Orquesta musicians also added new dance tunes, such as cha-cha-chas, danzones, boleros, and fox-trots. In the mid-1960s, the new generation of Tejano musicians modified the instrumentation and repertoire of what now was the older orquesta en-semble. They streamlined the brass section of these older orquestas and added the organ. They also eliminated most of the Latin American and Caribbean dance tunes while adding cumbias and new American tunes to the musical mix. The result was the creation of a new sound that came to be known as la Onda Chicana. Despite its increased popularity in the 1960s and 1970s, the orquesta disappeared as a viable musical tradition by the early 1980s because of changing musical tastes and other factors. It would ultimately be replaced by the grupo.

The grupo Tejano emerged in the early 1960s and increased in popularity during the following decade. This type of musical group emphasized the sounds of the keyboard. In the 1960s and early 1970s, the organ was the primary instrument featured in this music; by the latter part of the decade, the synthe-sizer assumed this central role. These groups also changed the musical reper-toire. They played fewer rancheras and more cumbias, baladas, and country tunes. They also played the new American tunes popular at that time, such as funk, soul, disco, rock, rap, and pop. The keyboard-driven grupos competed with the orquestas and other non-Tejano musical styles for dominance in the 1970s and won out during the 1980s. They became so popular that they effectively wiped out all the orquestas. In the early 1990s progressive conjuntos such as Emilio y Rio Band and La Tropa F increased in popularity and com-peted with grupos for fans. The primary response of grupos was to add the accordion selectively. Progressive conjuntos, in turn, also adjusted their mu-sic by using the synthesizer more extensively in their music. By the latter part of the 1990s, grupos and progressive conjuntos sounded very much alike. Few could distinguish between the grupo sounds of Mazz, La Mafia, or Jennifer y Los Jetz and the progressive conjunto music of Emilio, Elida y Avante, and Bobby Pulido. Whether grupos and progressive conjuntos survive as distinct ensembles into the next millennium depends on many factors, including the emergence of new groups with a different instrumental mix and with fresh approaches to playing música tejana. By the end of 1999, no such groups were on the horizon.[4] In early 2000, however, a new group emerged on the Tejano music scene and won several major awards at the Tejano Music Awards, in-cluding most promising band, album of the year (group) (*Amor, Familia y*

Los Kumbia Kings, 1999. *Left to right:* Roy "Slim" Ramirez,
Francisco "Cisko" Bautista, A. B. Quintanilla III, Alex Ramirez,
Robert Del Moral, Cruz Martinez, Andrew "Baby Drew" Maes, and
Jason "DJ Kane" Cano. *Courtesy Abraham Quintanilla amd Q Productions*

Respeto), show band of the year, and Tejano crossover song ("Azucar").[5] This
group, known as the Kumbia Kings, was the creation of A. B. Quintanilla,
Selena's brother. Unlike other Tejano groups, it did not play rancheras. Its
repertoire comprised cumbias, ballads, oldies (mostly rhythm and blues), and
hip-hop-style dance music. The Kumbia Kings was modeled after both American hip-hop and "boy bands" and utilized three- and four-part harmonies in
their songs.[6] Only time will tell whether the Kumbia Kings is the wave of the
future of música tejana—or only a passing fad.[7]

The Chicano country band was unique to música tejana in general and
border music in particular. Chicano country bands had at least three general
characteristics. First, they were small and depended on two important instruments for their sound: a violin and a steel guitar. Second, the vast majority of
vocalists sang with a country twang. Third, these bands played traditional
country music and traditional Mexican music—but in their own style. For the
most part, they "Mexicanized" traditional country music and "countrified"
traditional Mexican songs like "Los Laureles" or "Las Margaritas." The former
was done by singing the lyrics in Spanish or bilingually, the latter by playing
Mexican tunes with country instruments and singing them with a twang.

Little is known about the Chicano country bands or where they originated. Although the earliest recording of country music by a Tejano artist was
in 1949, the country twang and the use of the violin and steel guitar in these
songs probably originated sometime in the 1950s or 1960s along the lower Rio
Grande Valley. These groups probably became popular in the following two
decades.[8] In the 1970s Country Roland and several others had a significant
impact on Tejano groups. Among those most influenced by Chicano country
bands were Rudy Tee Gonzales y Sus Reno Bops, Snowball & Co., Roberto
Pulido y Los Clásicos, and Mazz.[9]

TRADITIONAL YET MODERN

This book has also shown that música tejana was traditional yet modern.
Música tejana was and continues to be rooted in Mexican musical traditions.
In the early part of the twentieth century, it was based on the diverse dances
popular in Mexico: polkas, schotises, mazurkas, redovas, valses, one-steps,
two-steps, huapangos, and others. In the post–World War II period, the musical
repertoire narrowed significantly and became limited mostly to polkas and
rancheras Tejanas (polkas with lyrics). Although Tejano groups played additional tunes such as baladas, huapangos, and valses, the majority emphasized
music with a polka beat. In the 1980s and 1990s, the repertoire again was
modified to include more cumbias, baladas, and country tunes.[10] Despite its
expansion, the musical repertoire of the 1990s was still less diverse than the
repertoire of the early decades of the century.[11]

The songs played by Tejano groups likewise were rooted in Mexican musical traditions. The primary songs in the repertoire were canciones típicas and
canciones románticas. On occasion, Tejano groups would record corridos.
For the most part, however, Mexican groups appealing to a Mexican immigrant audience, not Tejano artists, recorded corridos.

Although rooted in Mexican tradition, música tejana constantly received
influences from the United States. Throughout the decades, for instance, African American musical styles, such as jazz, rhythm and blues, soul, funk, rap,
and hip-hop, provided some of the rhythms that Tejano musicians selectively
incorporated into their music. Mainstream American music, including big
band, rock, country, dance, disco, and pop, also influenced música tejana. In
some cases, Tejano musicians incorporated the instrumentation used by American groups. This is true, for instance, of the wind and brass instruments used
by the big bands in the United States during the 1930s and 1940s, or of organs
and rhythm guitars used by rock groups during the 1960s. In most cases,

Tejano groups did not imitate the styles popular in the United States, as did Mexican-origin musicians in other parts of the country.[12] Instead they recorded jazz-influenced rancheras, rock-driven baladas, big band–style polkas, and pop cumbias. In those specific cases when English musical forms were recorded—say, fox-trots or rock and roll—the lyrics usually were in Spanish. Música tejana thus remained rooted in tradition but was consistently modernized over the years.

Música tejana also was influenced by musical cultures from Latin America and the Caribbean. Tejano musicians selectively adopted some of the dance forms and song types popular in these Spanish-speaking countries. In the post–World War II era, for instance, Tejano musicians, especially those involved with the orquestas, added canciones románticas from Mexico and Caribbean tunes such as mambos, cha-cha-chas, danzones, and boleros to the musical repertoire. In the post-1960 period, many groups added cumbias. In the last decade, Tejanos have begun to record the international sounds of mariachi music, música romántica, and "rock en español."

One final note pertaining to this music: it continued to be rooted in another Mexican tradition, the Spanish language. Some songs reflected the bilingual tradition of the Mexican-origin population living in the United States, but most were sung in Spanish.

MÚSICA TEJANA AND TEJANO LIFE

Tejano Proud has also indicated that música tejana was a particular form of border music developed by Tejanos for Tejanos. Because it is an indigenous creation, this music reflects the historical experiences, internal differences, and ethnic identity of the Mexican-origin population residing in Texas. Through its forms and lyrics, it mirrors the community's social subordination and its internal diversification. The various types of musical ensemble, for instance, reflect the emerging social differentiation of the Tejano community. The orquestas and grupos reflect the rise of the Tejano middle class, whereas the conjunto and the progressive conjunto reflects a working-class aesthetic. Vocal music, on the other hand, expresses the social subordination of the Mexican-origin population in Texas, the economic upheavals experienced by Mexicanos, the interethnic conflict between Anglos and Mexicans, and the patriarchal foundation of Tejano culture.[13]

More importantly, this music affirms and reinforces the distinct identity of the Mexican-origin population born or raised in Texas and compelled to live out the contradictions of being an ethnic American. Música tejana, in this case, can be viewed as an act of cultural affirmation by the Tejano population. Through this music the community is able to express its own aspirations, feelings, and sentiments about being Mexicano in a society that consistently denies them their language, culture, and dignity.[14] In other words, this music expresses the distinctive manner in which this particular ethnic group adjusted to living in a particular region of the United States and on the border of several different cultural fronts—the Tejano and the Anglo, the American and the Mexican, and, more recently, the national and the international. Although the geographical boundaries have changed in the last dozen years, música tejana continues to be border music for a border people.

CONCLUSION

Música tejana is complex, diverse, and ever changing. For most of the twentieth century it experienced significant changes, growing from a regional style to an international one. It also underwent several musical transformations. Despite these changes, música tejana remained rooted in Mexican culture and in the Spanish language; in other words, it remained culturally meaningful to Tejanos. The music, as Manuel Peña has noted, retained "its capacity to communicate a deeply felt aesthetic and other social meanings."[15] Throughout the entire twentieth century, Tejanos of all ages and from different parts of the state and country strongly identified with the various forms of música tejana because it reflected their ideals, sentiments, and desires. As one of the rising conjuntos of the twenty-first century, Los Garcia Brothers, recently said, música tejana *is* "nuestra música."[16]

Appendix A

Discography

NOTE: This is only a representative sample of artists. For each artist a compilation is included whenever possible and CD format if available. For the most recent groups, see a general music store such as Amazon.com or Ritmo Latino for details.

COLLECTIONS OF HISTORIC RECORDINGS

Mexican American Border Music, Vol.4: Orquestas Típicas—The First Recordings, 1926–38, Arhoolie CD7017, 1996.

Texas-Mexican Border Music, Vol. 1: An Introduction, 1930–60, Folklyric Records LP 9008, 1973 (reissued in an expanded format on CD as *Mexican American Border Music Vol. 1, An Introduction: The Pioneer Recording Artists, 1928–58,* Folklyric Records CD 7001, 1994).

Texas-Mexican Border Music, Vol. 2: Corridos, Part 1: 1930–34, Folklyric Records LP 9042, n.d.

Texas-Mexican Border Music, Vol. 3: Corridos, Part 2: 1929–36, Folklyric Records LP 9005, n.d.

Texas-Mexican Border Music, Vol. 4: Norteño Accordion, Part 1: The First Recordings, Folklyric Records LP 9006, n.d. (reissued in an expanded format on CD as *Mexican American Border Music Vol. 3: Norteño & Tejano Accordion Pioneers, 1929–39*, Arhoolie/Folklyric Records CD 7016, 1995).

Texas-Mexican Border Music, Vol. 5: The String Bands—End of a Tradition, Folklyric Records LP 9007, n.d. (reissued in an expanded format on CD as *Mexican American Border Music, Vol. 5: Orquestas de Cuerdas—The String Bands, The End of a Tradition, 1926–38*, Arhoolie CD 7018, 1996).

PRE–WORLD WAR II (1927–41)

Orquestas

Orquestas de Cuerda—The String Bands, Vol. 5, Arhoolie CD 7018.

Orquestas Típicas: Pioneer Mexican American Dance Orchestras, 1926–1938, Mexican American Border Music, Vol. 4, Arhoolie CD 7017.

Vocalists

Corridos y Tragedias de La Frontera: First Recordings of Historic Mexican American Ballads, Arhoolie CD 7019 and CD 7020.

Lydia Mendoza, 1928–1938, Arhoolie CD 7002.

Conjuntos

Norteño & Tejano Accordion Pioneers, Mexican American Border Music, Vol. 3, Arhoolie CD 7016.

POST–WORLD WAR II (1941–64)

General

Tejano Roots: Raíces Tejanas, Arhoolie CD 341 (conjunto, orquestas, vocalists).

15 Early Tejano Classics, Arhoolie CD 109 (orquestas, conjunto, vocalists).

Conjuntos

The Texas-Mexican Conjunto, Arhoolie audiocassette 9049.

Tejano Roots: Narciso Martínez, "Father of the Texas-Mexican Conjunto," Arhoolie CD 351.

Tejano Roots: Valerio Longoria, Arhoolie CD 358.

Tejano Roots: Conjunto Bernal, Arhoolie CD 344.

Tejano Roots: Tony de la Rosa, Arhoolie CD 362.

Esteban "Steve" Jordan: The Many Sounds of Steve Jordan, Arhoolie CD 319.

Tejano Roots: Los Pavos Reales, Early Hits, Arhoolie CD 410.

Tejano Roots: San Antonio's Conjunto in the 1950s, Arhoolie CD 376.

Orquestas

Tejano Roots: Orquestas Tejanas (1946–66), Arhoolie CD 368.

Tejano Roots: Beto Villa, "Father of the Tejano Orquesta," Arhoolie CD 364.

Tejano Roots: Isidro López, El Indio, Arhoolie CD 363.

Isidro López, *15 Hits,* Hacienda Records audiocassette SC161.

Vocalists

Tejano Roots: The Women, Arhoolie CD 343162.

Chelo Silva, La Reina Tejana del Bolero, Arhoolie CD 423.

BEFORE THE CORPORATE PRESENCE (1964–89)

General

Tejano—Back to the '70s, Freddie Records CD 2012, 1997 (orquestas and conjuntos).

Pura Onda: 16 Éxitos, Hacienda audiocassette 7016 (grupos and conjuntos).

Tejano Classics, Vol. 1, Hacienda CD SC205 (grupos and conjuntos).

Tejano Classics, Vol. 2: Recordando Los '80s, Hacienda CD SC209 (grupos and conjuntos).

Tejano Goldies, Lago Entertainment LC2000, 1996 (orquestas, progressive conjuntos, grupos, and country bands).

Conjuntos

Conjunto! Texas-Mexican Border Music, Vol. 2, Rounder CD 6024, 1988 (norteños and Tejanos).

Tony De La Rosa, Rubén Vela, and Gilberto Perez, *Bailando en Texas, Vol. 1,* Freddie Records audiocassette 1457 (Tejano conjuntos).

Legends of Conjuntos, Freddie Records CD 2028, 1998 (Tejano conjuntos).

Tex-Mex Conjuntos: Los Pinquinos del Norte and Fred Zimmerle's Trio San Antonio, Arhoolie CD 311, 1974.

Henry Zimmerle, *15 Hits,* Hacienda Records CD SC165.

Los Dos Gilbertos, *Vol. 2, 23 Hits,* Hacienda Records CD SC184 (Tejano conjunto).

Steve Jordan, *20 Hits,* Hacienda Records CD SC192 (Tejano conjunto).

Los Relámpagos del Norte, *20 Hits,* Hacienda Records CD SC190 (norteño).

Progressive Conjuntos

Roberto Pulido y Los Clásicos, *Un Rosal,* Freddie Records audiocassette 1326.

David Lee Garza y Los Musicales, *20 Super Golden Hits with Emilio Navaira and Ram Herrera,* Hacienda Records CD SC197.

Orquestas

Agustín Ramírez, Freddie Martínez, and Little Joe, *Los Dueños de la Música Tejana,* Freddie Records audiocassette RS5003.

Tejano Legend Series: Freddie Martínez, Freddie Records audiocassette 1556.

Tejano Legend Series: Little Joe, Freddie Records audiocassette 1557.

Tejano Legends Series: Agustín Ramírez, Freddie Records audiocassette 1558.

Tejano Legends Series: Sunny Ozuna, Freddie Records audiocassette 1559.

Tejano Legends Series: Joe Bravo, Freddie Records audiocassette 1560.

Leyendas y Raices, Freddie Records CD 1771, 1998.

The 4 Legends, Vol. 2: Freddie, Little Joe, Agustín, Sunny, Freddie Records CD 2006, 1996.

Grupos

Los Fabulosos, *Adiós Mi Juan,* Freddie Records audiocassette RS5017.

Laura Canales, *30 Hits,* Freddie Records CD 2046, 1999.

Mayo, *30 Greatest Hits,* Freddie Records CD 2041, 1999.

Los Chachos, *30 Greatest Hits,* Freddie Records CD 2042, 1999.

Ricky Smith y La Movida, *15 Éxitos,* Hacienda Records audiocassette SC164.

Vocalists

Lisa López, *20 Hits,* Hacienda Records CD SC169.

Freddy Fender, *Canta Hank Williams with Isidro López,* Hacienda Records audiocassette 7084.

Country Bands

Country Roland Band, *El Rey de Country,* Hacienda Records CD 7496.

Janie C. Ramírez y Cactus Country Band, *The Best of Cactus Country,* Hacienda Records CD 7482.

Jerry & the Ruf-Nex, *Oh Lonesome Me,* Hacienda Records CD 7320.

NEW DIRECTIONS (1989–2000)

General

Rodeo Tejano, Freddie Records CD 1751, 1997 (1970s–80s Tejano and norteño conjuntos; orquestas).

Video Jukebox, Vol. 1, Hacienda Records CD SC211 (1990s vocalists, Tejano rock, conjuntos, and grupos).

Freddie Fest '97, Freddie Records CD 2018, 1997 (Tejano and norteño conjuntos).

1995 Tejano Award Nominees, EMI Latin CD H2-7243-8-37690-2-5 (progressive conjuntos, grupos, norteño conjuntos).

Conjuntos

Rodeo Norteño, Freddie Records CD 1749, 1997.

Milenio Norteño, Freddie Records CD 1798, 2000.

Taquachito Nights: Conjunto Music, Smithsonian Folkways CD-40477, 1999 (Tejano and norteño conjuntos).

The Hometown Boys, *20 Hits,* Hacienda Records CD SC195 (Tejano conjunto).

Albert Zamora, *Albert Zamora y Talento en Concierto,* Hacienda Records CD 7461 (Tejano conjunto).

Los Palominos, *Lo Mejor de los Palominos,* Sony Discos CD B000002ER9, 1997 (Tejano conjunto).

Intocable, *Lo Mejor de Intocable,* EMI Latin CD B000000V7F, 1997 (norteño).

Ramón Ayala, Casas de Madera, Freddie Records CD B000001SJV, 1998 (norteño).

Limite, *En Concierto (Live),* Universal Music Latino CD B00001P4T2, 1999 (norteño).

Progressive Conjuntos

Emilio, *Mis Mejores Canciones: 17 Super Éxitos,* EMI Latin CD CAP0027654, 1993.

David Lee Garza, *Mis Mejores Éxitos,* EMI Latin CD B000001oRS, 1999.

La Tropa F, *Soldados de Plata,* EMI Latin CD B00004UAS6, 2000.

Bobby Pulido, *En Vivo . . . Desde Monterrey, Mexico,* EMI Latin CD B00000AF3P, 1998.

Elida y Avante, *Magico,* Tejas Records CSTR-9903, 1999.

Grupos

Selena, *All My Hits, Vol. 1,* EMI Latin CD B0000017XB, 1999; *Vol. 2,* CD B00004LMLG, 2000.

Mazz, *Anthology,* EMI Latin CD B00004VW4Y, 2000.

La Mafia, *Nuestras Mejores Canciones: 17 Super Éxitos,* EMI Latin CD B00000VNJ, 1993.

Gary Hobbs, *20 Hits,* Hacienda Records CD SC188.

Jennifer y Los Jetz, *Abrasame y Besame,* EMI Latin, 2000.

Kumbia Kings, *Amor, Familia, y Respeto,* EMI Latin CD B00001ABD, 1999.

CONTACT INFORMATION FOR RECORD COMPANIES
LISTED IN ÐISCOGRAPHY

1. Hacienda Records
1236 S. Staples
Corpus Christi, Tex., 78404
(361) 882-7066
www.haciendarecords.com
info@haciendarecords.com

2. Freddie Records
6118 S. Padre Island Dr.
Corpus Christi, Tex., 78412
(361) 992-8411
(361) 992-8428 *(fax)*

3. Arhoolie Records
Down Home Music Store
10341 San Pablo Ave.
El Cerrito, Calif., 94530
(510) 525-2129
www.arhoolie.com

4. Lago Entertainment, Inc.
5415 Bandera Road, Suite 504
San Antonio, Tex., 78238-1959

5. Tejas Records
2411 N. E. Loop 410
San Antonio, Tex., 78217
www.tejasrecords.com

6. Amazon.com (For EMI-Latin, Smithsonian Folkways, Sony Discos, and Universal Music Latino)

Appendix B

Tejano Music Awards, 1981–2000

	1981	1982	1983	1984	1985
Male Vocalist	Roberto Pulido	Jimmy Edward	Joe López	Little Joe	Roberto Pulido
Male Entertainer	Roberto Pulido	Little Joe	Little Joe	Little Joe	Oscar González
Female Vocalist	Lisa López	Laura Canales	Laura Canales	Laura Canales	Laura Canales
Female Entertainer	Lisa López	Lisa López	Laura Canales	Laura Canales	Laura Canales
Vocal Duo	Joe and Johnny Hernández	Joe and Johnny Hernández	Joe and Johnny Hernández	Oscar and Leonard González	Oscar and Leonard González

Tejano Music Awards, 1981–2000 *(cont.)*

	1981	1982	1983	1984	1985
Song of the Year	"Señorita Cantinera" (Roberto Pulido)	"Si Quieres Verme Llorar" (Lisa López)	"Oh Girl" (La Mafia)	"Ella" (Little Joe)	"Mi Loca Pasion" (La Mafia)
Single of the Year	"Señorita Cantinera" (Roberto Pulido)	"Si Quieres Verme Llorar" (Lisa López)	"Honey" (La Mafia)	"Tú Solo Tú" (La Mafia)	"Mi Loca Pasion" (La Mafia)
Most Promising Band	Mazz	La Mafia	David Lee Garza	Majic	La Sombra
Songwriter of the Year	Carlos Cardenas	Johnny Herrera	Luis Silva	Luis Silva	Luis Silva
Album of the Year— Orquesta (Grupo)	*Live for Schlitz* (Joe/ John/Familia)	*Prieta Linda* (La Familia)	*Honey* (La Mafia)	*Electrifying* (La Mafia)	*Hot Stuff* (La Mafia)
Album of the Year— Conjunto Traditional	*Por Una Mala Mujer* (Los Dos Gilbertos)	*Querida Reynosa* (Los Dos Gilbertos)	*Mi Golondrina* (Ramón Ayala)	*Especialmente Para Ti* (David Lee Garza)	*Award Winning Musicales* (David Lee Garza)
Album of the Year— Conjunto Progressive	n/a	n/a	n/a	n/a	n/a
Showband of the Year	n/a	n/a	n/a	n/a	n/a

	1981	1982	1983	1984	1985
Instrumental of the Year	n/a	n/a	n/a	n/a	n/a
Overall Album	n/a	n/a	n/a	n/a	n/a
Video of the Year	n/a	n/a	n/a	n/a	n/a
Tejano Norteño	n/a	n/a	n/a	n/a	n/a
Lifetime Achievement Award	n/a	n/a	n/a	n/a	n/a
Tejano Country	n/a	n/a	n/a	n/a	n/a
Tejano Crossover	n/a	n/a	n/a	n/a	n/a

	1986	1987	1988	1989	1990
Male Vocalist	Oscar González	Ram Herrera	Ram Herrera	Joe López	David Marez
Male Entertainer	Oscar González	Little Joe	Ram Herrera	Ram Herrera	Emilio Navaira
Female Vocalist	Laura Canales	Selena	Laura Canales	Selena	Selena
Female Entertainer	Laura Canales	Patsey Torres	Selena	Selena	Selena

Tejano Music Awards, 1981–2000 *(cont.)*

	1986	1987	1988	1989	1990
Vocal Duo	Joe López and Jimmy González	Rubén and Alonso Ramos	Joe López and Jimmy González	Joe López and Jimmy González	Joe López and Jimmy González
Song of the Year	"Las Isabels" (Little Joe)	"Si Tú Supieras" (La Mafia)	"Amor Querido" (Ram Herrera)	"Fijate" (David Marez)	"Ahora Quiero Que Me Quieras" (Mazz)
Single of the Year	"Un Rinconcinto en el Cielo" (Ramón Ayala)	"Entre Mas Lejos Me Vaya" (David Marez)	"Amor Querido" (Ram Herrera)	"Me Quieres Tú . . ." (David Lee Garza)	"Ay Mujer" (Latin Breed)
Most Promising Band	Montana Band	Fandango	Dirección	Los Dudes	Emilio Navaira
Songwriter of the Year	Luis Silva	Luis Silva	Luis Silva	Luis Silva	Joe López
Album of the Year— Orquesta (Grupo)	*No. 16* (Mazz)	*La Mafia 1986* (La Mafia)	*Beyond* (Mazz)	*Sold Out* (David Marez)	*Breaking the Rules* (Latin Breed)
Album of the Year— Conjunto Traditional	*Un Rinconcito en el Cielo* (Ramón Ayala)	*Cuantas Veces* (David Lee Garza)	*Dejame Quererte* (David Lee Garza)	*Tour 88* (David Lee Garza)	*Emilio* (Emilio Navaira y Grupo Río)

	1986	1987	1988	1989	1990
Album of the Year— Conjunto Progressive	n/a	n/a	n/a	n/a	n/a
Showband of the Year	n/a	n/a	n/a	n/a	n/a
Instrumental of the Year	n/a	n/a	n/a	n/a	n/a
Overall Album	n/a	n/a	n/a	n/a	n/a
Video of the Year	n/a	n/a	n/a	n/a	n/a
Tejano Norteño	n/a	n/a	n/a	n/a	n/a
Lifetime Achievement Award	n/a	n/a	n/a	n/a	n/a
Tejano Country	n/a	n/a	n/a	n/a	n/a
Tejano Crossover	n/a	n/a	n/a	n/a	n/a

	1991	1992	1993	1994	1995
Male Vocalist	Joe López	Joe López	Emilio Navaira	Emilio Navaira	Emilio Navaira

Tejano Music Awards, 1981–2000 *(cont.)*

	1991	1992	1993	1994	1995
Male Entertainer	Emilio Navaira	Emilio Navaira	Emilio Navaira	Emilio Navaira	Emilio Navaira
Female Vocalist	Selena	Selena	Selena	Selena	Selena
Female Entertainer	Selena	Selena	Selena	Selena	Selena
Vocal Duo	Joe López and Jimmy González	Joe López and Jimmy González	Emilio and Raul Navaira	Joe López and Jimmy González	Roberto Pulido and Emilio Navairo
Song of the Year	"No Te Olvidare" (Mazz)	"Que Me Lleven Canciones" (Mazz)	"Lo Voy Hacer Por Tí" (Mazz)	"La Charanga" (Fandango USA)	"Bidi Bidi Bom Bom" (Selena)
Single of the Year	"Amor con Amor" (Mazz)	"Ven Devorame Otra Vez" (Mazz)	"Lo Voy Hacer Por Tí" (Mazz)	"La Charanga" (Fandango USA)	"Amor Prohibido" (Selena)
Most Promising Band	La Fiebre	Xcelencia	Culturas	Estrella	La Diferenzia
Songwriter of the Year	Joe López	Joe López	n/a	n/a	n/a
Album of the Year—Orquesta (Grupo)	*No Te Olvidare* (Mazz)	*Para Nuestra Gente* (Mazz)	*Entre A Mi Mundo* (Selena)	*Selena-Live* (Selena)	*Amor Prohibido* (Selena)

	1991	1992	1993	1994	1995
Album of the Year— Conjunto Traditional	*Mi Acordeón y Yo* (Ramón Ayala)	*So Todas Fueran Como Tú* (Roberto Pulido)	*Right on Track* (La Tropa F)	*Unrivaled* (Los Chamacos)	*Bidi Bidi Bom Bom* (Selena)
Album of the Year— Conjunto Progressive	*Sensaciones* (Emilio Navaira)	*Shoot It* (Emilio Navaira)	*Unsung Highways* (Emilio Navaira)	*Southern Exposure* (Emilio Navaira)	*Ya Me Canse* (David Lee Garza)
Showband of the Year	n/a	n/a	David Lee Garza	Emilio Navaira[1]	Culturas
Instrumental of the Year	n/a	n/a	n/a	*Posse Polkas* (David Lee Garza)	*El Tren* (Los Chamacos)
Overall Album	n/a	n/a	n/a	n/a	n/a
Video of the Year	n/a	n/a	n/a	n/a	n/a
Tejano Norteño	n/a	n/a	n/a	n/a	n/a
Lifetime Achievement Award	n/a	n/a	n/a	n/a	n/a
Tejano Country	n/a	*South of the Border* (Emilio Navaira)[2]	*She's Not Alone* (David Lee Garza)	*I've Got a Never Ending Love* (Ram Herrera)	*She Can't Say I Didn't Cry* (Rick Treviño)

Tejano Music Awards, 1981–2000 *(cont.)*

	1991	1992	1993	1994	1995
Tejano Crossover	n/a	n/a	n/a	*La Charanga* (Fandango)	*Techno-Cumbia* (Selena)

	1996	1997	1998	1999	2000
Male Vocalist	Emilio Navaira	Michael Salgado	Bobby Pulido	Michael Salgado	Jay Perez
Male Entertainer	Emilio Navaira	Emilio Navaira	Bobby Pulido	Bobby Pulido	Bobby Pulido
Female Vocalist	Selena	Selena	Shelly Lares	Jennifer Peña	Elida Reyna
Female Entertainer	Selena	Jennifer Peña	Jennifer Peña	Jennifer Peña	Elida Reyna
Vocal Duo	Emilio and Raul Navaira	Emilio and Raul Navaira	n/a	n/a	n/a
Song of the Year	"Tú Solo Tú" (Selena)	"Siempre Hace Frío" (Selena)	"Mundo Sin Guitarras" (La Diferenzia)	"Te Quiero Te Amo" (A. B. Quintanilla)	"Duele" (Elida y Avante)
Single of the Year	n/a	n/a	n/a	n/a	n/a

	1996	1997	1998	1999	2000
Most Promising Band	Pete Astudillo	Bobby Pulido	Jennifer y Los Jetz	Elida y Avante	Kumbia Kings
Songwriter of the Year	n/a	n/a	n/a	n/a	n/a
Album of the Year— Orquesta (Grupo)	*Solo Para Tí* (Mazz)	*Como Te Extrano* (Pete Astudillo)	*Llegaste A Mi Vida* (Bobby Pulido)[5]	*Cuantas Veces* (Mazz)	*Amor, Familia, y Respeto* (Kumbia Kings)
Album of the Year— Conjunto Traditional	*Cruz de Madera* (Michael Salgado)	*En Concierto* (Michael Salgado)	*Un Recuerdo Especial* (Michael Salgado)	*Intocable* (Intocable)	*Contigo* (Intocable)
Album of the Year— Conjunto Progressive	*Sound Life* (Emilio)	*A Un Nuevo Nivel* (La Tropa F)	n/a	n/a	n/a
Showband of the Year	Selena y los Dinos	La Tropa F	Eddie González	La Tropa F	Kumbia Kings
Instrumental of the Year	*David Lee's Favorites* (David Lee Garza)	*Joe's Special No. 10* (Hometown Boys)	n/a	n/a	n/a
Overall Album	*Dreaming of You* (Selena)	*Como Te Extrano* (Pete Astudillo)	n/a	n/a	n/a

Tejano Music Awards, 1981–2000 *(cont.)*

	1996	1997	1998	1999	2000
Video of the Year	"Lucero de mi Alma" (Emilio Navaira)[3]	"Hay Unos Ojos" "Paloma Negra", tie	"Le Pedire" (Bobby Pulido)	"Como Un Suspiro" (Ruben Ramos)	"De Bolon Pin Pon" (Flaco Jiménez)
Tejano Norteño	n/a	n/a	Grupo Limite	Grupo Limite	"Duele" (Elida y Avante)[4]
Lifetime Achievement Award	n/a	n/a	n/a	La Mafia	Sunny Ozuna
Tejano Country	*It's Not the End of the World* (Emilio)	*Mi Vida Eres Tú* (Rick Treviño)	n/a	n/a	n/a
Tejano Crossover	"I Could Fall In Love" (Selena)	"No Quiero Saber" (Selena)	"Donde Estes" (Bobby Pulido)	"Cowboy Cumbia" (Javier Molina)	"Azucar" (Kumbia Kings)

Sources: La Prensa de San Antonio (1996), 6; "List of the Winners," *Que Onda* (March 4, 1997), 13; Ramiro Burr, "Pulido Rules Tejano Show with Five Wins," *Houston Chronicle* (March 15, 1998); "Ganadores Entrega XIX: Tejano Music Awards," *Hola* (March 25, 1999), 20; "20th Annual Tejano Music Awards," *Tejano Yearbook* (March 11, 2000).

[1]Tejano Yearbook mistakenly lists David Lee Garza in this category.
[2]"20th Annual Tejano Music Awards" failed to list this song in its publication.
[3]Tejano Yearbook fails to list this title.
[4]Category renamed "Mexican Regional Song."
[5]Category renamed "Album of the Year–Grupo" (dropped "orquesta").

Notes

PREFACE

1. Manuel Peña, *Música Tejana.*
2. His most important works include *"With His Pistol in His Hand": A Border Ballad and Its Hero; A Texas-Mexican Cancionero;* and *Folklore and Culture on the Texas-Mexican Border.*
3. Peña's major works include *The Texas-Mexican Conjunto: History of a Working-Class Music; Música Tejana;* and *The Mexican American Orquesta.*
4. Ramiro Burr, *The Billboard Guide to Tejano and Regional Mexican Music.*
5. Los García Brothers, *Cuatro Paredes,* Zaz Records, 1999, liner notes.

CHAPTER I

1. Manual Peña, *Música Tejana,* 3–14.
2. Ramiro Burr, "Conjunto Faithful to Converge at San Antonio Festival," *Houston Chronicle,* May 11, 1997.
3. For different definitions of "Tejano," see Jon Pareles, "Niche Music . . . ," *New York Times,* Sunday, May 14, 1995, late edition; Burr, "Conjunto Faithful,"; Marty Racine, "Making the Music," *Houston Chronicle,* August 16, 1992; and Thaddeus Herrick, "Go Tejano!/ Music's Appeal Oversteps Traditional Boundaries," *Houston Chronicle,* February 9, 1995.
4. Peña, *Música Tejana,* xi, 184–186.
5. Vilma Maldonado, "Defining Tejano Hard Because It Encompasses So Much," *McAllen Monitor,* October 14, 1997.
6. Ibid.
7. This definition is the one used by Peña in his most recent study. Peña, *Música Tejana.*
8. Richard L. Nostrand, *The Hispano Homeland,* 99.
9. For an overview of the distinctiveness of the border in Tejano history, see Paredes, *"With His Pistol in His Hand,"* 7–32.
10. Armando C. Alonzo, *Tejano Legacy: Rancheros and Settlers in South Texas, 1734–1900,* 3.
11. Joe Nick Patoski, *Selena: Como La Flor,* 12.
12. Sam Suniga, interview by author, San Antonio, Texas, November 18, 2000.
13. Alice, Texas, a rural community forty-five miles west of Corpus Christi, in fact, was officially declared as the "birthplace" of música tejana by the state legislature in August 2000. Carlos Truan, state senator from the Corpus Christi area, discussed this legislative proclamation at an induction ceremony honoring artists and pioneers of the Tejano music industry. The author was in attendance at that ceremony and was chosen to be one of the presenters. The induction ceremony was held on Friday, August 25, 2000, at the Knights of Columbus Hall in Alice, Texas.
14. Gloria Anzaldua, *Borderlands/La Frontera: The New Mextiza,* preface.
15. Manuel Peña, *Texas-Mexican Conjunto,* 24.

16. For a historical overview of Mexican Americans in Texas, see Arnoldo De León, *Mexican Americans in Texas: A Brief History,* 2d ed.; and David Montejano, *Anglos and Mexicans in the Making of Texas, 1836–1986.*

17. Peña, *Texas-Mexican Conjunto,* 24.

18. Dan William Dickey, *The Kennedy Corridos: A Study of the Ballads of a Mexican American Hero,* 7. On corridos in general, see also Paredes, *"With His Pistol in His Hand."*

19. Paredes, *"With His Pistol in His Hand,"* 129–50.

20. Peña, *Música Tejana,* 30.

21. This, as well as other corridos, can be found in *Corridos y Tragedias de la Frontera: First Recordings of Historic Mexican American Ballads,* Arhoolie CD 7019 and CD 7020. For an analysis of "The Corrido of Gregorio Cortez," see Paredes, *"With His Pistol in His Hand."*

22. Peña, *Música Tejana,* 77.

23. Peña notes that in the latter part of the century a new type of ranchera emerged. He argues that this "Texo-centric" ranchera was a variant of the ranchera that accepted the Texan myth of bigness. Ibid., 39.

24. Peña argues that the canción típica was also known as a *canción mexicana* in the early part of the century. Ibid., 50.

25. Ibid., 39.

26. Peña argues that the treacherous woman theme was a form of ideology displacement that transposed issues of class relations to the gender domain. Ibid., 54. Lydia Mendoza bucked the practice of casting women as deceitful lovers. Refer to the collection of her hits from the 1930s. Lydia Mendoza, *Mal Hombre,* Arhoolie CD 7002, 1992.

27. Peña, *Música Tejana,* 50–51.

28. The cancíon romántica or música romántica acquired the label of *música moderna* in the post–World War II era. Ibid., 60.

29. The ranchera and the romántica illustrated a much larger relationship between the country and the city and its ideological articulation. The concepts of lo ranchero and "jaitón" encapsulated the ideological contradictions embodied in the concepts of the city (capitalism) and the country (feudalism), an idealized rural communitarian experience accompanied by backward, uncivilized peon and an idealized modernizing urban middle-class experience. Ibid., 63.

30. Herrick, "Go Tejano!".

31. Burr, *Billboard Guide,* 105.

32. See *Texas-Mexican Border Music, Vol. 4: Norteño Accordion, Part I: The First Recordings,* Folklyric Records LP 9006, n.d. (ca. 1973).

33. Sordo Sodi notes that there are various types of ranchera songs. One of these is the canción norteña, played by norteño groups. These songs were at one time accompanied on the *vihuela.* Beginning in 1850, harp, vihuela, and psaltery were used in the accompaniment of these songs. Around 1890 the *jarana* and guitar came into use; the accordion appeared still later. Canciones norteñas became popular in the capital in the 1920s. From there they radiated all over the country. The norteño ensemble, as it was known in the 1970s, is little more than twenty-five years old. Antonio González, *Mexican American Musicians: A History,* 98.

34. Peña, *Música Tejana,* 51–53. He argues that the canción ranchera, sung primarily by vocal duets, became powerfully charged with class and gender implications in the second quarter of the twentieth century. The songs were gender biased and coalesced around the theme of the treacherous woman.

35. For examples of the relative increase in cumbias during the 1990s, see Intocable, *Intocable,* Capitol-EMI (CD H2724349517820), 1998, and Selena, *Baila Esta Cumbia,* Capitol-EMI (audiocassette 40779905240), 1992.

36. Little Joe, for instance, recorded the song "Las Nubes" bilingually in the late 1970s. Ram Herrera recently recorded "A Never Ending Love," a ranchera with English lyrics. For a sophisticated cultural and musical analysis of "Las Nubes" and several other songs by Little Joe, see Peña, *Mexican American Orquesta,* 244–59.

37. These processes have been called "bimusicality" by Peña and "hybridity" by Burr. For a complex analysis of the former, see Peña, *Mexican American Orquesta,* 227–74. For more on hybridity, see Burr, *Billboard Guide,* 15–39.

38. Letty Guval, *Miles de Suenos,* A. B. Wick Records 001, 1994.

39. Conjunto Bernal, *Aurora,* GS Records 160, 1983. (The 1983 date of this recording is probably that of a reissue. I originally heard the album in the summer of 1978 when I moved to Santa Barbara, California. My cousin, Elias Soto, a displaced Tejano living in California, had bought the album in Texas. He introduced me to it the first day I visited him in Santa Barbara. This album, then, must have been recorded in the late 1970s.)

40. To hear some of his original recordings issued between 1948 and 1954, refer to *Beto Villa: Father of Orquesta Tejana,* Arhoolie CD 364, 1992.

41. For examples of this type of music, refer to Sunny & the Sunliners, *Little Brown Eyed Soul,* Key-Loc KL-3005, n.d.; and Little Joe and the Latinaires, *Unbeatable!,* Tomi Records TLP1002, n.d. All songs on these albums are in English and were recorded during the early 1960s.

42. In 1957, for instance, Conjunto Bernal recorded a rock and roll song entitled "La Novia Antonia." This selection can be found on *Tejano Roots: Raices Tejanas,* Arhoolie CD 341, 1991.

43. Peña refers to this development as the "triumph of the anti-ranchero." See Peña, *Mexican American Orquesta,* 166–99.

44. Some musicians "Tejano-ized" other styles so that they reflect the experiences of Mexican Americans in the barrio but did not rearrange the tunes so that Tejanos can dance to them. One of these is Randy Garibay, the great Tejano bluesman. He records old-time blues music with lyrics that reflect the experiences of Mexican Americans in the barrios of San Antonio. Randy Garibay, *Barbacoa Blues,* Angelita Mía Production (cd number not available), 1997; and *And Cats Don't Sleep,* Angelita Mía Production RGCD 3943, n.d.

45. The song can be found on *Steve Jordan: The Many Sounds of Steve Jordan,* Arhoolie CD 319, 1990.

46. This song can be heard on *The Best of the 11th Annual Tejano Conjunto Festival, 1992,* (Videocassette), San Antonio: Guadalupe Cultural Arts Center Production, 1992.

47. Refer to "Sobrevivire" on Priscila y Sus Balas de Plata, *Todo Por Tí,* FonoVisa B00009R4V, 1999.

48. Throughout the fall of 1999, I constantly heard this song on KQQK 106.5 FM in Houston, and on several radio stations in Corpus Christi, including KUNO 1400 AM, KSAB 99.9 FM, and KMIQ 105.1 FM.

49. For an example of three-part harmony in the orquesta style of música tejana, refer to Los Dinos, *Los Dinos,* Falcon FLP 2057, n.d.

50. Burr, *Billboard Guide,* 135.

51. Pulido has countless albums and CDs illustrating his unique combination of the orquesta and conjunto sounds. For an example from the late 1970s, refer to Roberto Pulido y Los Clásicos, *El Primo,* Falcon ARVLP 1056, 1979.

52. Refer to Emilio Navaira & Río Band, *Sensaciones,* CBS CRC 80329, 1990.

53. Country Roland recorded a large number of albums in the 1970s and early 1980s. For one example of his music, refer to Country Roland, *Mr. Chicano Country,* Falcon ARVLP 1062, 1980. For an example of the variety of Chicano country bands that recorded during

the latter part of the 1970s and the early 1980s, refer to *The Best of Chicano Country, Vol. 2,* Falcon ARVLP 1075, 1982. This album has songs by Roberto Pulido y Los Clásicos, Texas Country Band, Cactus Country Band, Country Roland, and Country Roland, Jr.

54. For an excellent analysis of this process as reflected in the modern orquesta, see Peña, *Mexican American Orquesta,* 227–74.

55. One other type of group is the banda. Bandas utilized mostly wind-based or brass instruments such as the clarinet, cornet, flute, trumpet, trombone, and tuba. Many of them also had one or two sets of drums. Although some banda groups have been popular in the Tejano community, especially along the border, no banda group recorded Tejano music during the twentieth century. The association of banda music with military functions or marching bands among the popular imagination probably accounts for this lack of popularity among Tejanos.

56. Américo Paredes, *A Texas-Mexican Cancionero: Folksongs of the Lower Border.*

57. Guadalupe San Miguel, Jr., "The Rise of Recorded Tejano Music in the Post–World War II Years, 1946–64," 26–49.

58. Several scholars have used the term "Tejano" synonymously with what I call "grupo." "Tejano," however, is a confusing term that encompasses all groups currently playing música tejana. Even Peña provides two definitions of "Tejano." He argues that Tejano is composed of "the most recent crop of synthesizer-driven ensembles and their styles." Later, he expands this definition and argues that Tejano is composed of "the various Texas-Mexican musical groups and their styles" played in the 1990s. Peña, *Música Tejana,* xi, 184. Ramiro Burr, the well-known music columnist for the *San Antonio Express News,* argues that Tejano includes all types of musical styles, including the orquestas that originated in the post–World War II era and the progressive conjuntos. Burr, *Billboard Guide,* 197.

59. Strachwitz, *Tejano Roots/Raices Tejanas,* Arhoolie CD 341, 1991, liner notes; Strachwitz, *Mexican American Border Music: Vol. 5, Orquestas de Cuerdas: The End of a Tradition,* Arhoolie CD 7018, 1996, liner notes; Strachwitz, *Mexican American Border Music: Vol. 4, Orquestas Típicas, The First Recordings, 1926–38,* Arhoolie CD 7017, 1996, liner notes; Peña, *Música Tejana,* 118–27.

60. The songs and dances played by these orquestas also changed over time. The changing repertoire will be discussed in further detail later.

61. Peña argues that it most likely originated in Mexico. Violent confrontations between Anglos and Mexicans in the San Antonio area discouraged its use in the Mexican community. German settlers, especially workers in Monterrey, probably introduced it to the community. Peña, *Texas-Mexican Conjunto,* 33.

62. Strachwitz, *Texas-Mexican Border Music, Vol. 4, Norteño Accordion, Part I: The First Recordings,* Folklyric Records, LP 9006, n.d. (ca. 1973), liner notes.

63. Adrian Treviño, *Tejano Music, 1830–1930: An Informal History.*

64. The bajo sexto has a thicker neck than a regular guitar and has a feature called a "cutaway," which improves resonance. The electric bass replaced the bajo sexto's bass function in many conjuntos in the 1950s, and today the bajo sexto mainly serves as a rhythm instrument. Burr, *Billboard Guide,* 58.

65. They also do not give billing to any members of the group. Burr, *Billboard Guide,* 102.

66. Patoski, *Selena,* 23.

67. For a sampling of this music, refer to the following recordings: Country Roland, *Las Margaritas,* Falcon, ARVLP 1057, 1979; Country Roland Band, *Rancho Grande,* Falcon, ARVLP 1052, 1978; Country Mingo, *The Outlaw,* Falcon, FLP 5041, 1980; The Texas Country Band, *Valle de Palmas,* Falcon, ARVLP 1065, 1980; Country Roland, Jr., *Mucho Macho,* Falcon, ARVLP 1064, 1980; *The Best of Chicano Country, Vol. 2,* Falcon, ARVLP 1075, 1982.

68. For a sampling of the country music recorded by these artists, refer to Rudy Tee Gonzales y Sus Reno Bops, *Country,* Teardrop, TD 2030, n.d. (ca. 1972); Snowball & Co., *Snowball & Co.,* Fireball, FLP 1001, n.d. (especially the song "Just Because," a Chicano country ballad); Roberto Pulido on *The Best of Chicano Country, Vol. 2,* Falcon, ARVLP 1075, 1982; and Mazz, *Perfect 10,* Cara, CA-10B, 1977. Mazz recorded three country songs on their first album in 1977, "Algo Bonito" (Something Pretty), "El" (He), and "Laura Ya No Vive Aquí" (Laura Doesn't Live Here Anymore). Unlike other Tejano artists, Mazz abandoned the use of the steel guitar and violin and played these songs using the synthesizer and rhythm guitar as its primary instruments.

CHAPTER 2

1. Strachwitz, *Tejano Roots/Raices Tejanas,* Arhoolie CD 341, 1991.

2. For a listing of these songs, see Richard K. Spottswood, *Ethnic Music on Records: A Discography of Ethnic Recordings in the United States, 1894–1942.*

3. According to Peña, vocal singing—especially with regards to phrasing, articulation, and ability—was stylistically developed. Two modes of singing developed: the *bel canto* style popularized in Mexico after the introduction of the Italian opera, and the nasalized, pinched style of the working class. The former was most popular, but the nasalized singing became popular by the early twentieth century. Peña, *Texas-Mexican Conjunto,* 34–35.

4. For information on the definition, structure, and content of the modern corrido, see Merle E. Simmons, *The Mexican Corrido as a Source for Interpretive Study of Modern Mexico (1870–1950),* 3, 16–27.

5. In Mexico, the canción romántica gained popularity several decades earlier than in Texas. It began to flourish by the 1870s and 1880s rather than by the end of the century. Peña, *Música Tejana,* 38. See also Juan S. Garrido, *Historia de la música popular en Mexico.*

6. Peña, *Música Tejana,* 34–38.

7. Ibid., 37.

8. Peña argues that male musicians focused on the treacherous woman theme due to what he calls ideological displacement. Mexican men, in other words, were socially, economically, and politically subordinate to the male members of the predominantly Anglo rulers in Texas. Able to do little about their public oppression in larger society, working-class men transferred this resentment to the domestic domain in general and to Mexican women in particular. He states, "The perennial conflict between men and women was reinforced by the resentment these working-class men harbored as a result of their economic oppression; in a gender relation in which, historically, they had enjoyed overwhelming dominance, working-class men were free to unleash their frustrations upon more or less defenseless women." Peña, *Música Tejana,* 58.

9. This song can be found on *Tejano Roots: The Women (1946–70),* Arhoolie, CD 343, 1991.

10. "Mi galán," she sings, "era tan falso" (My man was untrue). Both of these songs can be found on Lydia Mendoza, *Mal Hombre and other Original Hits from the 1930s,* Arhoolie CD 7002, 1992.

11. Peña, *Música Tejana,* 59.

12. Ibid., 39.

13. Peña aptly noted that corridos reflected "the deeper transformations being wrought within the culture by the modernizing impact of a capitalist political economy." Ibid.

14. For an elaboration of the corrido tradition and its significance to Mexican Americans, see Paredes, *"With His Pistol in His Hand."*

15. The process of the development of the romance tradition in the colonial period and its evolution into the modern corrido is unclear. Some romances were sung during the conquest of the Americas, and some corrido-like poems and ballads were written during this period, but inadequate data exists to clarify the presence and evolution of corridos. Simmons, *Mexican Corrido,* 11–12.

16. This is in contrast to the traditional interpretation of the rise and fall of the corrido in Mexico. According to historian Vicente Mendoza, the corrido had three historical stages: 1875–1910, the period of ascent; 1910–30, the height of the corrido during the Mexican Revolution era; and 1930–present, a period of decadence. For a brief history of the corrido, see Philip Sonnichson, *Texas-Mexican Border Music, Vols. 2–3, Corridos, Part I, II,* Arhoolie/Folklyric Records, 1975, LP booklet.

17. Simmons argues that the corrido became the dominant form of canción by the first decade of the twentieth century, but he provides no evidence of its dominance. He also notes that there were other musical traditions in Mexico, including the canción, *son,* huapango, and *zandunga,* but these became subordinate to the corrido by the early twentieth century. Simmons, *Mexican Corrido,* 16, 26. The definition, structure, and content of the modern corrido are given on 3, 16–27.

18. Ibid., 33.

19. See *Texas-Mexican Border Music, Vol. 2: Corridos, Part I: 1930–34,* Folklyric Records LP 9042, n.d., and *Texas-Mexican Border Music, Vol. 3: Corridos, Part II: 1926-1936,* Folklyric Records LP 9005, n.d.

20. De León, *The Tejano Community,* 182–83.

21. Ibid.

22. Américo Paredes notes that individual singing at public events was usually a male-only activity. Females sang primarily at family celebrations. See Paredes, *A Texas-Mexican Cancionero,* xix–xxiv.

23. Los pastores and las pastorelas were based on the birth of Christ. These musical dramas, noted Steven Loza, "depicted the journey of the shepherds to the Nativity manger." Las pastorelas were often enacted at churches or private homes in conjunction with the "posada" (inn), "a social, religious gathering where songs celebrating the Christmas season were sung." The last time vocal singing was used for las pastorelas in Los Angeles was in the 1860s. Steven Loza, *Barrio Rhythm: Mexican American Music in Los Angeles,* 11.

24. See *Texas-Mexican Border Music, Vol. 1: An Introduction, 1930-1960,* Folklyric Records LP 9008, 1973; *Texas-Mexican Border Music, Vol. 5: The String Bands—End of a Tradition,* Folklyric Records LP 9007, n.d.; *Texas-Mexican Border Music, Vol. 2: Corridos, Part I, 1930–34,* Folklyric 9042, n.d.; *Texas-Mexican Border Music, Vol. 3: Corridos, Part II, 1929–36,* Folklyric 9005, n.d.; *Texas-Mexican Border Music, Vol. 4: Norteño Accordion, Part I, The First Recordings,* Folklyric 9006, n.d.

25. Peña estimated that perhaps two-thirds of the music recorded by the major labels during the years from the late 1920s to the early 1940s, as indicated by the comprehensive discography by Richard K. Spottswood, was of the vocal duet variety. Peña, *Música Tejana,* 51. For a listing of all these recordings during these years, see Spottswood, *Ethnic Music.*

26. For a sampling of music by Lydia Mendoza, refer to *Lydia Mendoza—Mal Hombre and Other Original Hits from the 1930s,* Arhoolie, CD 7002. See also Chris Strachwitz and James Nicolopulos, comps., *Lydia Mendoza: A Family Autobiography.*

27. In the early 1950s Berlanga joined el Conjunto Trio San Antonio, one of the most popular conjuntos of this decade. Strachwitz, *Mexican American Border Music, Vol. 1: An Introduction: The Pioneer Recording Artists, 1928–58,* Folklyric Records CD 7001, 1994, liner notes 18–19, 21–22.

28. Refer to *Texas-Mexican Border Music, Vol. 5: The String Bands—End of a Tradition,* Folklyric LP 9007, n.d.

29. Orquestas occasionally played other popular dance forms including the following: the minuet, the *lancera,* the redowa, and the quadrille. Some of these dance steps—for example, the Viennese waltz, the German schottische, and the French cotillion—were brought by the French during the occupation of Mexico in the 1860s. Others were imported to Mexico by Germans who immigrated to the United States in the early and mid-1800s. Antonio González, *Mexican American Musicians: A History,* 93.

30. Strachwitz, *Mexican American Border Music, Vol. 4.*

31. According to Peña, some instruments, such as the mandolin and contrabass, originally were used in musical groups that performed for upper-class social functions, but they soon found their way into the working-class plazas and fiestas. Peña, *Texas-Mexican Conjunto,* 32.

32. See *Songs of the Homeland,* a documentary film produced and directed by Hector Galán (Austin: Galán Productions, 1995), for an example of late nineteenth century orquestas. Two pictures are found about 6 mins. after the video starts.

33. Peña, *Música Tejana,* 125–26.

34. The first orquesta típica was organized in 1884 by students and teachers from the National Conservatory in Mexico City under the direction of Carlos Curti. Their repertoire consisted of arrangements of a great variety of popular dance music. The musicians in the group wore charro costumes similar to those favored by mariachis in the 1990s. The most famous of the early national orquestas típicas was formed in 1901 under the direction of Miguel Lerdo de Tejada. Although based in Mexico City, his orquesta toured widely throughout Mexico and the United States, always with government support. Strachwitz, *Mexican American Border Music, Vol. 4: Orquestas Tipicas, 1996,* liner notes.

35. Peña, *Música Tejana,* 121.

36. Ibid., 122.

37. The group was under the direction of Timotéo Gloria. *Corpus Christi Caller Times,* May 27, 1883.

38. A commentator praised Persio's group for his excellent music in 1891. *San Antonio Express,* July 13, 1891.

39. González, *Mexican American Musicians,* 93.

40. Strachwitz, *Mexican American Border Music: Vol. 5,* Arhoolie CD 7018, 1996, liner notes.

41. For a picture of the group, see Thomas Kreneck, *Del Pueblo: A Pictorial History of Houston's Hispanic Community,* 70.

42. For a picture of this group, see Peña, *Mexican American Orquesta,* 84.

43. This group was directed by José López. The members of the group in 1933 were Rebecca Aguirre, Eliz Aguirre, Janie Cervantes, Agapita Marquéz, Florinda Smith, Susie Cortez, Lily Cortez, Angelita Pérez, and Esther Luna. Picture from Mr. and Mrs. Fernando Salas Collection, Houston Metropolitan Research Center, Public Library, Houston, Texas. For a picture of the Salases, see Kreneck, *Del Pueblo,* 100.

44. Strachwitz, liner notes, *Mexican American Border Music, Vol. 4,* Arhoolie CD 7017, 1996.

45. De León, *The Tejano Community,* 177.

46. Peña, *Música Tejana,* 122.

47. Strachwitz, *Mexican American Border Music, Vol. 4,* Arhoolie CD 7017, 1996, liner notes.

48. For a picture of the Southern Pacific Lines Band and the Our Lady of Guadalupe Church Band, see Kreneck, *Del Pueblo,* 54, 61.

49. Peña, *Texas-Mexican Conjunto*, 33.

50. Food, sports, and games were also part of these large community celebrations; De León, *Tejano Community*, 174–76.

51. Ibid., 174.

52. De León refers to these as *funciones* or fiestas, which were popular from the 1880s to 1930. De León, *Tejano Community*, 176.

53. De León, *Tejano Community*, 181.

54. No banda group recorded until the 1940s. In this decade a group by the name of Banda Típica Mazatlán was recorded. See *Mexican American Border Music, Vol. 4., 1996*.

55. See Strachwitz, *Mexican American Border Music: Vol. 5*, Arhoolie CD 7018, 1996, liner notes.

56. See *Texas-Mexican Border Music, Vol. 1: An Introduction, 1930–60*, Folklyric LP 9008, n.d. Included in the Mendoza family singers was Lydia Mendoza, who would soon become known as "La Cancionera de los Pobres." For more information on Lydia Mendoza, see Strachwitz and Nicolopulos, comps., *Lydia Mendoza*.

57. Strachwitz, *Mexican American Border Music: Vol. 5*, Arhoolie CD 7018, 1996, liner notes.

58. Ibid.

59. Ibid.; Peña, *Texas-Mexican Conjunto*, 51.

60. For a discussion of these theories, see chapter 1 of this book. See also Strachwitz, *Tejano Roots/Raíces Tejanas*, Arhoolie CD 341, 1991, liner notes; Peña, *Texas-Mexican Conjunto*, 33; and Adrian Treviño, *Tejano Music*.

61. Jeremy Marre and Hannah Charlton, *Beats of the Heart* (New York: Pantheon Books, 1985), 110.

62. Peña, *Texas-Mexican Conjunto*, 36.

63. Ibid., 37.

64. There were several other accordionists and conjuntos in addition to the ones represented in the historical recordings. Some, like Pedro Ayala, started playing in the 1930s but did not record until 1947. The recordings by Ayala in the late 1940s signaled new changes in conjunto. It was more "snappy" and had more contrabass; Peña, *Texas-Mexican Conjunto*, 64–69.

65. Ibid., 52.

66. Strachwitz, *Texas Mexican Border Music, Vol. 3: Norteño & Tejano Accordion Pioneers, 1929–39*, Arhoolie CD 7016, 1995, liner notes.

67. Peña, *Texas-Mexican Conjunto*, 43, 53.

68. After the war, he recorded under the Ideal label. He began to tour outside Texas in 1952; Ibid., 52.

69. Ibid., 60.

70. Ibid., 60–62.

71. This was the beginning of what Strachwitz referred to as the end of a musical tradition in the Tejano community. See Strachwitz, *Mexican American Border Music: Vol. 5*, Arhoolie CD 7018, 1996, liner notes.

72. This is only true for Texas. In California mariachi music became extremely popular. Loza, *Barrio Rhythm*, 32–39.

73. Strachwitz, *Mexican American Border Music: Vol. 5*, Arhoolie CD 7018, 1996, liner notes.

74. Ibid.

75. In the mid-1930s mariachi music was transformed when a trumpet was added to a mariachi band during a radio broadcast. Since then this music and its instrumentation has become highly stylized. The flute was added earlier, in the 1920s. Ibid.

76. Peña, *Texas-Mexican Conjunto,* 73.

77. For information on the definition, structure, and content of the modern corrido, see Simmons, *Mexican Corrido,* 3, 16–27.

78. Loza, *Barrio Rhythm,* 21.

79. Ibid.

80. Peña, *Texas-Mexican Conjunto,* 20–39.

81. George S. Sanchez, *Becoming Mexican American* (Oxford: Oxford University Press, 1993). For examples of touring circuses and vaudeville, see Nicolás Kanellos, *Mexican American Theater: Legacy and Reality.*

82. See Strachwitz, *Mexican American Border Music: Vol. 5,* Arhoolie CD 7018, 1996, liner notes.

83. Peña, *Texas-Mexican Conjunto,* 54.

84. Ibid., 53.

85. The bajo sexto was not new to the conjunto ensemble, of course, but in the past it had to compete with the bass-chord elements of the accordion itself, an arrangement that masked its peculiar sonority. Ibid., 54.

86. Ibid., 53.

87. Ibid.

88. Ibid., 25.

89. Peña argues that these dance forms became popular because of the evolution of the opera into the contemporary canción and the popularity of salons. Ibid.

90. Ibid., 57.

CHAPTER 3

1. Peña, *Texas-Mexican Conjunto,* 70–71.

2. Strachwitz, *Tejano Roots: The Women (1946–70),* Arhoolie CD 343, 1991.

3. Ibid., 6.

4. Ibid.

5. Ibid., 5.

6. Ibid.

7. Ibid.

8. Strachwitz, *Tejano Roots/Raices Tejanas: The Roots of Tejano and Conjunto Music,* Arhoolie CD 341, 1991, liner notes.

9. Peña, *Texas-Mexican Conjunto,* 75.

10. Some females were also part of male-female duets, including Victor y Lolita, who recorded for Falcon Records, and Martín y Malena. This latter group recorded for a while with Azteca Records. Almost no information, however, is available about these females—not even their first names—about the música groups, or about the recording companies. For further information, see Terese Paloma Acosta, "Tejana Singers," *The Handbook of Texas Online, http://www.tsha.utexas.edu.*

11. Strachwitz, *Tejano Roots/Raices Tejanas: The Roots of Tejano and Conjunto Music,* Arhoolie, CD 341, 1991, liner notes.

12. "Se Me Fue Mi Amor," ranchera, Carmen y Laura, on *Tejano Roots/Raices Tejanas: The Roots of Tejano and Conjunto Music,* Arhoolie, CD 341, 1991.

13. Women were cultural "negotiators" and negotiated the Americanizing influences of mainstream institutions, popular consumer culture, and institutional mistreatment. They also played key roles in community formation, labor organizing, social activism, and electoral issues. On the diverse roles played by Mexican-origin women in the twentieth century,

see Vickie Ruiz, *From Out of the Shadows;* Sarah Deutsch, *No Separate Refuge: Culture, Class, and Gender on the Anglo-Hispanic Frontier in the American Southwest, 1880–1940;* and Cynthia Orozco, *Beyond Machismo, La Familia, and Ladies Auxiliaries: A Historiography of Mexican-Origin Women's Participation in Voluntary Associations and Politics in the United States, 1870–1990.*

14. It is unclear how long female vocal singing has been popular along the border, but Charles Loomis of the Southwest Museum made over forty noncommercial cylinder recordings of the Villa Sisters, Rosa and Luisa, accompanying themselves on guitar and mandolin in Los Angeles as early as 1904. Strachwitz, *Tejano Roots/Raíces Tejanas: The Roots of Tejano and Conjunto Music,* Arhoolie CD 341, 1991, liner notes.

15. A group known as the Herrera Sisters recorded for the Sunset label in Los Angeles in the mid–1920s. By the early 1930s the Posada Sisters, Lupe and Virginia, recorded locally. A group known as the Aguilar Sisters from Mexico also made frequent appearances in Los Angeles during these years. Ibid. See also Loza, *Barrio Rhythm,* 34–35.

16. For a listing of male musicians playing a variety of musical styles, refer to *Texas-Mexican Border Music, Vol. 1: An Introduction,* Arhoolie LP 9003; *Texas-Mexican Border Music, Vol. 2: Early Corridos—Part I,* Arhoolie LP 9004; *Texas-Mexican Border Music, Vol. 3: Early Corridos—Part II,* Arhoolie LP 9005; *Texas-Mexican Border Music, Vol. 4: Norteño Acordeón—Part I, The First Recordings,* Arhoolie LP 9006.

17. One other possible recording artist in the pre–World War II period is Rosita Fernández. Originally from Monterrey, Mexico, Fernández began to sing with her uncle's group, El Trio San Miguel, after the family moved to San Antonio around 1916 or 1917. She was extremely popular in San Antonio and was regularly featured on radio during the 1920s and 1930s. She also toured South Texas during this period and performed in a variety of places, like Robstown, Alice, and Falfurrias. She might have recorded some songs during the 1930s, but I have not come across any of them. The only recordings by Fernández located were done in the 1950s. For several songs by Fernández as a soloist and as part of a duet, refer to the *Tejano Roots: The Women (1946–70),* Arhoolie, CD 343. For general information on Fernández, see Kelly Shannon, "San Antonio's Premier Singer Rosita Fernández Still Charms Texas Listeners after 65 Years," *Corpus Christi Caller-Times,* December 25, 1995.

18. For the early recordings by Mendoza and her family, see *Mexican American Border Music, Vol. 2: Lydia Mendoza, 1928–38,* Arhoolie CD 7002.

19. Strachwitz, *Tejano Roots/Raíces Tejanas,* Arhoolie CD 341, 1991, liner notes.

20. Peña, *Texas-Mexican Conjunto,* 7.

21. Isaac Figueroa, a neighbor, played the accordion on the first recordings. Narciso Martínez and Paulino Bernal played the accordion in later years. See Strachwitz, *Tejano Roots/Raíces Tejanas,* Arhoolie CD 341, 1991, liner notes.

22. Ibid. Although no exact figures are available, their records sold quickly.

23. Ibid.

24. Ibid.

25. For a sampling of this diversity, hear the songs on *Tejano Roots: The Women,* Arhoolie CD 343, 1991.

26. All of these groups are featured on *Tejano Roots: The Women,* Arhoolie CD 343, 1991.

27. The Hermanas Fraga, for instance, recorded the song "Amor Pendiente" in 1948 with a group called Mariachi Mexico del Norte. The Hermanas Segovia recorded "No Quiero Esperar" in 1950 with Mariachi Ideal, a house band at Ideal Studios. All of these songs can be found on *Tejano Roots: The Women,* Arhoolie CD 343, 1991.

28. For a picture of Carmen y Laura with Narciso Martínez, refer to Strachwitz, *Tejano Root/s Roots/Raíces Tejanas,* Arhoolie CD 341, 1991, liner notes.

29. For an excellent oral history of her trials and tribulations in the music business, see Lydia Mendoza, "The Lark of the Border," in the American Folklife Center's *Ethnic Recordings in America: A Neglected Heritage*, 119–31. See also Strachwitz and Nicolopulos, comps., *Lydia Mendoza*, 1994.

30. Strachwitz, *Tejano Roots/Raices Tejanas*, Arhoolie CD 341, 1991, liner notes. Peña notes that the company originally was called Mira Records. He gives no date as to when it was renamed Falcon. However, he does state that this label "eventually became the largest and most successful Chicano recording company ever." Peña, *Texas-Mexican Conjunto*, 66–67.

31. Refer to Silva's "Si Acaso Vuelves" (In Case you Return). In this song, an accordion is used as part of the orchestral accompaniment. *Tejano Roots: The Women, 1946–70*, Arhoolie CD 343, 1991.

32. Strachwitz, *Tejano Roots/Raices Tejanas*, Arhoolie CD 341, 1991, liner notes.

33. Fernández, known simply as Rosita, made four motions pictures and many sound recordings, but she was best known in San Antonio for her participation in the Fiesta Noche del Rio, an annual San Antonio River festival. From the mid-1970s to the 1990s, Rosita performed at this fiesta. She also performed for movie stars, presidents, and the pope. Shannon, "San Antonio's Premier Singer Rosita Fernández."

34. Ibid.

35. To hear this song, refer to *Tejano Roots: The Women*, Arhoolie, CD 343, 1991.

36. Carol Rust, "Queen of the Accordion," *Houston Chronicle*, August 14, 1996.

37. In addition to playing in the band, Ventura Alonzo also took tickets at the door, washed and ironed her husband's "white starched band shirts he wore onstage," and negotiated all contracts with bands during the dozen years they ran the dance hall. Rust, "Queen of the Accordion."

38. Much of this limited information is taken from Terese Paloma Acosta, "Tejana Singers," *The Handbook of Texas Online, http://www.tsha.utexas.edu.*

39. Manuel Peña, *Orquestas Tejanas: The Formative Years*, Arhoolie CD 368, 1992, liner notes.

40. Ibid.

41. Ibid. Many of these musicians were formally trained at home or at school. The two kings of orquesta Tejana during this period, Beto Villa and Isidro López, both learned to play the saxophone at school.

42. This argument expands on Peña's views by emphasizing the urban and acculturated aspects of orquesta Tejana. For his interpretation of orquesta as mostly a "middle-class" alternative to conjunto, see Peña, *Orquestas Tejanas: The Formative Years*, Arhoolie CD 368, 1992, liner notes; and Peña, *Texas-Mexican Conjunto*, 134–62.

43. In the mid-1800s, orquestas típicas were working-class musical groups, but in the late nineteenth century, the Mexican elite appropriated this name for its own ensembles. Thus, the orquestas típicas, which had been associated with the peasants and the working class, now became part of government-sponsored elite culture. Although they appealed to increasing numbers of working-class groups, their primary base of support was the middle and upper classes of Mexico. The orquestas of the working class, in the meantime, struggled to survive. In many ways, these continued to be smaller and more ad hoc in nature, but because of their dependence on string instruments such as the violin, guitar, and mandolin, they became known as orquestas de cuerda by the end of the 1800s. Peña, *Música Tejana*, 125–26.

44. Peña, *Orquestas Tejanas: The Formative Years*, Arhoolie CD 368, 1992, liner notes.

45. Nothing is known about the fate of the Sonny Boys or their impact on local society. Ibid.

46. Ibid.

47. Peña notes that in the 1940s and 1950s musical sophistication was occasionally equated with "high-class" snobbery, which working-class people usually ascribed to the upwardly mobile. The term "jaitón," a derisive Hispanicized cultural label coming from "high-tone," came into use to distinguish this style of orquesta, its musicians, and its fans from the conjunto. The conjunto style, in turn, was referred to by scholars as "lo ranchero." In my view, the term "jaitón" is loaded and does not reflect the orquesta musicians' own notion of the type of music they played. Historians need a less derisive cultural label to denote the complexity of the music played by these musicians. Most importantly, historians need a positive term that the orquesta musicians themselves used to define their music. In the absence of one, I have developed the term "moderno" to indicate the opposite of "ranchero" and in keeping with the orquesta musicians' need or desire to play more-sophisticated, urban sounds. On the use of "jaitón" see Peña, *Mexican American Orquesta,* 122–65; Peña, *Música Tejana;* Peña, *Orquestas Tejanas: The Formative Years,* Arhoolie CD 368, 1992, liner notes; and Peña, *Texas-Mexican Conjunto,* 117, 139.

48. Chris Strachwitz and Manuel Peña, *Beto Villa: Father of Orquesta Tejana,* Arhoolie CD 364, 1992, liner notes.

49. Peña, *Orquestas Tejanas: The Formative Years,* Arhoolie CD 368, 1992, liner notes.

50. Ibid.

51. Ibid.

52. A significant number of songs recorded by these individuals may be found on *Orquestas Tejanas: The Formative Years,* Arhoolie CD 368, 1992.

53. The instrumental nature of orquesta music and the use of the accordion in this emerging style is illustrated in these tunes by Beto Villa: "Rosita Vals," and "Las Delicias," on *Orquestas Tejanas: The Formative Years,* Arhoolie CD 368, 1992.

54. Peña, *Orquestas Tejanas: The Formative Years,* Arhoolie CD 368, 1992, liner notes.

55. Strachwitz, *Tejano Roots/Raices Tejanas,* Arhoolie CD 341, 1991, liner notes.

56. Some of his old songs are available on *Orquestas Tejanas: The Formative Years,* Arhoolie CD 368, 1992.

57. Eugenio Gutiérrez, from a small town called Runge, was unique in that he recognized the importance of the accordion for Tejanos. Gutiérrez recorded several orquesta hits with Pedro Ayala, a notable accordionist of the 1940s and 1950s. Some of his songs can be found on *Orquestas Tejanas: The Formative Years,* Arhoolie CD 368, 1992.

58. Rust, "Queen of the Accordion."

59. Peña, *Orquestas Tejanas: The Formative Years,* Arhoolie CD 368, 1992, liner notes.

60. The themes of canciones rancheras often focused on abandoned lovers and treacherous women. In all these cases, the rancheras were sung to music played by mariachi groups. For some samples of canciones rancheras, refer to *Jorge Negrete, 15 Éxitos,* Orfeon C068; and *Pedro Infante, Boleros de Oro, Vol. 1,* Orfeon C0055.

61. For a sampling of these tunes, refer to *Orquestas Tejanas: The Formative Years,* Arhoolie, CD 368, 1992; *Tejano Roots/Raices Tejanas,* Arhoolie CD 341, 1991; and *Beto Villa,* Arhoolie CD 364, 1992.

62. Peña, *Orquestas Tejanas: The Formative Years,* Arhoolie CD 368, 1992, liner notes.

63. González's bolero was entitled "No Te Preocupies Por Mí," and Lydia Mendoza's was titled "Feliz Sin Tí." Both of these were recorded in the 1950s. Refer to *Orquestas Tejanas: The Formative Years,* Arhoolie, CD 368, 1992.

64. Ibid.

65. For a history of musical developments in Southern California, see Loza, *Barrio Rhythm;* and David Reyes and Tom Waldman, *Land of a Thousand Dances: Chicano Rock 'n' Roll from Southern California.*

66. The Flores Orchestra used to play at the White Swan Cafe on Navigation Boulevard during the late 1940s. For a picture of this group in 1949, see Monica García Coll, Houston Metropolitan Research Center (HMRC), cited in Thomas H. Kreneck, *Del Pueblo,* 142. Eloy Pérez and the Latinaires at one point had three saxophones, one tololoche, one drum, two trumpets, and one set of maracas. For a picture of the group taken during the late 1940s, see Kreneck, *Del Pueblo,* 143. Gaston Ponce used to play in several nightclubs around Houston, including the Pan American Nite Club in the late 1950s. For a photo of this group in the late 1950s, see G. T. Valerio Coll, in Kreneck, *Del Pueblo,* 146. Alonzo y Sus Rancheros was composed of the Alonzo family, including Ventura Alonzo (female, piano accordionist), Frank Alonzo (guitarist), and Frank Alonzo, Jr. (bass fiddle). In the 1950s it had three saxes, two trumpets, one drummer, one guitar, one tololoche, and two singers. For a photo of them in the 1950s, see Kreneck, *Del Pueblo,* 147.

67. I can remember as a young child growing up in the 1950s in Corpus Christi seeing the Galván Orchestra, formed by the Galván brothers, a talented group of siblings who played a variety of instruments. The Galván Orchestra did not record their music but, like other groups throughout Texas, were extremely popular for several decades in that city.

68. Valentine gave Martínez his nickname, "El Huracán Del Valle" (the Hurricane of the Valley). Strachwitz, *Texas-Mexican Border Music, Vol. 1: An Introduction, 1930–60,* Arhoolie LP 9003, 1974, liner notes.

69. Strachwitz notes that Martínez was not the first accordion player to record, though he was the first to appeal to a large audience, perhaps largely due to his approach to playing conjunto music. He played mostly the high end of the accordion and left the bass work to his bajo sexto player. See Strachwitz, *Texas-Mexican Border Music, Vol. 1,* Arhoolie LP 9003, 1974, liner notes. For the initial recordings by several other accordionists, refer to *Texas-Mexican Music, Vol. 4,* Folklyric LP 9006.

70. Both songs can be found on *Tejano Roots/Raices Tejanas,* Arhoolie CD 341, 1991.

71. For a list of these groups and their recordings, see *Arhoolie Catalogue,* (El Cerrito, Calif.: Arhoolie Productions, Inc. 1996).

72. Peña argues, without any evidence, that in the late 1940s Valerio Longoria introduced boleros, a song type originally from the Caribbean, into conjunto music. Peña, *Texas-Mexican Conjunto,* 83.

73. Ibid., 82

74. His first pieces in 1947 were a polka called "Cielito" and a corrido, "Jesus Cadena." That same year, he recorded one of his most successful songs, the canción ranchera "El Rosalito." Ibid.

75. Longoria's popularity declined after he left Texas in 1959. He went to Chicago for eight years and then to San Jose, California. Although he made some records for local companies in Illinois and California, he was not able to duplicate his earlier success. Ibid., 84–85.

76. Ibid., 82.

77. Peña argues that Longoria was responsible for popularizing what he called the canción corrida among conjuntos, as well as the canción ranchera in vals tempo. Because of the confusion of terms, I refer to the former as a ranchera and the latter as a ranchera vals. A ranchera, in my view, is a polka with lyrics, whereas a ranchera vals is a waltz with lyrics. The ranchera Tejana is different from the ranchera in Mexico in that the former is an accordion-based song with a polka beat while the latter is vocal singing with mariachi accompaniment. For an example of the labeling of the ranchera as a polka with lyrics and the vals ranchera as a waltz with lyrics, refer to *Narciso Martínez: Father of the Texas-Mexican Conjunto,* Arhoolie CD 361, 1993, songs 10 and 15.

78. Guide González, "Tony De La Rosa: No More Time to Fish," *Corpus Christi Sun,* January 19, 1978.

79. His first recordings were a pair of polkas, "Sarita" and "Tres Rios." Peña, *Texas-Mexican Conjunto,* 86.

80. To hear some of his most popular hits during the 1950s and 1960s, refer to *Tejano Roots: Tony De La Rosa, Atotonilco,* Arhoolie CD 362, n.d.

81. Peña, *Texas-Mexican Conjunto,* 87.

82. González, "Tony De La Rosa," 21.

83. Cited in "A Tribute to Tony de la Rosa: Conjunto Music Pioneer," *La Voz de Uvalde County,* June 1997, 5. Peña recognized the impact de la Rosa had on Tejano dancing in the mid–1980s: "For audiences the drums added a much more solid pulse that in my estimation had much to do with hastening the adoption of the new dance style of el tacuachito"; Peña, *Texas-Mexican Conjunto,* 87. On a comparison of techniques used by de la Rosa and Longoria in playing their accordions, see Peña, *Texas-Mexican Conjunto,* 88.

84. For a sampling of all of these styles from one conjunto, refer to *Narciso Martínez: Father of the Texas-Mexican Conjunto,* Arhoolie CD 361, 1993. Most of the songs in this CD were recorded between 1946 and 1957.

85. Juan López acquired the name of "El Rey de la Redova" (The King of the Redova). For this conjunto's songs, refer to *Tejano Roots: Juan López "El Rey de la Redova,"* Arhoolie CD 407, n.d.

86. Chris Strachwitz has collected twenty-four original de la Rosa hits from the years 1953 to 1964 on *Tejano Roots: Tony De La Rosa, Atotonilco,* Arhoolie CD 362, n.d.

87. For a more extensive view of this group's origins and evolution, see Burr, *Billboard Guide,* 74–75; Peña, *Texas-Mexican Conjunto,* 100–10; Peña, *Música Tejana,* 102–105.

88. Conjunto Bernal also was unique in adding rock and roll to its repertoire. See "La Novia Antonia," *Tejano Roots: Raices Tejanas,* Arhoolie, CASS-341, 1991. For a collection of Bernal hits from 1954 through 1960, see *Tejano Roots: Conjunto Bernal, "Mi Unico Camino,"* Arhoolie CD 344, n.d.

89. One of the longest surviving cantinas was Mary's Place in Corpus Christi, Texas. This cantina originally opened in 1951. It closed its doors thirty years later. The owner, Mary Gutierrez, was an astute and professionally minded Tejana originally from Richmond, Texas, but was raised in Berclaire, a hamlet in Goliad County. Interview with Mary Gutierrez conducted by Roberto Gutierrez on behalf of the author, March 16, 2001, Corpus Christi, Texas.

90. Strachwitz, *Texas-Mexican Border Music, Vol. 1,* Arhoolie LP 9008, 1974, liner notes.

91. Ibid. For the songs of Los Hermanos Torres-García, refer to *Tejano Roots: Los Pavos Reales, Early Hits,* Arhoolie CD 410 or audiocassette 410, n.d.

92. With a few minor exceptions, Los Alegres de Terán made most of its records for Falcon and Discos Columbia. For a list of some of these albums, see Strachwitz, *Texas-Mexican Border Music, Vol. 1,* Arhoolie LP 9008, 1974, liner notes.

93. Ibid. Several additional norteño groups were formed in the 1960s, including Los Tremendous Gavilanes, Los Norteños de Nuevo Laredo, Los Hermanos Prado, El Palomo y El Gorion; Los Huracanes de Terán, and Los Relámpagos del Norte. For a list of these groups, see ibid.

94. Los Alegres de Terán did not incorporate the dance-band drum or the electric bass into the group. Peña, *Texas-Mexican Conjunto,* 98, footnote 8.

95. Ibid., 140–41. I remember the overwhelming popularity of conjunto music in 1950s Corpus Christi. Although Beto Villa and Corpus Christi's own Isidro López were popular, more conjunto music was heard at Tejano weddings, *quinceañeras,* community dances, and public celebrations.

96. For a list of these companies, see *Tex Mex Border Music, Vol. 1: An Intro, 1930–60,* Folklyric Records LP-9008, 1973. Strachwitz, *Texas-Mexican Border Music, Vol. 1,* Arhoolie LP 9003, 1974, liner notes.

97. Strachwitz, *Texas-Mexican Border Music, Vol. 5: The String Bands, End of a Tradition,* Folklyric LP 9007, liner notes.

98. Peña, *Texas-Mexican Conjunto,* 87.

99. The *bracero* program was a binational agreement between the U.S. and Mexico. Its purpose was to recruit cheap Mexican labor for American agricultural and industrial interests. Over 4.5 million Mexicans were recruited to work in the U.S. between 1942 and 1964. For a brief overview of the bracero program, see Manuel G. González, *Mexicanos: A History of Mexicans in the United States,* Bloomington, Ind.: Indiana University Press, 1999, 170–78.

CHAPTER 4

1. The word *pachucos* historically has referred to groups of juvenile delinquents, but in many cases, especially in South Texas, pachucos were merely rebellious working-class Tejano youth. For further information on pachucos and their portrayal in American society, especially during World War II, see Rudy Acuña, *Occupied America: A History of Chicanos,* 254–57; and De León, *Ethnicity in the Sunbelt,* 105–10.

2. The first five groups were initially founded in the 1950s but continued to be popular into the 1960s. The latter were formed during the 1960s. For a brief history of these groups, see Burr, *Billboard Guide.*

3. For a selected discography of norteño and Tejano conjuntos, see Strachwitz, *Texas-Mexican Border Music, Vol. 1,* Arhoolie LP 9003, 1974, liner notes.

4. In 1957, for instance, the group recorded a rock and roll song in Spanish called "La Novia Antonia." See song 17 on *Tejano Roots/Raices Tejanas,* Arhoolie CD 341, 1991.

5. For a sampling of groups such as Los Dos Gilbertos, Rubén Vela, Tony de la Rosa, Mingo Saldívar, and others, refer to *Tejano Conjuntos,* Hacienda Records CAS3397-4, 1995; and *Conjunto: Texas-Mexican Border Music, Vol. 1,* Rounder CAS6023, 1992.

6. One example of the lack of popularity of conjuntos can be found in the top-ten list of Tejano hits in Houston for the fall of 1970. According to a newspaper column, only two of the "Chicano Top Ten" hits in that city were by conjuntos, the song "Sufro Por Tí" by Los Relámpagos del Norte and "Cappillito de Rosas" by Conjunto Bernal and Cristo Salinas. "Chicano Top Ten," *Papel Chicano,* October 10–23, 1970, Vol. 1, ed. 5, p. 16. The other hits were by orquestas or grupos Tejanos.

7. For two examples of increased interest in the youth-based orquestas at the expense of conjuntos, see Guile González, "Big Name Bands Seek New Talent," *Corpus Christi Sun,* May 15, 1978; and Guile González, "Little Joe Returns to Alice," *Corpus Christi Sun,* February 23–March 1, 1978.

8. See Sunny's comments about two-thirds into *Songs of the Homeland,* a documentary film produced and directed by Hector Galán (Austin: Galán Productions, 1995).

9. Patoski, *Selena,* 14.

10. Ramiro Burr, "Accordion's Jimi Hendrix: Nothing Stodgy About Steve Jordan's Wail," *Houston Chronicle,* June 17, 1990.

11. In the 1960s and 1970s, Jordan recorded a Spanish composition of "You Keep Me Hanging On" ("Me Traes Colgando"), and songs by Ray Charles ("Georgia On My Mind") and Buck Owens ("Together Again"). For the Buck Owens song and another country song, called "More Pretty Girls Than One," refer to *Esteban "Steve" Jordan: The Many Sounds of Steve Jordan,* Arhoolie CD 319, 1996. The politically inspired song is called "Corrido del

Aceite." It deals with the explosion of an oil well in the Gulf of Mexico and the effects of the oil spill. This corrido can be found on *Conjunto! Texas-Mexican Border Music, Vol. 1,* Rounder C-6023, 1992.

12. He stated this several times in a conversation I had with him when we first met in September of 1969. We sat side by side in an airplane as I was going to college in New York and had the most wonderful and memorable conversation. He invited me to his gig in Central Park, where he played the lead guitar for Willie Bobo, a popular Latin jazz group.

13. Burr, *Billboard Guide,* 73–74.

14. Peña, *Música Tejana,* 159–63.

15. Teresa Palomo Acosta, "Tejano Conjunto Festival," *The Handbook of Texas Online,* *http://www.tsha.utexas.edu.*

16. For an elaboration of the differences between these styles, see Guy Bensusan, "A Consideration of Norteña and Chicano Music," 158–64.

17. For an example of the type of music played by this group, refer to *Los Chachos,* Freddie Records RS-5006, 1976.

18. Refer to Los Relámpagos del Norte, *Estamos en algo,* Bego B6-1040, n.d.; and *Hoy, Manana, Y Siempre,* Marsol MSLP-108, n.d. (reissued as GS107, 1978).

19. From 1972 to 1992 Ramón Ayala recorded over fifty-seven albums. For more information on him, see Burr, *Billboard Guide,* 55–57.

20. His most recent hit CD was called *Quémame los Ojos* (Burn My Eyes Out) and recorded by Freddie Records in 2000 (JMCD 1805). For a catalog of all his hits under Freddie Records, refer to *Freddie Presenta El Catalog Discografico de Ramón Ayala y sus Bravos del Norte* (Corpus Christi, Texas: Freddie Records, 2000).

21. This type of musical group emphasized the use of the keyboard in Tejano music. Although it emerged in the early 1970s, the grupo did not become a powerful force in Tejano music until the 1980s.

22. Patoski, *Selena,* 25.

23. See *Songs of the Homeland,* a documentary film produced and directed by Hector Galán (Austin: Galán Productions, 1995)

24. Patoski, *Selena,* 14.

25. Reyes and Waldman, *Land of a Thousand Dances,* 3–34.

26. De León and Griswold del Castillo, *North to Aztlán,* 123. See also George Lipsitz, "Chicano Rock and Roll from East Los Angeles: A Research Discography," in Guillermo Rojas, ed., *Chicano Studies: Nuevos Horizontes-Midwest Foco Proceedings,* (Minneapolis, MN: published by the Prisma Institute in Cooperation with the Institute for the Study of Ideologies and Literature, 1987), 67–71.

27. Reyes and Waldman, *Land of a Thousand Dances,* 35–44.

28. De León and del Castillo, *North to Aztlan,* 123.

29. During this period, Mexican Americans also recorded more mainstream English-language music for adults. Three of the most popular performers were Andy Russell, Vicki Carr, and Trini López; Matt Meier and Feliciano Ribera, *Mexican Americans/American Mexicans,* 242.

30. The recording by Beto Villa can be found on *Tejano Roots/Raices Tejanas,* Arhoolie CD 341, 1991. Ornelas's recording is on *Orquestas Tejanas: The Formative Years,* Arhoolie CD 368, 1992.

31. This song can be found on *Tejano Roots/Raices Tejanas,* Arhoolie CD 341, 1991.

32. These two recordings can be found on *Tejano Roots/Raices Tejanas,* Arhoolie CD 341, 1991.

33. Patoski, *Selena,* 14.

34. See ibid., 10–11. Quintanilla originally was with a group called The Gumdrops, an informal group of choir members at Miller High School formed in 1957. Los Dinos' original members were Perales, Lira, and Guadalupe Barrera. Around 1958 Barrera left the group, and Quintanilla asked to be his replacement. According to Patoski, some of these groups had the assistance of other musicians, such as Johnny Olenn and his Disciples, Sonny Ace, and Doug Sahm (later the Sir Douglas Quintet). Los Dinos recorded one song in 1960, three in 1961, and six more during the 1959–61 period. Their known songs include "Give Me One Chance" (1960), "Twistin' Irene" (1961), "Ride Your Pony" (1961), and "Lover's Holiday" (1961). Ibid., 19–20.

35. Patoski also includes Question Mark and the Mysterians as one of the Tejano groups recording American pop music. This was actually a Michigan band of Latinos with South Texas roots. Ibid., 16. Little Joe played rock and soul tunes. Two of the songs he recorded in the early 1960s are "Tell It Like It Is" and "Kansas City." The former was a popular slow rock song, the latter a soul tune. In both cases, his group utilized the pitos and the organ as key instruments. Refer to Little Joe, *The Incredible Little Joe,* Tomi Records TLP 1002, 1963.

36. Sunny was influenced by Randy Garibay, a blues singer from San Antonio, and was guided by Huey P. Meaux, a Houston record producer. Patoski, *Selena,* 15.

37. Refer to the following early albums by Sunny and the Sunglows: *Little Brown-Eyed Soul,* Key-Loc KL3005, n.d; *Smile Now, Cry Later,* Big Star BS7017, 1983 (originally recorded in the 1960s by Key-Loc Records).

38. Patoski notes that the emerging Chicano movement in the mid-1960s encouraged the youth to turn to their roots and record Mexican music. I have not found any evidence in support of this statement, though it appears that the Chicano Movement may have *encouraged* further development of Mexican music. Racism and other factors, however, probably account for the switch to Spanish-language music among the rock and roll generation. For a brief overview of the impact of racism and community pressures on the music of Los Dinos during this same period, see Patoski, *Selena,* 18–20.

39. Little Joe included one cumbia on his first Spanish-language album in 1968, "Cumbia de la Media Noche." See Little Joe and the Latinaires, *Arriba,* Buena Suerte Records LP 1001, 1968.

40. Little Joe and the Latinaires, *Por Un Amor,* Super Tex CASS-8439, 1964 (reissued in 1994 by Roy Sales); *Arriba!* Buena Suerte Records LP-1001, n.d. In later years, Little Joe continued to record some "activist" songs. In 1971, he recorded "Que Bruto." The following year he recorded "Las Nubes." The latter became the anthem for the Chicano movement because of its references to continual struggle in this country. Burr, *Billboard Guide,* 132–33.

41. *Con Esta Copa,* Falcon FLP 2019, 1964.

42. Potoski, *Selena,* 19–26.

43. Abraham Quintanilla, interview by author, August 25, 2000.

44. For examples of this music, refer to the following: The Latin Breed, *The Latin Breed: USA,* Guerra Company Productions (GCP) LP 115, 1975; Freddie Martínez, *El Nuevo Rey Texano,* Freddie Records LP 1005, 1972; and Agustín Ramírez, *Sangre de Indio,* El Zarape SLP 1040, n.d. See also the following compilations of música tejana from the 1960s to the early 1980s: *Tejano Goldies,* Lago LC 1006, 1995; and *Tejano Goldies II,* Lago LC 2000, 1996.

45. See "Chicano Top Ten," *Papel Chicano,* October 10–23, 1970, Vol. 5, p. 16.

46. Ramos originally picked the name "The Mexican Revolution" because of the emerging Chicano movement and its search for a militant identity. By 1981 he changed the name to the "Texas Revolution" because he felt Tejanos did not need such a militant image, and they "were getting an identity in Texas." Burr, *Billboard Guide,* 174.

47. A few record labels and promoters tried to revive interest in orquesta music in the late 1980s and 1990s, but without much success. For instance, at least four popular orquestas issued reunion albums in this period: Latin Breed (1989), Little Joe y la Familia (1996), the Royal Jesters (1996), and the Tejano Legends (Sunny Ozuna, Agustín Ramírez, Carlos Guzman, and Freddie Martínez) (1998). A handful of new groups likewise were formed to play this type of music. The most ambitious was Bob Gallarza and Friends. In all these cases, the music was updated by introducing the accordion and composing new arrangements. None of these efforts, however, succeeded in reviving orquestas Tejanas. Refer to Bob Gallarza and Friends, *On the Edge,* Sony Discos DIS80620, 1991. On the Latin Breed reunion, see Ramiro Burr, "Latin Breed Returns with Updated Sound," *Houston Chronicle,* March 31, 1989. On the Tejano legends, see Burr, "Compilations Bring Together Best Work of Legendary Groups," *Houston Chronicle,* June 7, 1998. Refer also to *Leyendas y Raices,* Freddie Records, 1998.

48. The synthesizer, created in the late 1970s, is a particular type of electronic instrument that produces thousands of sounds, including accordionlike tones to mariachi-style sounds. The synthesizer was incorporated into Tejano music in the late 1970s. Its use led to the enhancement of a new type of musical ensemble that came to be known as the grupo Tejano.

49. The saxophone, for instance, was an integral part of Los Tigres del Norte, a norteño outfit formed in 1968. For more information on this group, see Burr, *Billboard Guide,* 200–201.

50. Burr, *Billboard Guide,* 171–72.

51. It's quite possible that Cecilio Garza y Los Kasinos was the originator of the progressive conjunto sound since Pulido played with this group in the early 1970s and his later albums use the same instrumentation as Pulido's. Much more research needs to be done on these two groups, however. For an example of Cecilio Garza's music, see Cecilio Garza y Los Kasinos, *El Muchacho Alegre,* Freddie Records LP-1145, 1979. On Cali Carranza y Los Formales see the two albums done in the early 1980s: Los Formales de Cali Carranza, *Cuando Te Hayas Ido,* Supremo LP5047, 1980, and Los Formales de Cali Carranza, *Manana, Seimpre Manana,* Scorpio Productions LP2017, n.d.

52. Burr, *Billboard Guide,* 98.

53. For examples of this style, see David Lee Garza, *Los Musicales,* Hacienda 1008, 1982; Los Formales de Cali Carranza, *Cuando Te Hayas Ido,* Supremo LP5047, 1980; Los Formales de Cali Carranza, *Manana, Seimpre Manana,* Scorpio Productions LP2017, n.d.

54. Burr, *Billboard Guide,* 99.

55. See "Previous Winners (of Tejano Music Awards, 1980–95)," *La Prensa de San Antonio,* 1996, appendix.

56. Ronald L. Davis, *A History of Music in American Life, Volume III: The Modern Era, 1920–Present,* (Malabar, Florida: Robert Krieger Publishing Company, 1981), 371. On Freddy Fender and his country hits during the mid–1970s, see Nelson Allen, "Look Who's Living on Ocean Drive!" *Corpus Christi Sun,* January 19, 1978; and Anissa R. Hernandez, "El Be-bop Kid Gets His Star," *La Onda of Corpus Christi,* Monday, Feb. 1, 1999, *www.caller.com/autoconv/laonda99/laonda27.htm.* On Johnny Rodriguez's history of country hits during the 1970s, see Associated Press, "No More Drugs, R & R Johnny Rodriguez says bad times are behind him," Houston Post, January 11, 1988; and Bob Claypool, "This Country Singer Holds Nothing Back," *Houston Chronicle,* January 29, 1989, Zest section.

57. For samples of country music performed by this group, refer to *Rancho Grande,* ARV International LP 1052, 1978; *Las Margaritas,* ARV International LP 1057, 1979; *Mr. Chicano Country,* ARV International LP 1062, 1980; *The Legend,* ARV International LP 1072, 1982.

58. For a collection of these artists' songs, refer to *The Best of Chicano Country, Vol. 2,* ARV International LP 1075, 1982.

59. See Rudy Tee Gonzalez, "Mandame Tu Cariño" (Send Me Your Love), *Country,* Tear Drop TDLP-2030, 1972. On Pulido, see the section on progressive conjuntos. For further information on Canales and Mazz, see the next section of this chapter.

60. One scholar recently referred to them as combos. Antonio González, "Latino Music," talk given at the Latino/Latina Unity Conference, University of Houston, Houston, Texas, November 18, 1996.

61. José Reyna, a well-known Tejano music scholar, has noted that the groups that used the organ as their key instrument during this period did not refer to themselves as conjuntos or as orchestras. He said that there was no particular label for the groups. José Reyna, "Notes on Tejano Music," *Aztlan* 13, 1982, 81–94.

62. Rudy R. Treviño, "Tejano Music: A Historical Perspective," *Music World Magazine,* February, 1997, 32–33.

63. Burr notes that the term "grupo" had its origins in the 1960s. In the 1980s and 1990s grupos expanded their repertoire to include cumbias, baladas, and country. Burr, *Billboard Guide,* 102.

64. For general information on Los Fabulosos Cuatro, see ibid., 89; and Armando Gutiérrez, "Los Fabulosos Cuatro," *http://www.ondanet.com/tejano/artists/Los.Fabulosos/ fabulosos.htm.*

65. The group was called Carlos Guzman y Su Conjunto. All the members—Baldemar "Balde" Muñoz (drummer), Armando "Chore" Hinojosa (accordion), Gamaliel "Mel" Villarreal (bass), Ramiro "Snowball" de la Cruz (electric guitar), and Carlos Guzman (lead vocals)—came from the Lower Rio Grande Valley. Soon after the group began to play in public, Balde was drafted into the army. Juan Hinojosa, the roadie for the group and Chore's uncle, assumed his position; Armando "Chore" Hinojosa, interviews by author, August 4, 2000 and September 16, 2000. See also Guile González, *Corpus Christi Sun,* June 15–18, 1978.

66. The two songs on which the bajo sexto was used was "No Nacisté Para Mí" and "Es Necesario." Chore Hinojosa played the bajo sexto in both songs. Armando "Chore" Hinojosa, interview by author, October 10, 2000.

67. Ramiro "Snowball" de la Cruz was the guitar player for Los Fabulosos Cuatro. He was a superb talent who experimented with the chords used in playing música tejana. Carlos Guzman stated that Snowball had "a certain way of playing a guitar." This was one of the reasons the group hired him. Armando "Chore" Hinojosa, interviews by author August 4, 2000 and September 16, 2000. See also Guile González, *Corpus Christi Sun,* June 15–18, 1978.

68. See José Reyna, "Tejano Notes," and Treviño, "Tejano Music: A Historical Perspective," 33, 32. Another scholar, Antonio González, referred to them as combos, but this term is not used by Tejano music leaders in the contemporary period. For this reason, I favor the term used by Rudy Treviño.

69. Peña, *Música Tejana,* 198.

70. La Movida is unique among these groups in its use of the guitar. Ricky Smith, its lead guitarist, experimented with guitar-driven, rock-oriented rancheras with much success. Refer to "La Movida Theme," "Jugador del Amor," and other songs on *La Movida Classics: Es Amor,* Hacienda Records HC206, 1980 (renewed 1997). For a sampling of Arturo Montes y Ternura, refer to *Tejano Goldies,* Lago LC1006, 1995; *Tejano Goldies II,* Lago LC2000, 1996; Mayo, *Oh Darling,* Freddie Records RS5024, 1979 (reissued 1985); and La Movida, *La Movida,* Hacienda audiocassette 7925, 1980.

71. Burr, *Billboard Guide,* 71.

72. Ramiro Burr notes that prior to joining Snowball and Company's group, she played with Conjunto Bernal in his article "Pura Vida Awards Honor Classics in Texas Music," *Houston Chronicle,* June 2, 1996.

73. Ibid.

74. See appendix B, Tejano Music Awards, 1981–2000.

75. "Grupo Mazz Signs Tour with Miller Lite," *Houston Post,* June 11, 1993.

76. Peña notes that Mazz played mostly baladas and cumbias. He ignores the importance of their canciones with a country beat. Nonetheless, he is accurate in arguing that Mazz projected a "non-tejano aesthetic"—i.e., deviating from the traditional polka-ranchera reper-toire of most Tejano musicians. Peña, *Música Tejana,* 198.

77. Mazz, *Perfect 10,* Cara CA10B, 1977.

78. Mazz, *Mazz,* Cara Santos4000, 1978.

79. Mazz, *Album of the Year,* Cara CARA012, 1979.

80. Refer to the following albums by Mazz: *Class,* Cara CA23, 1980; *1980,* Cara CA17, 1980; *Perfect 10, Vol. 2,* Cara M10-2, 1980; and *Look of Mazz,* Cara CA028, 1981.

81. In 1986 and 1988 Mazz won the awards for vocal duo and album of the year (orquesta). In 1989 the group won the male vocalist and vocal duo categories. See appendix 2, Tejano Music Awards, 1981–2000.

82. "Previous Winners," *La Prensa de San Antonio,* 6.

83. See the polka "Los Jalapeños," on *Magnificent 7,* Diana Discos, Big Star 7032, 1981.

84. See "Camino Pal Circo," *Only in Texas,* Diana Discos LP 1005, 1981.

85. See "Parece Que Fue Ayer," *Magnificent 7,* Diana Discos, Big Star 7032, 1981.

86. The album *Honey,* for instance, did not have a single song that used the accordion. The *Xplosive* album was synthesizer-driven, with pito accompaniment, though La Mafia used the accordion on one song ("Un Million de Rosas"), if only for a couple of seconds. See *Honey/Carino,* CBS CRC84317, 1986; and *Xplosive,* CBS CRC80072, 1988.

87. La Mafia was "officially" formed in 1978. It recorded its first Tejano album in 1978 under Diana Discos, an independent label. In 1980 the band signed with Cara Records, led by Luis Silva and Bob Grever. It greatly benefitted when, in 1986, Cara entered into a five-year promotion and distribution deal with CBS Discos. When EMI Latin bought Cara Records in 1990 and signed Mazz, La Mafia opted to jump ship and signed on with rival CBS/Sony Discos. However, La Mafia still owed two CDs to Cara/EMI Latin. It delivered these two CDs, but not without some controversy. Burr, *Billboard Guide,* 139.

88. Rick Mitchell, "Pride of the North Side," *Houston Chronicle,* February 11, 1996.

89. Rick Mitchell, "La Mafia and Its Snazzy, High-Tech Tejano Houston Group Plays Summit for First Time," *Houston Chronicle,* July 14, 1991.

90. Ibid.

91. The group initially recorded three albums for the tiny Diana label in Baytown, Texas, between 1980 and 1981. They then recorded eight albums for Cara Discos. In 1986 the group switched to CBS International Records and recorded for them until 1990. The following year, they made a seven-record deal with Sony Discos. Their four gold records were recorded under CBS. See discography for more information.

92. In 1982 La Mafia won the award for most promising band. In 1983 they won song of the year ("Oh Girl"), single of the year, and album of the year *(Honey).* The following year they won vocal duo, single of the year ("Tú solo Tú"), and album of the year *(Electrifying).* In 1986 and 1987 they won two awards, male vocalist and male entertainer in the former year, and song of the year ("Si Tú Supieras") and album of the year *(La Mafia 1986)* in the latter. See appendix B, Tejano Music Awards, 1981–2000.

93. The categories were vocal duo, male entertainer, single of the year ("Mi Loca Pasion"), album of the year *(Hot Stuff)*, and song of the year ("Mi Loca Pasion"). See appendix 2, Tejano Music Awards, 1981–2000.

94. Patoski also argues that Selena took over the Tejano music industry between 1985 and 1989 and became an international star from 1989 through 1995. However, he provides no real evidence for these statements. Patoski, *Selena.*

95. Peña refers to this changed repertoire as a "non-Tejano aesthetic"; Peña, *Música Tejana,* 198. In my view, this is too judgmental and implies that the music played by these groups was not Tejano anymore. It *was* Tejano music. Unlike the repertoire of earlier years, there were fewer rancheras and more baladas and cumbias. It was a *new* Tejano aesthetic rather than a non-Tejano one.

96. Selena, *Mis Primeras Grabaciones,* Freddie Records C1294, 1985.

97. Selena, *Alpha,* Manny Music-BMI GPLP1002, 1985; *Dulce Amor,* Manny R. Guerra RPLP8803, 1988.

98. In 1992 Selena recorded an album on which half the songs were cumbias. See *Baila Está Cumbia,* Capitol-EMI H242635, 1992. She continued recording a variety of cumbias that became regional and international hits until her death in 1995. Her biggest hits were cumbias, such as "Techno-Cumbia," "Como La Flor," and "La Carcacha." The most popular, as indicated by record sales, was "Amor Prohibido." This was the lead song from her album by the same name. Refer to Selena, *Amor Prohibido,* Capitol EMI H2724382880325, 1994.

99. These two songs can be found on Selena, *Mis Primeras Grabaciones,* Freddie Records C1294, 1985.

100. Rick Mitchell, "Selena: In Life, She Was the Queen of Tejano Music, in Death, the 23-Year-Old Singer is Becoming a Legend," (part 1 of 2), *Texas Magazine,* May 21, 1995), 4, 7.

101. See the following songs: "Con Esta Copa," on *Alpha,* 1986; and "No Llores Mas Corazón" and "La Puerta Se Cerro," both on *Dulce Amor,* Manny R. Guerra RPLP8803, 1988.

102. Patoski, *Selena,* 155.

CHAPTER 5

1. The term "progressive conjunto" was first used by the Texas Talent Musician Association, sponsors of the Tejano Music Awards, in 1991. The TTMA developed the category "album of the year (progressive conjunto)" to distinguish it from the existing "album of the year (traditional conjunto)" category. For a brief historical overview of progressive conjuntos and other major musical ensembles in Tejano music during the twentieth century, see Rudy R. Treviño, "Tejano Music: A Historical Perspective," *Music World Magazine,* February 1997, 32–33.

2. Peña, *Música Tejana.*

3. For examples of this style, refer to David Lee Garza, *Los Musicales,* Hacienda 1008, 1982; Los Formales de Cali Carranza, *Cuando Te Hayas Ido,* Supremo LP 5047, 1980; and Los Formales de Cali Carranza, *Mañana, Siempre Mañana,* Scorpio Productions LP 2017, n.d.

4. In each year from 1985 to 1989, Los Musicales won the album of the year (conjunto) award at the annual Tejano Music Awards. In 1989 it won two awards, one for album of the year (conjunto) *(Tour 88)* and the other for single of the year ("Me Quieres Tú"). See appendix B, Tejano Music Awards, 1981–2000.

5. Emilio, *Sensaciones,* CBS CRC80329, 1990.

6. For an example of the old look of Tejano Country, see the album cover of *Los Musicales,* Hacienda 1008, 1982.

7. Emilio's impact on his fans was quite apparent by December 1990, when I attended one of his dances at the Fort Bend County Fairgrounds in the Houston area. A large proportion of the males and females attending this same dance, anywhere between 30 and 60 percent, were wearing the new country fashions in imitation of Emilio's look. Even my nephews, nieces, and cousins in Corpus Christi, as I found out the following month at several additional dances, were beginning to wear Wrangler jeans, Stetson hats, brightly colored country and western shirts, and ropers.

8. For a brief review of this album and how Navaira was incorporating rock and country into música tejana, see the insightful but all too brief article by Ramiro Burr, "Emilio Navaira's Change Is for the Better," *Houston Chronicle,* August 30, 1992.

9. *Shoot It,* Capitol-EMI, 1991; *Southern Exposure,* Capitol-EMI H2542838, 1993.

10. *Life is Good,* Nashville-Capitol CDP-7243-8-32392-2-1, 1995; *Its on The House,* Nashville-Capitol 7243-852180-2-6, 1997.

11. Emilio, *Emilio y Rio Band,* Cara, 1989; *Sensaciones,* CBS CRC-80329, 1990; *Shoot It,* Capitol-EMI, 1991; *Shuffle Time,* Capitol-EMI H242675, 1992.

12. Refer to *Southern Exposure,* EMI H2542838, 1993; *Sound Life,* EMI H2529116, 1994; *Emilio,* CEMA-Capitol S21-18085, 1994; *Quedate,* EMI H2724383776528, 1996; *A Mi Gente,* EMI H2724385911125, 1997; and *Mi Primer Amor,* EMI H472434-9919044, 1999.

13. Rick Mitchell, "Stepping Out," *Houston Chronicle,* August 27, 1995.

14. In 1990, Emilio won three awards: male entertainer, most promising band, and album of the year (conjunto). In 1991 and 1997 he won two awards: male vocalist and male entertainer; in 1993 and 1994, he won four; and in 1995 he won three. See appendix B, Tejano Music Awards, 1981–2000.

15. For a discussion of this album and some of its songs, see Alfredo Alvarado, "Sweet Sounds of Tejano, Attendance a Record for Second-Sunday Show," *Houston Chronicle,* February 27, 1990.

16. Burr, "Hot Emilio Succeeds at Dual Careers," *Houston Chronicle,* July 1, 1997.

17. The other two artists were Roberto Pulido y Los Clásicos and Vickki Carr. Alvarado, "Sweet Sounds of Tejano."

18. Burr and Herrick initially reported lower attendance figures for 1995 and 1997. See Burr, "Hot Emilio Succeeds at Dual Careers," and Herrick, "Go Tejano!". For an official listing of attendance figures, see table 9 in chapter 6, or the Houston Livestock Show and Rodeo website, *www.hlsr.com.*

19. Bobby Pulido, for instance, won the male entertainer of the year award at the TMA in 1998 and 1999, single of the year in 1998, most promising band in 1997, and male entertainer of the year in 2000. Elida won most promising band in 1999, and song of the year, female entertainer of the year, and female vocalist of the year in 2000. See appendix B, Tejano Music Awards, 1981–2000.

20. Other minor groups, such as Los Pekadorez, had a limited impact on música tejana and quickly faded from view.

21. "Jaime y Los Chamacos," *Tejano Reporter,* December 1997, 3.

22. Ramiro Burr, "Flashy Los Chamacos Draws Crowds," *Houston Chronicle,* September 27, 1992.

23. Burr, *Billboard Guide,* 116.

24. *Del Norte al Sur* (1992), 50,000 sold; *Corazón de Cristal* (1993), 115,000 sold; *El Ganador* (1995), 115,000 sold; *Duele el Amor* (1996), 140,000 sold; *Lo Mejor de los Palominos* (1997), 50,000 sold; and *Te Seguire* (1998), 100,000 sold. For further information on this group, see the extremely informative article by Alfredo de los Santos, "An Interview con Los Palominos," *La Voz de Uvalde County,* August 1998, 14–17.

25. Los Palominos, *Por Eso Te Amo*, Sony TET-83022-4-475041, 1999. For a discussion of the 1999 Latino Grammy winners, see Gustavo Lafarge/Terra, "La Noche del Grammy Latino: Santana y Otras Figuras," *Semana*, March 2–8, 2000, 18–19.

26. Burr, *Billboard Guide*, 164.

27. Ibid., 109.

28. Ibid. In October 1997, the group's percussionist, Roman, Jr., died of unknown causes. Shortly afterward, Joe Martínez left the band because of a contractual disagreement with the record label, but the band continued producing music. On January 22, 1998, Joe Martínez died of a massive heart attack while playing several songs with his old group, the Hometown Boys.

29. Ibid., 115.

30. Ramiro Burr, "Viva Norteño," *Houston Chronicle*, September 16, 1998.

31. Rick Mitchell, "Intocable Deaths Are Mourned," *Houston Chronicle*, February 2, 1998.

32. The group included his brother, Ernie, Jr., on bajo sexto, his uncle James on drums, and his cousin Joe Tanguma on bass. Michael sang and played the accordion. Burr, *Billboard Guide*, 184.

33. "La Union Es Parte de Nuestro Éxito: Michael Salgado," *Que Onda*, February 25, 1997, 13.

34. Ibid.

35. Burr, *Billboard Guide*, 185.

36. Refer to the songs on *En Concierto*, Joey International Joey3427, 1995; and *Puro Pueblo*, Joey International JRT-8292514-469979, 1998.

37. "Grupo Limite," *Houston Chronicle*, February 13, 1997.

38. Ramiro Burr, "No Limits," *Houston Chronicle*, February 23, 1997.

39. Frank Dalo, "Sentimientos," *Que Onda*, October 7, 1997, 11.

40. Ramiro Burr, "Grupo Limite Still Shows the Spirit," *Houston Chronicle*, December 13, 1998.

41. Ibid.

42. Ibid.

43. Burr, *Billboard Guide*, 31–39.

44. "Grupo Mazz Signs Tour with Miller Lite," *Houston Post*, June 11, 1993.

45. "Terco Corazón" is on Selena, *Baila Esta Cumbia*, EMI 407-799052-4, 1992. Refer also to *Entre a Mi Mundo*, EMI H242635, 1992; and *Selena Live*, EMI H2-0777-7-4277-20, 1993. On the former, she used the accordion on three songs; on the latter, on four out of eleven songs.

46. In 1989, for instance, Elsa García recorded an album with ten songs, the accordion was used on none of them. In 1990 her ten-song album included six songs with the accordion as a lead instrument. Refer to Elsa García, *Fresh*, Puma 1007, n.d.; and Elsa García, *Simplemente*, Polygram 846-847-4, 1990.

47. By the late 1990s, this dual marketing strategy changed to one called "cross-marketing," in which Latino artists would be simultaneously marketed in the Latino and non-Latino markets. On this new marketing strategy, see Ramiro Burr, "'98 Brought Latin Scene Big Changes," *Houston Chronicle*, December 1998.

48. In one specific case, a major recording label encouraged Mazz to add banda songs to their recordings. Banda, a style that utilizes a large number of brass instruments, including the tuba, was extremely popular in certain parts of Mexico and California. Few Tejanos, however, enjoyed this type of music, and many complained about the banda songs. Mazz has not recorded any banda songs since that initial effort.

49. Marty Racine, "La Mafia Hits Mexico: Houston Band's Bold Move South is Paying Off Big," *Houston Chronicle*, March 14, 1993.

50. Ibid.

51. Ramiro Burr, "Musical Growth Earns La Mafia the View from Top," *Houston Chronicle,* July 18, 1993.

52. La Mafia, *Enter the Future,* CBS International CRL80341, 1990; *Estás Tocando Fuego,* Sony Discos DIC80660, 1991; *Vida,* Sony Discos DCC81215, 1994.

53. *Estás Tocando Fuego,* Sony Discos DIC80660, 1991; *Vida,* Sony Discos DCC-812154-469641, 1994.

54. Mitchell, "La Mafia and Its Snazzy, High-Tech Tejano."

55. Racine, "La Mafia Hits Mexico."

56. In early December 1998, La Mafia announced that it was splitting up. Joey Guerra, "Breaking Up Is Hard to Do for La Mafia," *Houston Chronicle,* December 3, 1998.

57. For an overview of Mazz's shift toward boleros and experimentation with other styles, including banda, see Ramiro Burr, "Mazz Displays Bent for Banda on LP," *Houston Chronicle,* August 1, 1993.

58. In 1986 and 1988 the group won awards for best vocal duo and album of the year (orquesta). In 1989 it won the male vocalist and vocal duo awards. See appendix B, Tejano Music Awards, 1981–2000.

59. *Houston Post,* Friday, June 11, 1993.

60. In early November 1998, the group officially split up into two groups. Ramiro Burr, "No More Mazz," *Houston Chronicle,* November 8, 1998.

61. Other groups in the 1990s soon joined the trend toward a new Tejano aesthetic—that is, away from rancheras and toward cumbias, baladas, and mariachi music. Although no Tejano group repeated La Mafia's brash move of recording an album without a ranchera on it, a few, such as David Olivarez and Elida y Avante, recorded mostly cumbias and baladas. Elida's 1999 CD, for instance, contained only two rancheras, "Dejame" and "Amorcito" (the other songs were cumbias and baladas); Elida y Avante, *Magico,* Tejas Records CSTR-9903, 1999.

62. Selena y Los Dinos, *Baila Está Cumbia,* Capitol-EMI 407-7990524, 1992.

63. This was the lead song from her album by the same name. Selena, *Amor Prohibido,* Capitol-EMI H2724382880325, 1994.

64. On her 1992 album, five out of ten songs were rancheras. Her live album of 1993 contained seventeen songs; nine were rancheras. See *Entre a Mi Mundo,* Capitol-EMI H242635, 1992; and *Selena Live,* EMI H2-0777-74277020, 1993.

65. For an excellent history of Selena's impact on the music industry on both sides of the border, see Patoski, *Selena.*

66. These two songs can be found on Selena, *Mis Primeras Grabaciones,* Freddie Records C1294, 1985.

67. Selena, "Enamorada de Tí," personal cassette recording in author's collection, 1991.

68. Selena with the Barrio Boys, *Dondequieras Que Estes* (promotional copy), Capitol-EMI DPRO79043 (CD Single), 1993.

69. Two of her best-known mariachi songs were "Que Creias" and "Tú Solo Tú." The former can be found on *Entre a Mi Mundo,* Capitol-EMI H242635, 1992; the latter on *Dreaming of You,* Capitol-EMI H2724333412327, 1995. For a discography of Selena's recordings, see Patoski, *Selena,* 282–89.

70. Refer, for instance, to the following songs: "Con Esta Copa," *Alpha,* 1986; and "No Llores Mas Corazón" and "La Puerta Se Cerro," *Dulce Amor,* 1988.

71. For more on her accomplishments, see appendix B, Tejano Music Awards, 1981–2000. See also Patoski, *Selena,* 125.

72. Ramiro Burr, "Teamwork Produces Hits for Brownsville's Mazz," *Houston Chronicle,* September 6, 1992.

73. Patoski, *Selena,* 125.

74. Ramiro Burr, "Few New Voices," *Houston Chronicle,* December 9, 1996.

75. To this date, nobody has broken Selena's record. For the official attendance figures, see *www.hlsr.com.* See also Patoski, *Selena,* 155.

76. As late as 1999, Selena had a collection of hits in the top twenty albums of *Billboard*'s Hot Latin Tracks. See the information provided on Selena's website at *http://www.neosoft.com/SELENA/discgrfy.html.*

CHAPTER 6

1. In the late 1970s René and René recorded Spanish-only songs geared toward a Tejano and Mexican audience, but they also expanded their repertoire to include cumbias, disco, and a few Caribbean tunes. Refer to *Quisiera Ser,* Falcon ARVLP-1050, 1978; and *Crei,* Falcon ARVLP-1005, 1978.

2. Burr, *Billboard Guide,* 133.

3. Patoski, *Selena.*

4. Ramiro Burr, "Emilio Navaira, A Country Boy," *Houston Chronicle,* February 16, 1992.

5. In 1996 and 1997 Emilio toured with two popular country artists, Alan Jackson and Clay Walker, and performed at more than seventy concerts with each. Ibid.

6. Anissa R. Hernández, "Award-Winning Emilio Hoping for More Good Luck," *La Onda,* January 1998, 9.

7. "Emilio Navaira Regresa a Raices Hispanas con Nuevo Album," *El Mexica,* July 22, 1999, 3.

8. Emilio also experienced problems in his personal life and in his career as a Tejano musician. In October 1999 he filed for divorce from his wife of twelve years. In early January 2000 he was arrested on allegations of assault and resisting arrest. Later that month he left EMI, his recording company. He soon signed a multiyear contract with BMG and released an album in the spring of 2000. Ramiro Burr, "Facing Many Changes, Emilio Remains Unfazed," *Houston Chronicle,* January 30, 2000.

9. Ramiro Burr, "Houston-Based La Mafia Signs with CBS Discos," *Houston Chronicle,* January 16, 1990.

10. Burr, *Billboard Guide,* 150; Guerra, "Breaking Up Is Hard"; Joey Guerra, "Recordings: Leaving on Its Own Terms," *Houston Chronicle,* September 5, 1999.

11. Ramiro Burr, "Record Companies Scramble to Fill Demand for Latin Stars," *Houston Chronicle,* November 7, 1999; Joey Guerra, "Regarding Ricky," *Houston Chronicle,* November 4, 1999.

12. For this comment, see *Songs of the Homeland,* a documentary film produced and directed by Hector Galán (Austin: Galán Productions, 1995).

13. Elida y Avante's manager, Nikki Sandoval, recalls how sexism was still prevalent in the Tejano music industry as late as 1996. She recalled that there were many times when male promoters refused to deal with her because she was female. "They would go around me and talk to the musicians about booking," she said. "But luckily, they [musicians] would send them back to me." Ramiro Burr, "Women Tap Regional Mexican Music," *Houston Chronicle,* August 25, 1996.

14. Guile González, "The Brown Express: Rolling to Glory," *Corpus Christi Sun,* March 23–26, 1978; Burr, *Billboard Guide,* 73–74.

15. Burr, *Billboard Guide,* 136.

16. One other female artist should be noted here, Janie C. Ramírez. Ramírez played Chicano country with a group called Cactus Country Band. She was known professionally as the "First Lady of Chicano Country." More research, however, needs to be done on her role in and influence on the Chicano country genre in particular and música tejana in general. For a sampling of her music, refer to Cactus Country Band, *Untitled,* Falcon ARVLP-1063, 1981.

17. Burr, *Billboard Guide*, 203.

18. Rick Mitchell, "Tejano Star Lares Now Getting Her Due," *Houston Chronicle,* May 28, 1998.

19. Burr, *Billboard Guide*, 128. See also *Shelly Lares Bio, www.ondanet.com:1995/tejano/ MannyMusic/shelly.htm.*

20. Burr, *Billboard Guide,* 99. Russell Contreras argues that by 1999 García was resentful and angry for being excluded from the music scene. Russell Contreras, "Roll Over Selena and Tell Emilio the News," *Houston Press,* May 6–12, 1999.

21. Burr, *Billboard Guide,* 71–72.

22. See appendix B, Tejano Music Awards, 1981–2000.

23. In 1996, Canales was inducted into the Tejano Music Hall of Fame at the Pura Vida Music Awards held in San Antonio, Texas. See Burr, "Pura Vida Awards."

24. For an excellent account of Selena's career and her rise to the top, see Patoski, *Selena.*

25. Burr, "Women Tap Regional Mexican Music."

26. Ibid.

27. Larry Rohter, "Pop Music: Latin Music Crosses New Borders," *New York Times,* September 19, 1993, late edition.

28. Herrick, "Go Tejano!"; Ramiro Burr, "Tejano Getting Its Due But Must Seize Its Future," *Houston Chronicle,* February 12, 1995.

29. Angelique Siy, "Parade Celebrates Cinco de Mayo," *Houston Chronicle,* May 2, 1999.

30. Ernesto Cruz, "Tejano Fever Catching on in Texas," *Viva,* June 2, 1991, 17.

31. I attended that first large dance with my wife, Alicia. Pulido, once he got on stage, commented on the size of the dance floor: "Hijole! [Whew!] This place is so big that you need a taxi just to get to the other side!"

32. Rick Mitchell, "Stylistic Diversions Blur with Bronco," *Houston Chronicle,* May 31, 1993; Ramiro Burr, "Tejano Milestone: El Baile," *Houston Chronicle,* June 13, 1994.

33. In 1990 the festival was extended to seven days, but it was cut down to five in 1994. See Ramiro Burr, "Top Old, New Conjunto Groups Assembled for 7-Day Festival," *Houston Chronicle,* May 13, 1990; and Ramiro Burr, "Tejano Bands Energize Conjunto Format," *Houston Chronicle,* May 25, 1997.

34. For an overview of the conjunto festival's evolution during these twenty years, see the following articles by Ramiro Burr, all of which appeared in the *Houston Chronicle:* "Festival of Conjunto Music Set," May 12, 1988; "Top Old, New Conjunto Groups Assembled"; "Conjunto Plays Big in Alamo City/30,000 Expected To Attend 7-Day Festival," May 16, 1991; "Tejano Bands Energize Conjunto Format"; "Tejano Festival To Promote Young Talent," May 3, 1998.

35. Ramiro Burr, "Houston Band Leads Mexican Concert Bill," *Houston Chronicle,* April 8, 1992.

36. Carol Juarez G [*sic*], "KQQK Sets Airwaves Ablaze with Tejano Music," *Viva,* December 4, 1992; Ramiro Burr, "Spanish Station Tops the Market in San Antonio," *Houston Chronicle,* November 8, 1992.

37. Treviño was a native of Beeville, Texas, and a sixth-generation Tejano. He started as a disk jockey but later switched to reporting after graduating from George Washington University with a degree in broadcast journalism. For additional information on *Tejano Gold,* see Ramiro Burr, "Radio Spreads Tejano Gold," *Houston Chronicle,* March 16, 1997.

38. Anissa R. Hernández, "Here It Is—All-Tejano Music Video Channel," *La Onda,* November 1997, 9.

39. Guile González, "Annual Mike Chavez Awards at Memorial Coliseum," *Corpus Christi Sun,* March 2–8, 1978.

40. Janie López, "Potpourri," *El Sol,* November 1985; Maribel Maldonado, "Houston Celebrates its 5th Annual Chicano Music Awards," *El Sol,* newspaper clippings given to the author by Dr. Antonio González, September 1995.

41. Ramiro Burr, "Voting Ends Saturday for Tejano Music Stars," *Houston Chronicle,* January 23, 1987.

42. Ibid.

43. Herrick, "Go Tejano!"; Ramiro Burr, "Emilio Navaira, Selena Sweep Tejano Music Awards Again," *Houston Chronicle,* March 13, 1993; Burr, "TMA: The Good, the Bad, the Tacky," *Houston Chronicle,* March 20, 1994.

44. Renee Haines, "Tejano Music Awards Growing in Stature," *Houston Chronicle,* January 29, 1988.

45. The TMA, for instance, eliminated a few awards categories, such as song and single of the year, and developed several new ones, such as songwriter, video, and Tejano norteño of the year. Ramiro Burr, "TMA," *Houston Chronicle,* March 20, 1994; Benjamen Frieventh, "Las Nuevas Estrellas," *Semana,* March 12–18, 1998, 12.

46. This overview is gleaned from the following articles: Haines, "Tejano Music Awards Growing in Stature"; Burr, "Voting Ends Saturday"; Ramiro Burr, "Latin Labels to Secede from Tejano Awards in Protest," *Houston Chronicle,* April 9, 1992; Burr, "Tejano Awards Move Forward," November 22, 1992; Burr, "Emilio Navaira, Selena Sweep Tejano Music Awards,"; Burr, "TMA: The Good, the Bad, the Tacky,"; Frieventh, "Las Nuevas Estrellas," 12.

47. Little Joe was awarded the Grammy in 1992 for his album *El 16 de Septiembre,* Selena in 1993 for *Selena Live,* and La Mafia in 1997 and 1998 for *Un Million de Rosas* and *En Tus Manos,* respectively; Ramiro Burr, "Grammy Officials Vote To Include Exclusive Tejano Category," *Houston Chronicle,* July 5, 1998.

48. Ibid.

49. Flaco Jiménez received the Grammy for his album *Said and Done.* Los Palominos won it for their album *Por Eso Te Amo;* Olivia P. Tallet, "Siete Gramofonos Para los Latinos," *Semana,* March 4–10, 1999, 12; Gustavo Lafarge/Terra, "Santana y Otras Figuras," *Semana,* March 2–8, 2000, 19.

50. For further elaboration of the causes and consequences of the recording of Mexican music by the major record labels during the interwar years, see chapter 1.

51. Ramiro Burr, "Cara Sales Sees Tejano Music Outgrow Its Texas Borders," *Houston Chronicle,* January 16, 1990.

52. The dominance of Capitol-EMI led to a protest by several other Latin labels. See Burr, "Latin Labels To Secede."

53. Arista/Latin originally signed several Tejano acts, including Freddie Fender and Flaco Jiménez, two Tejano crossover veterans, and Joel Nava and La Diferenzia, two new acts. In 1998 it shifted direction by releasing Fender and Jiménez and by signing several non-Tejano acts, including mariachi songstress Nydia Rojas, pop sensation Angelica, and ex-Menudo member Rubén Gómez. Abel Salas, "Record Label Abandons Tejano Experiment," *Hispanic,* September 1998, 14. Independent recording companies, such as Freddie Records, Manny Music, Voltage, and others, contributed to this growth by also signing new acts during the 1990s. For an overview of the increased activity among the major and indie labels, see Ramiro Burr, "Manny Music Signs Deal with BGM International," *Houston Chronicle,* August 2, 1992; Ramiro Burr, "Tejano Labels Mushrooming," *Houston Chronicle,* August 6, 1995.

54. It also included Roberto Zenteno and Orchestra; see "Música: A Celebration of Hispanic Music and Dance," *Houston Chronicle,* April 26, 1987.

55. Ramiro Burr, "Texas Stops/Mexican Pop Ballad Group Touring the United States," *Houston Chronicle,* May 3, 1992.

56. See, for instance, the alarmist view offered by Contreras in his article "Roll Over Selena."

57. Burr, *Billboard Guide,* 39.

58. Ibid.

CONCLUSION

1. Peña, *Música Tejana,* xi.

2. Albert Zamora y Talento, a conjunto from Corpus Christi, for example, added a keyboard in the mid-1990s. This keyboard, however, was used only on a limited number of songs. For a brief history of this group, see Guadalupe San Miguel, "Albert Zamora y Talento: Leading the Pack," *Tejano Times,* September 10–24, 1997, 4.

3. For a brief overview of these early orquestas, see *Mexican American Border Music, Vol. 4,* Arhoolie CD 7017, 1996; and *Mexican American Border Music, Vol. 5,* Arhoolie CD 4984, 1996.

4. One type of ensemble that has not been tried in the contemporary period is a guitar-driven group. These types of groups are becoming increasingly popular, as indicated by the emergence of "rock en español." However, none of these recent musicians, including Chris Perez, former guitar player from Selena y Los Dinos, is playing música tejana. For an example of one group that occasionally used the guitar as a lead instrument in rancheras during the early 1980s, refer to La Movida, *Es Amor,* Hacienda Classics SC206-4, 1997. Ricky Smith was the lead guitarist for this group. La Movida disbanded sometime during the mid- or late 1980s. In the late 1990s, the band regrouped, but without Ricky Smith.

5. Vanessa A. Conner and J. Carlos Silva, "Tejano Music Awards Shines Over the Lone Star State," *Que Onda,* March 14, 2000, 14.

6. "Boy bands" were generally composed of four or five young males who sang various types of pop and rhythm and blues songs in three– or four–part harmony. One of the original "boy bands" was the Philadelphia-based quartet Boys II Men. For a brief history of this group and a review of their 2000 CD, see Jake McKim, "Boys II Men's Latest Effort Reaffirms Group's Talent," (University of Houston) *Daily Cougar,* October 23, 2000.

7. "Kumbia Kings: New Dimensions with No Limits in the Latin Scene," *Tejano Times,* September 1998; "Los Kumbia Kings, 'Down with the Kings'", *Tejano Times,* September 1998, 5.

8. In 1949, Johnny Herrera, from Corpus Christi, recorded the country music standard "Jealous Heart" in English and in Spanish for the Melco label. Two years later he recorded the same song as "Corazón Celoso" for Decca Records. The recording was made with saxophones, trumpets, and the accordion, not the traditional violin and steel guitar of the later Chicano country groups. Patoski, *Selena,* 23. For a sampling of this music, refer to the following LPs: Country Roland, *Las Margaritas,* Falcon ARVLP-1057, 1979; Country Roland Band, *Rancho Grande,* Falcon ARVLP-1052, 1978; Country Mingo, *The Outlaw,* Falcon FLP-5041, 1980; The Texas Country Band, *Valle de Palmas,* Falcon ARVLP-1065, 1980; Country Roland, Jr., *Mucho Macho,* Falcon ARVLP-1064, 1980; *The Best of Chicano Country, Vol. 2,* Falcon ARVLP-1075, 1982.

9. For a sampling of the country music recorded by these artists, refer to Rudy Tee Gonzales y Sus Reno Bops, *Country,* Teardrop TD-2030, ca. 1972; Snowball & Co., *Snowball & Co.,* Fireball FLP-1001, n.d. (especially "Just Because," a Chicano country ballad); Roberto Pulido on *The Best of Chicano Country, Vol. 2,* Falcon ARVLP-1075, 1982; and Mazz, *Perfect 10,* Cara CA-10B, 1977. Mazz recorded three country songs on their first album in 1977, "Algo Bonito" ("Something Pretty"); "El" ("He"); and "Laura Ya No Vive Aquí"

("Laura Doesn't Live Here Anymore"). Unlike other Tejano artists, Mazz did not use the steel guitar and violin but played these songs using the synthesizer and rhythm guitar as primary instruments.

10. Two-steps are usually associated with American country music but have been an integral part of música tejana since the early decades of the twentieth century. For further elaboration, see chapters 2, 4, and 5.

11. Although the repertoire expanded during the 1990s, the number of rancheras performed and recorded declined. In late 1999 and early 2000, at least two popular groups, Jennifer y Los Jetz and Los Kumbia Kings, each recorded a CD without any rancheras. It is too early yet to see if this is a trend or only a coincidence. Refer to Jennifer y Los Jetz, *Besame y Abrasame,* EMI Latin, 2000; and Los Kumbia Kings, *Amor, Familia, y Respeto,* EMI Latin, 1999.

12. See Reyes and Waldman, *Land of a Thousand Dances;* and Steven Loza, *Barrio Rhythm.*

13. For further elaboration of how música tejana reflected the community's social subordination and its social differentiation, see Peña, *Música Tejana,* especially chapters 1 and 2.

14. Herrick, "Go Tejano!".

15. Peña, *Música Tejana,* 11.

16. Los García Brothers, *Cuatro Paredes,* ZAZ Records, 1998, liner notes.

Bibliography

Acuña, Rudy. *Occupied America: A History of Chicanos,* 3d edition. New York: Harper
  Collins, 1988.
Alonzo, Armando C. *Tejano Legacy: Rancheros and Settlers in South Texas, 1734–1900.*
  Albuquerque: University of New Mexico Press, 1998.
Anzaldua, Gloria. *Borderlands/La Frontera: The New Mextiza.* San Francisco: Aunt Lute
  Books, 1987.
Bensusan, Guy. "A Consideration of Norteña and Chicano Music," *Studies in Latin
  American Popular Culture* 4 (1985): 158–64.
Burr, Ramiro. *The Billboard Guide to Tejano and Regional Mexican Music.* New York:
  Watson-Guptill Publications, 1999.
De León, Arnoldo. *Ethnicity in the Sunbelt: A History of Mexican Americans in Houston.*
  Houston: Center for Mexican American Studies, University of Houston, 1989; 2d
  edition, College Station: Texas A&M University Press, 2001.
———. *Mexican Americans in Texas: A Brief History,* 2d ed. Wheeling, Ill.: Harlan
  Davidson, 1999.
———. *The Tejano Community.* Albuquerque: University of New Mexico Press, 1982.
———, and Richard Griswold del Castillo, *North to Aztlán.* New York: Twayne Publishers,
  1996.
Deutsch, Sarah. *No Separate Refuge: Culture, Class, and Gender on the Anglo-Hispanic
  Frontier in the American Southwest, 1880–1940.* New York: Oxford University Press, 1987.
Dickey, Dan William. *The Kennedy Corridos: A Study of the Ballads of a Mexican American
  Hero.* Austin: Center for Mexican American Studies, University of Texas, 1978.
Garrido, Juan S. *Historia de la Música Popular en Mexico.* Mexico City: Editorial
  Contemporanees, 1974.
González, Antonio. *Mexican American Musicians: A History.* Houston: Privately printed, n.d.
Kanellos, Nicolás. *Mexican American Theater: Legacy and Reality.* Pittsburg: Latin American
  Literary Review Press, 1987.
Kreneck, Thomas H. *Del Pueblo: A Pictorial History of Houston's Hispanic Community.*
  Houston: Houston International University, 1989.
Lipsitz, George. "Chicano Rock and Roll from East Los Angeles: A Research Discography,"
  in Guíllermo Rojas, ed., *Chicano Studies: Nuevos Horizontes-Midwest Foco Proceedings,*
  Minneapolis, Minn.: Published by the Prisma Institute in Cooperation with the Institute
  for the Study of Ideologies and Literature, 1987.
Loza, Steven. *Barrio Rhythm: Mexican American Music in Los Angeles.* Chicago: University of
  Illinois Press, 1993.
Meier, Matt, and Feliciano Ribera. *Mexican Americans/American Mexicans.* New York: Hill
  and Wang, 1993.
Mendoza, Lydia. "The Lark of the Border," in American Folklife Center, *Ethnic Recordings
  in America: A Neglected Heritage.* Washington, D.C.: Library of Congress, 1982.

Montejano, David. *Anglos and Mexicans in the Making of Texas, 1836–1986.* Austin: University of Texas Press, 1987.

Nostrand, Richard L. *The Hispano Homeland.* Norman: University of Oklahoma Press, 1992.

Orozco, Cynthia. *Beyond Machismo, La Familia, and Ladies Auxiliaries: A Historiography of Mexican-Origin Women's Participation in Voluntary Associations and Politics in the United States, 1870–1990.* Renato Rosaldo Lecture Series Monograph 10 (1992–93).

Paredes, Américo. *Folklore and Culture on the Texas-Mexico Border.* Austin: Center for Mexican American Studies, University of Texas, 1993.

———. *A Texas-Mexican Cancionero: Folksongs of the Lower Border.* Austin: University of Texas Press, 1976.

———. *"With His Pistol in His Hand": A Border Ballad and Its Hero.* Austin: University of Texas Press, 1958.

Patoski, Joe Nick. *Selena: Como La Flor.* New York: Little, Brown, and Company, 1996.

Peña, Manuel. *The Mexican American Orquesta.* Austin: University of Texas Press, 1999.

———. *Música Tejana.* College Station: Texas A&M University Press, 1999.

———. *The Texas-Mexican Conjunto: History of a Working-Class Music.* Austin: University of Texas Press, 1985.

Reyes, David, and Tom Waldman. *Land of a Thousand Dances: Chicano Rock 'n' Roll from Southern California.* Albuquerque: University of New Mexico Press, 1998.

Ruíz, Vickie. *From Out of the Shadows.* New York: Oxford University Press, 1998.

Sánchez, George S. *Becoming Mexican American.* Oxford: Oxford University Press, 1993.

San Miguel, Guadalupe, Jr. "The Rise of Recorded Tejano Music in the Post–World War II Years, 1946–1964," *Journal of American Ethnic History* 19 (fall, 1999): 26–49.

Simmons, Merle E. *The Mexican Corrido as a Source for Interpretive Study of Modern Mexico (1870–1950).* New York: Draus Reprint Co., 1969.

Spottswood, Richard K. *Ethnic Music on Records: A Discography of Ethnic Recordings in the United States, 1894–1942.* Urbana: University of Illinois Press, 1990.

Strachwitz, Chris, and James Nicolopulos, comps. *Lydia Mendoza: A Family Autobiography.* Houston: Arte Público Press, 1993.

Treviño, Adrian. *Tejano Music, 1830–1930: An Informal History.* Albuquerque: Trellis Publishing Company, 1990.

Treviño, Rudy R. "Tejano Music: A Historical Perspective," *Music World Magazine* (February, 1997): 30–32.

Index

Note: References to illustrations appear in *italics*.

Las Abajenas, 41
Abrego, Eugenio, 57
accordion: American drum impact on, 54; in conjunto groups, 30, 31, 55; electrification of, 83; German origin of, 17, 30; in grupos Tejanos, 102, 104; and orquestas, 32, 48; and popularity of mùsica Tejana, 125; post-WWII popularity of, 38, 41; resurgence of, 97–102; Villa's dropping of, 48–49; and vocal singing popularity, 33
Los Alegres de Terán, 57
Alice, Tex., 6, 56, 153*n* 13
Alonzo, Ventura (née Martínez), 43, 45, 50
Alonzo y Sus Rancheros, 45
American Bandstand, 73
American influences: drums in conjunto groups, 53–54; mainstreaming of música tejana, 71, 113–15. *See also* Anglos; popular American music
amplification, 54
Andres Huesca y Su Trio Huracán, 30
Angelini, Bill, 118
Anglos: big band influences on orquestas, 46–47, 51–52; definitional issues, 4–5; greater acceptance of música tejana, 118; mainstreaming of música tejana, 71, 113–15; popularity of pop music with Mexican American youth, 70; Tejano use of Anglo tunes, 14; theme of conflict with, 7. *See also* popular American music
Arhoolie Records, 10, 21
Arista/Latin, 179*n* 53
Arreola brothers, 98
awards, music. *See* music awards
Ayala, Ramón, *68, 69*

bajo sexto, 17, 35, 36, 54, 55
baladas (ballads), 7, 85, 90, 105
bandas. *See* orquesta de pitos (bandas)
bel canto singing style, 157*n* 3
Berlanga, Andres, 24
Bernal, Paulino, 55
Betancourt, Paco, 38, 39, 48
big band music, 47, 49, 51–52
bilingual radio, 122
bimusicality, 48
Bluebird Records, 32, 52
bolero songs, 43, 44, 50
border music, 5–6
bracero program, 58–59, 167*n* 99
brass instruments. *See* wind/brass instruments
Los Bravos del Norte, 69
Brown Express, 64, 65–66, 116
Burr, Ramiro, 99, 102, 123, 127–28

Campos, Mario Alberto, 123
Canales, Laura, 85, *87,* 117
canciones: norteñas, 4, 154*n* 33; rancheras, 10–11, 21; románticas, 8, 21, 22, 154*n* 29; típicas, 8, 21, 22, 33;
cantadores, 23
cantinas, 56, 58, 166*n* 89
cantineras (prostitutes), 64
Cantú, Jesus, 101
Cantú, Laura Hernández, 42, 45
Capital Nashville, 114
Capitol-EMI Latin, 99, 125–26
Cara Records, 125
Caribbean influences, 49, 50–51
Carlos Guzman y su Conjunto, 83, 171*n* 65
Carmen y Laura, 39, 42
Casiano, Jesús (El Gallito), 32, 35

Castillon, Ricardo, 14
CBS International, 125
CBS-Sony Discos, 114, 115
Los Chamacos, 98
Chavela y Brown Express, 64, 65–66, 116
Chicano country bands: development of,
    15; and diversity of ensembles, 18;
    emergence of, 78, 80–82; historical
    summary of, 133–34; and Janie Ramírez,
    177n16
Chicano movement, 66, 169n38
Chicano Wave, 46, 77
El Ciego Melquiades, 30, 33
Cinco de Mayo, 120
classes, 8–9. See also elite classes; middle
    class; working class
commercialization, 3, 104, 118, 122–24, 125–
    26
concerts: Emilio, 96; expansion of venues,
    121; La Mafia, 104–105; Selena, 110
Concha's Band, 27
El Conjunto Bernal, 13, 55, 61, 62
conjunto groups: and Chavela Ortíz, 116;
    and diversity of ensembles, 16–17; in
    early twentieth century, 30–32, 34–36;
    grupos Tejanos as originating from, 83;
    longevity of, 130; and música ranchera,
    47; and post-World War II era, 52–59;
    and resurgence of traditional, 97–102;
    rise and fall of (1960s-1980s), 61–69;
    San Antonio as center of, 5; traditional-
    ism in, 14; urban influences on, 4; and
    vocal singing, 14, 24, 50. See also
    norteño conjunto; progressive conjunto
    groups
Corona Records, 53
corporate involvement, 104, 118, 122–24,
    125–26
corporate sponsorship, 126
Corpus Christi, Tex., 6, 56, 166n89
corridos: and Anglo-Mexican conflict
    theme, 7–8; Longoria's influence on,
    165n77; nineteenth century dominance
    of, 21; and norteño conjunto, 57;
    popularity of accordian in, 33;
    popularizers of, 5; and romantic
    tradition, 158n15–17; themes in, 22–23
Cortez, Gregorio, 7, 22
country and western music: and Emilio,

94–96, 114–15; fashion in, 94; and
    influence on música tejana, 4; and
    instruments for grupos, 13; in progres-
    sive conjunto, 78. See also Chicano
    country bands
Country Roland Band, 15, 18, 81, 82
crossover projects, 71, 113–15. See also
    country and western music; popular
    American music
Cuarteto Carta Blanca, 24
cuerda, orquesta de, 16, 27–28, 32, 46
cultural issues: and conjunto music, 64, 66,
    97; and country vs. city in song, 154n
    29; and metamorphosis of mùsica
    Tejana, 134–36; música tejana as
    expression of, 7–9; and origins of
    música tejana, 9–12; Tejano definition
    of, 4–5; and Tejano festivals, 120; and
    youth rejection of parental music, 70.
    See also women
cumbia: and grupos Tejanos, 17, 85, 105; in
    orquestas, 74; and ranchera, 11; Selena's
    focus on, 90, 108

dance halls, 56, 120
dancing: American drum impact on, 54;
    early twentieth century types of, 36; and
    el taquachito, 58; and Emilio, 96; and
    gran bailes, 120; and origins of música
    tejana, 10; orquesta types for, 29, 159n
    29; and Selena, 90, 109; and two-steps,
    181n10. See also cumbia; instrumental
    dance music
David Lee Garza y Los Musicales, 79–80,
    93
de Anda, Jaime, 98
de la Cruz, Ramiro (Snowball), 171n67
de la Rosa, Oscar, 98
de la Rosa, Tony, 54, 56, 63
del Castillo, Richard Griswold, 71
de Léon, Arnoldo, 23, 70–71
de León, R., 31
Díaz, Porfirio, 26–27, 28
La Diferenzia, 14
Los Dinos, 71, 72, 74–75, 169n34
discography, 137–42
Discos Falcon, 42, 81
Discos Ideal. See Ideal Records
discrimination, 73, 114

drums, 53–54
duets: female, 41, 42, 53; male-female duets, 161*n* 10

Eddie Con Los Shades, 71
Eighth Cavalry Mexican Band, 28
electric bass guitar, 53
electric guitar, 70, 73, 83
elite classes: appeal of orquestas to, 26–27, 29; and bandas, 28; early twentieth century music for, 27; mid-twentieth century decline of, 34; and musical sophistication, 163*n* 43, 164*n* 47; vocal singing popularity for, 23. *See also* middle class
El Paso, Tex., 27
EMI Latin, 118
Emilio Navaira y el Grupo Río, 15, 17, 93–97, 114–15. *See also* Navaira, Emilio
English-language market, 71, 113–15, 117
entrepreneurs and importation of Mexican music, 34–35
ethnic identity, 9, 135–36. *See also* cultural issues
Eugenio Gutiérrez y Su Orquesta, 42, *49,* 50, 51
European influences: and canción romántica, 8; on conjunto groups, 31; on corridos, 23; and French, 10, 28; and German, 17, 30. *See also* polka

Los Fabulosos Cuatro, 17, 83–84, 171*n* 67
Falcon Records, 42, 81
Farrington, Curtis, 28
females. *See* women
Fender, Freddie, 71
Fernández, Rosita, 43, 44, 162*n* 17
fiestas patrias, 120
Flores, Robin, 99
Flores Orchestra, 165*n* 66
folk, 8
Fono Visa Records, 99, 118
Freddie Records, 6, 98, 99
French influences, 10, 28

Gabriel, Juan, 14
Galán, Héctor, 9
Galván Orchestra, 165*n* 67
García, Elsa, 117

García, Juanita, 43, 45
Garcia, Roland, 81
Garza, Cecilio, 170*n* 51
Garza, David Lee, 79–80, 93
geographical range of música tejana, 5–6
German influences, 17, 30
Gloria's Band, 27
González, Antonio, 123
González, Balde, 49, 51, 71
González, Jimmy, 86–87
González, Oscar and Leonard, 88
Go Tejano Rodeo, *121*
Grammy Awards. *See* music awards
gran bailes, 120
Grever, Bob, 125
grupo, 171*n* 63
grupos Tejanos: in Alice, Tex., 6; and appeal to middle class, 8; emergence of, 82–91; historical development of, 132–33; instruments in, 12–13, 17–18; and progressive conjunto, 93; rhythms in, 13–14; transformation and dominance of, 102–11
guitars, 17, 53, 70, 73, 83
Gutiérrez, Delia, 43, 45, *49*
Gutiérrez, Eugenio, 42, *49,* 50, 51
Guval, Letty, 13
Guzman, Carlos, 83, 171*n* 65

Hacienda Records, 6
harmonies, 55, 62, 98
Hermanas Guerrero, *43*
Los Hermanos Torres-García, 57
Hernández, Carmen, 39
Hernández, Laura, 39, 45
hero. *See* male hero
Herrera, Johnny, 18
Herrera, L'il Julian, 70
Herrera, Ramiro, 80
Hinojosa, Armando (Chore), 83
Hometown Boys, 98–99
Houston, Tex.: dance halls in, 120; early twentieth century music in, 29; and gran bailes, 120; Livestock Show and Rodeo in, 110, 121; and post-WWII orquestas, 52; and radio, 122; and Ventura Alonzo, 45
Houston Tejano Music Awards (HTMA), 122

huapango, 15
Huerta, Balderama (Bebop Kid), 71
Huesca, Andres, 30

Ideal Records: in Alice, Tex., 6; establish-
    ment of, 33, 37–39; Longoria's impact
    on, 53; and música ranchera, 50;
    orquesta recordings by, 47, 48; and
    Tony de la Rosa, 54
identity, ethnic, 135–36. See also cultural
    issues
immigration, 34
Las Incomparables Hermanas Ortiz, 65–66
instrumental dance music: and Chicano
    country bands, 81; and class differences,
    8; diversity of ensembles in, 16–17; vocal
    singing additions in, 14–15. See also
    conjunto groups; dancing; orquestas
instruments: and bajo sexto, 17, 35, 36, 54,
    55; in Chicano country bands, 81; and
    class distinctions, 159n 31; and conjunto
    developments, 35–36, 47–48, 53–54, 62,
    66; and ensemble diversity, 15–18; and
    grupos Tejanos, 82–83, 86, 93, 102, 104;
    and keyboards, 17, 82–83, 125; modern-
    izing influences on, 12–13; and norteño
    conjunto, 67; and organ, 69, 70, 73, 82,
    171n 61; and orquesta developments, 16,
    26–27, 47–48, 73; and progressive
    conjunto, 78, 93; and string, 16, 26, 47, 58.
    See also accordion; wind/brass instruments
internationalization, 104, 105–6, 115–16, 124
Intocable, 99, 100
Isidro López y Su Orquesta, 51
Italian influences, 8

J. W. Fox Records, 71
Jaime y Los Chamacos, 98
jaitón music, 164n 47. See also música
    moderna
jarocho groups, 27, 30
Jiménez, Cha Cha, 67
Jiménez, Santiago (Flaco), 30, 32, 35
Jordan, Steve (El Parche), 14, 64–65
jukebox, 38, 39

Los Kasinos, 79
keyboards, 17, 82–83, 125
Los Kumbia Kings, 133

language: English, 71, 113–15, 117; Ozuna's
    return to Spanish, 73; Spanish as
    primary for singing, 9, 11–12, 42, 49, 52.
    See also radio, Spanish-language
Lares, Shelly, 117
Lares, Tony, 117
Latin American influences, 8, 13–14, 46, 49,
    50–51
Latin soul music, 73
Laura Canales and Encanto, 85
Lichtenberger, Mando, 88, 98, 104
Limite, Grupo, 101–2
Lira, Bobby, 71
Little Joe, 12, 14, 114
Little Joe and the Latinaires, 74, 75
Llamaz, Beatriz, 44, 45
Longoria, Valerio, 5, 50, 53, 165–66n 77,
    165n 75
Loomis, Charles, 162n 14
López, Isidro, 12, 15, 47, 50
López, Joe, 86–87
López, Lisa, 116
Los Angeles, 14
love themes, 8, 22
Loza, Steven, 34
lyrical songs. See típicas, canciones; vocal
    singing

La Mafia, 6, 88–89, 104–5, 172n 87, 172n 92
mainstream, 71, 113–15. See also country and
    western music; popular American music
Maldonado, Vilma, 4
male domination: of conjunto groups, 30;
    and origins of música tejana as cultural
    voice, 7; and treacherous woman
    theme, 8; of vocal singing, 16, 24; and
    women's musical role, 41, 116
male-female duets, 161n 10
male hero, 22
Manny Music, 117
marching band music, 28–29
Mariachi Acosta, 30, 33
Mariachi Coculense Rodríguez, 30
mariachi groups, 11, 27–28, 30, 33, 47
Mario, Luis, 101
Marroquín, Armando, 33, 38–39, 47, 55
Martínez, Freddie, 12
Martínez, Narciso, 5, 32, 35, 36, 52
Martínez, Rene, 99

Martínez, Ricky and Joe, 99
Mazz: and bandas, 175n 48; development of, 105–6, *107, 108;* and internationalization vs. mainstreaming, 115; and new rhythms, 14; non-Tejano aesthetic of, 172n 76
Medina River Boys, 33
Mendoza, Lydia, *40,* 43, 51; post-WWII popularity of, 42; and women's voice in música tejana, 22, 24, 41
Mexican Americans, 4–5
Mexican Brass Band, 27
Mexican Orchestra (Solis), 29
Mexicanos. *See* norteño conjunto
Mexican Social Club, 27
Mexico: concert expansion in, 121; grupos Tejanos in, 104–105; Mazz in, 105–106. *See also* norteño conjunto
middle class: and conjunto music, 62, 66; and expansion of música tejana, 118; and orquesta music, 6, 8, 16, 26–27, 46, 69
Mike Chavez Awards, 122
Montalvo, Francisco, 24
Morales, Santiago, 30, 33
La Movida, 171n 70
MTV, 89
las mujeres. *See* women
Muñoz, Ricardo (Ricky), 99
música moderna, 47, 48–49
música tejana: definition of 4–5; multiple influences of, 3
music awards: Los Chamacos, 98; David Lee Garza, 93; La Mafia, 89, 172n 92; Laura Canales, 85, 117; list of winners, 143–52; Mazz, 87–88, 106; Michael Salgado, 100; progressive conjunto, 80; Selena, 90, 110; Shelly Lares, 117; types of Tejano, 122–24
music hybridity, 48
musicians: and conjunto groups, 31; of early twentieth-century, 30; and orquesta Tejana development, 46–47; and touring, 35. *See also* individual musicians

Navaira, Emilio: and instruments, 15, 17; introduction of, 80; new rhythms of, 14; and personal life, 177n 8; and popularity, 173–74n 7; success of, 93–97, 114–15

norteña, canción, 4, 154n 33
norteño conjunto: and conjunto Tejano, 61; emergence of, 57; growth of, 66–69; and La Mafia, 88; popularity of, 62; resurgence of, 99–102
norteño culture, 9
Nostrand, Richard, 5

Oberstein, Eli, 52
La Onda Chicana, 46, 77
organ, 69, 70, 73, 82, 171n 61
orquesta de cuerda, 16, 27–28, 32, 46
orquesta de pitos (bandas), 16, 28–29; decline of, 46; and Mazz, 175n 48; origins of, 156n 55
orquestas Tejanas: in Alice, Tex., 6; and appeal to middle class, 8; revival of, 170n 47; decline of, 32–33; diversity of dance forms in, 159n 29; historical development of, 24–30, 131–32; instruments in, 12, 16; and post-World War II era, 46–52; rise and fall of, 69–77; vocal singing addition to, 14; women's role in, 41–42
orquesta típica, 16; elite classes' preference for, 163n 43; origins of, 24, 26–27, 159n 34; popularity of, 29–30; replacement of, 46
Orquesta Típica Laredo, 28
La Orquesta Típica Torres, 28
Ortíz, Isabela Salaiza (Chavela), 64, 65–66, 116
Ortíz, Tomás, 57
Our Lady of Guadalupe Church, 29
Ozuna, Sunny, 12, 14, 69–70, 72–73, 75

pachucos, 61, 64, 167n 1
Padilla, Gerado, 101
Los Palominos, 98
patriarchal culture. *See* male domination
Los Pavos Reales, 57
Payen, Encarnación, 28
Peña, Jennifer, *127*
Peña, Manuel, 4, 54; and accordion usage, 17; and grupos Tejanos, 85; song styles of, 21; on types of mùsica Tejana, 129; on Villa, 48
Perales, Seff, 71
piano accordion, 31, 32

pitos, orquesta de. *See* orquesta de pitos (bandas)

playing styles, early twentieth century, 35. *See also* rhythms

political activism, 8, 22–23

polka: American drum impact on, 54; in conjunto groups, 53, 98–99; de la Rosa's dominance of, 55; as dominant rhythm, 10–11, 30, 36

Ponce, Sergio, 101

popular American music: and big band influence on orquestas, 47, 49, 51–52; and influence on grupos Tejanos, 85; and mainstreaming of música tejana, 71, 113–15; and popularity with Mexican American youth, 70

preservation of old recordings, 21

Priscila y sus Balas de Plata, 14

progressive conjunto groups: and Emilio, 93–97; historical development of, 77–82, 132–33; and Los Kasinos, 170*n* 51; and origins of term, 173*n* 1; and traditional conjunto, 16–17

Pulido, Roberto, 15, 17, 77–78, 93, 170*n* 51

Pura Vida Awards. *See* music awards

Quintanilla, Abraham, 71, 75, 133, 169*n* 34

Quintanilla, Selena. *See* Selena

radio, Spanish-language: and conjunto popularity, 34, 61, 97; and corridos popularity, 23; declines in, 126; growth of, 122

Ramírez, Arnaldo, 42

Ramírez, Carlos, 101

Ramírez, Janie, 177*n* 16

Ramón Ayala y Los Bravos del Norte, 69

Ramos, Rubén, 77

rancheras, canciones, 10–11, 21

ranchera Tejana: in conjunto groups, 55; and country vs. city in song, 154*n* 29; and moderna, 48–50; and post-WWII development, 47; and vals, 53

El Ranchero, 30

recordings, discography, 137–42

recording studios, 6, 20–36, 57, 58, 97, 102, 104, 114, 115, 118, 123, 125–26, 179*n* 53; Arhoolie Records, 10, 21; Arista/Latin, 179*n* 53; Bluebird Records, 32, 52;

Capital Nashville, 114; Capitol-EMI Latin, 99, 125–26; Cara Records, 125; CBS International, 125; CBS-Sony Discos, 114, 115; contact information, 142; Corona Records, 53; EMI Latin, 118; Falcon Records, 42, 81; Fono Visa Records, 99, 118; Freddie Records, 6, 98, 99; Hacienda Records, 6; J. W. Fox, 71; Manny Music, 117. *See also* Ideal Records

Refugee Management Agency, 114

Los Relámpagos del Norte, 67, 69, 100–101

religion: and church-based bands, 29; and musical dramas, 158*n* 23; vocal singing popularity for, 23–24, 33–34

Reyna, Cornelio, 69

Reyna, José, 171*n* 61

rhythm and blues influences, 13, 14, 71

rhythms, 10, 50–52, 64–65, 94–95, 106, 108, 125; American influences, 73–74; conjunto, 53, 54–55; grupos Tejanos, 83, 87, 93, 104, 105, *107*; modernizing influences, 13–14; norteño conjunto, 67, 99; progressive conjuntos, 93; rock and roll, 13, 14, 69–73, 94–95, 180*n* 4; vals tempo, 53, 165*n* 77. *See also* corridos; country and western music; cumbia; polka

Roberto Pulido y Los Clásicos, 78

rock and roll, 13, 14, 69–73, 94–95, 180*n* 4

rodeos, 120–21

Rodríguez, Minerva, *49*

románticas, canciones, 8, 21, 22, 154*n* 29

rural communities, 7, 8, 11

Saldívar, Mingo, 14

Salgado, Michael, 100–101

salones de baile. *See* dance halls

San Antonio, Tex.: and conjunto festival, 120–21; early twentieth- century music in, 27, 28, 29; and origin of música tejana, 5–6; radio promotion of música tejana in, 122

Sandoval, Nikki, 177*n* 13

saxophone, 47

Selena: impact of, 89–91, 117; main-streaming plans of, 114; new rhythms of, 14; promotion of, 104, 106–11

Selena y Los Dinos, 89–91, 104

"Se Me Fue Mi Amor," 39–40, 41

Serna, Sergio, 99

sexism, 177*n* 13. *See also* male domination; women

Shelly Lares Band, 117

showmanship: Los Chamacos, 98; Emilio, 96; La Mafia, 88–89; Selena, 90, 109

Silhouettes, 70–71

Silva, Chelo, 42–43, *44*

singing. *See* vocal singing

Smith, Ricky, 171*n* 70

Snowball & Co., 85

Sodi, Sordo, 154*n* 33

Solis, Aurelio L., 29

La Sombra, 6

sones Mexicanos, 26

Sonny Boys, 47

Sony Discos, 118

sound effects, 88–89

Sousa, John Philip, 28–29

Southern Pacific Lines Band, 29

South Texas: and bandas of early twentieth century, 28–29; and Chicano country bands, 82; and origins of música tejana, 9–10; popularity of conjunto music in, 57–58

stage presence: 94; Emilio, 96; La Mafia, 89; Limite, 102; Selena, 90, 109

Steve Jordan y El Rio Jordan, 14, 64–65

Strachwitz, Chris, 17, 31, 38, 41, 57

studios. *See* recording studios

styles. *See* rhythms

Sunglows, 69–70, 72–73

Suniga, Sam, 5–6

super dances, 120

synthesizer: addition of, 15; background of, 170*n* 48; and grupos Tejanos, 77, 82–83, 86, 105; influence of, 4; in progressive conjunto, 93

Tamaulipas, 15

tambora de rancho, 35, 54

el taquachito, 54, 58

Tejano: definition of, 4–5, 156*n* 58; sound of, 41

Tejano Conjunto Festival, 66

Tejano Gold, 122

Tejano Music Awards, 122, 123, 143–52. *See also* music awards

television programming, bilingual, 122

Texachi, 15

Texas: and bandas of early twentieth century, 28–29; and Chicano country bands, 82; decline of mariachi in, 33; origins of música tejana in, 5–6, 9–10; orquestas origins in, 27; popularity of conjunto music in, 57–58

Texas-Mexican music, 4. *See also* música tejana

Texas Revolution (orquesta), 77

Texas Talent Musician's Association (TTMA), 123

típica, orquesta. *See* orquesta típica

típicas, canciones, 8, 21, 22, 33

tololoche, 35, 36

Torres, Albino, 28

Torres, James, 123

Torres, Patsy, 116

Tosti, Don, 70

touring, 35. *See also* concerts

traveling shows, 35

treacherous woman theme, 8, 22, 154*n* 26, 154*n* 34, 157*n* 8

Treviño, Reymundo, 49

Treviño, Rudy, 123

El Trio San Miguel, 44

trovadores, 23

TTMA (Texas Talent Musician's Association), 123

two-steps, 181*n* 10

urbanization: and conjunto popularity, 58–59, 61; and música moderna, 47; and orquesta developments, 46, 69; and transformation of music, 7

Valenzuela, Richard (Ritchie Valens), 70–71

vals tempo, 53, 165*n* 77

Vaquero dress, 94

Vela, Rubén, 58, 63

venues, 45, 56, 120; closure of, 126; and conjunto groups, 31; and early twentieth century orquesta, 29; and popularity of música tejana, 120–21; post-WWII changes in, 56

Villa, Beto: and female duets, 42; innovations of, 12, 13–14, 18, 47, 48–49; and musical influences, 51, 71

Villalobos, L., 31

Villareal, Alicia, 101, 102

Villareal, Bruno (El Azote del Valle), 5, 32, 35

vocal singing: in conjunto music, 31, 53, 55, 62, 98; decline in, 58; and diversity of ensembles, 15–16; historical development of, 21–24, 33–34, 131, 157n 3; in post-WWII orquestas, 50

wind/brass instruments: in conjunto music, 17, 78; in orquestas, 16, 41, 47, 73

women: and addition of vocalists, 16; as cultural negotiators, 161–62n 13; in early twentieth century groups, 28; and female duets, 41, 42, 53; and increasing influence in música tejana, 115–18; and male-female duets, 161n 10; and post-World War II era, 39–45; and sexism in

Tejano culture, 177n 13; and vocal singing, 53, 66, 162n 14. *See also* individual musicians

working class: conjunto popularity in, 8, 32, 34, 58–59, 61; dance music for, 28; and elite's musical tastes, 164n 47; and increase in purchasing power, 38; and orquestas, 26, 29, 46, 69; transformation of imported music by, 35; vocal singing popularity in, 23

World's Industrial and Cotton Centennial Exposition, 28

World War II, 37

youth: conjunto popularity with, 61; orquesta popularity with, 69; and rejection of conjunto music, 62–63, 66

Zimmerle, Henry, 63

ISBN 1-58544-159-7